French Feminist Theory

French Feminist Theory

An Introduction

Dani Cavallaro

continuum
LONDON • NEW YORK

Continuum
The Tower Building, 11 York Road, London SE1 7NX
15 East 26th Street, NY 10010
www.continuumbooks.com

British Library Cataloguing-in-Publication Data
A catalogue record for this book is available from the British Library.

ISBN: 0-8264-5885-8 (hardback) 0-8264-5886-6 (paperback)

Typeset by Acorn Bookwork, Salisbury, Wiltshire
Printed and bound in Great Britain by MPG Books Ltd, Bodmin, Cornwall

To Paddy, with love and gratitude

Contents

Introduction

gender precedes sex ... sex itself simply marks a social division.

(Delphy 1996: 35)

we must move on to the rhetoric of women, one that is anchored in the organism, in the body.

(Duras in Marks and Courtivron 1980: 238)

our enemy isn't man but phallocracy; that is, the imperialism of the phallus.

(Fouque 1987: 52)

theft, swindling, and embezzlement are done covertly; and to appropriate male people requires a war; but not so the appropriation of female people ... for they are already property.

(Guillaumin 1996: 72)

history cannot do without the existence of two human subjects, man and woman, if it is to get away from master–slave relationships.

(Irigaray 1996: 5)

a feminist is a woman who does not allow anyone to think in her place.

(Le Doeuff in Kemp and Squires 1997: 142)

This book offers an introductory investigation of key concepts in French feminist thought, exemplified with reference to a range of representative theorists and texts. French feminism is assessed in terms of both its philosophical and its political dimensions. Developments in the field are historically situated in relation to the particular cultural and social contexts in which they have emerged and unfolded. The book's approach, however, is fundamentally *thematic*. Thus, each chapter addresses a theme or cluster of themes reflecting the principal concerns of French feminist theory. The main areas thereby explored encompass ongoing debates on the cultural construction and defini-tion of sexual and gendered identities; the relationship between subjectivity and language; the roles played by both private and public institutions in the shaping of sexual relations; the issue of embodiment; the relationship between gender, sexuality and race. Within each chapter, a range of positions put forward by critics of diverse theoretical and political orientations is dis-cussed. These positions are arranged according to two basic criteria, namely analogy and opposition, so as to convey a sense of both interconnections and divergences within the field under consideration.

The gallery of illustrative figures recurrently discussed throughout *French Feminist Theory: An Introduction* features primarily the following authors (here listed in alphabetical order):

Hélène Cixous
Christine Delphy
Colette Guillaumin
Luce Irigaray
Sarah Kofman
Julia Kristeva
Michèle Le Doeuff
Nicole-Claude Mathieu
Paola Tabet
Monique Wittig

Additional authors are brought into play as consolidating illustrations and examples: for instance, Marguerite Duras, Antoinette Fouque, Annie Leclerc, Françoise Picq, Monique Plaza.

Certain theorists and examples are explored in greater depth than others so as to enable readers to engage closely with representative issues and debates in the discourse. This is the case, for instance, with the segments on 'Equal-ity versus Difference', where the writings of Michèle Le Doeuff and Sarah Kofman are foregrounded; 'Subjects-in-Process', which focuses on Julia Kristeva; 'Decoding the Codes', where particular emphasis is placed on the work of Luce Irigaray; '*Écriture Féminine*', which concentrates on the the-ories of Luce Irigaray and Hélène Cixous; and 'The Stranger Within', where priority is given to Julia Kristeva and Hélène Cixous. Even in parts of *French Feminist Theory* where a range of theorists are panoramically cited and dis-cussed, especially cogent examples are accorded greater prominence than others in order to help the reader identify and situate distinctively influential voices and perspectives. At the same time, the book considers less renowned authors whose contributions to the principal topics here addressed are of a more marginal character. Their inclusion, however, is an important aspect of the book insofar as it challenges the reductivist trend that fosters narrow and exclusionary approaches to French feminism, by engaging with positions which have been hitherto scarcely considered within anglophone circles and hence contributing a novel perspective on the field. Concurrently, it encourages readers to pursue further lines of enquiry in the course of their own research careers, specifically *vis-à-vis* the interconnection between French feminism and Anglo-American models. Pursuing this lead, the book's *Appendix* draws attention to at times obvious, at times implicit, connections between debates specifically initiated by French feminists in their particular sociohistorical contexts and the writings of Anglo-American critics bearing relevant affinities to those debates.

The exploration of French feminist thought must take into consideration the specificity of women's conditions in France and grapple with the ambiguities of its culture. On the one hand, in France, as in many other Catholic countries, woman has been traditionally relegated to the private sphere of the family and hence to the realm of fundamentally domestic responsibilities. This segregational move has conventionally stemmed from deeply ingrained suspicions about the public display of femininity as a potential indicator of immodest behaviour. On the other hand, French history does not by any means lack prestigious female figures who have influenced deeply the intellectual climate of their days. Simone de Beauvoir is a case in point and this twentieth-century philosopher will be discussed in detail in *Chapter 1*. No less remarkable were the achievements, in earlier epochs, of women conducting and co-ordinating the artistic and critical activities of lively *salons* – centres for the production, confrontation and exchange of often revolutionary aesthetic and political ideas. Madame de Staël in the eighteenth and early nineteenth centuries, and Gertrude Stein in the period between the two World Wars are eminent examples, in this respect. Madame de Staël's *salon* was a distinguished centre of political debate both before and after the French Revolution of 1789. Promoting a spirit of tolerance and fidelity to the ideals of the Enlightenment, she both gained access to otherwise exclusively masculine political circles and herself organized in Paris, in Switzerland, indeed throughout Europe, sites of intellectual resistance to imperial power: that is, the negation of all the liberties she staunchly defended. Stein, for her part, was a revered critic in the world of experimental arts and letters, whose judgement was held capable of both making and destroying entire reputations. She was also among the first collectors of works by the Cubists and other experimental painters of the period, such as Pablo Picasso (who painted her portrait), Henri Matisse and Georges Braque. At her *salon*, these artists mingled with expatriate American writers, such as Ernest Hemingway, and other visitors drawn by Stein's reputation.

These cursory examples indicate that there exists a tension within French culture between contrasting models of femininity. This tension is replicated, significantly, at the level of party politics. While it might be tempting to assume that the left is on women's side and the right is inimical to women's emancipation, it would be quite misleading to take this assumption for granted. There have, indubitably, been times when the left has advanced women's rights. For instance, it was in 1981, when 'the left came to power for the first time in twenty-five years, with a Socialist President and a major-ity of Socialists in parliament' that 'a Ministry for Women's Rights' was founded under the direction of Yvette Roudy, and it was with 'the return of the right to power in 1986' that the Ministry was 'abolished' (Duchen 1987: 21–2). However, taking a broader historical spectrum into account, it should also be remembered that the left was for long opposed to women's enfranch-isement, abiding by the belief that female subjects were particularly suscep-tible to clerical influence and that an electorate – a large proportion of which might be malleable by the Church – could only, ultimately, serve con-servative and reactionary interests. The extension of the franchise to women, in other words, was held to mean 'a great accession of strength to the Catho-lic interest' (Cobban 1965: 203).

Even when female members started featuring conspicuously in the ranks of left-wing parties, especially the *Parti Communiste Français* (PCF), in the 1970s, this did not automatically guarantee the promulgation of feminist causes, or indeed sustained consciousness-raising among male members of the organization. These same men, after all, had until very recently been ardently antagonistic to the legalization of contraception and abortion. Indeed, contraception was legalized in 1967 and abortion, where this was deemed appropriate, in 1975. During attempts to expand the Communist Party's political agenda to women's advantage, feminist members met a major obstacle in the form of a rather rigid and thoroughly centralized organization that tended to discourage departures from the majority line. As Maurice Duverger observes, 'the Communist Party values its structure more highly than its doctrine' (Duverger 1963: 209). Structural cohesion, moreover, goes hand in hand with the doctrine of absolute doctrinal adherence: 'The Com-munist Party demands of its members a total engagement: to be a Communist does not only entail a political attitude but also a religious, scientific, ethical, familial attitude' (p. 210). In light of these comments, it may be unsurprising that when a collective of Communist women called *Elles Voient Rouge* pub-lished an article in *Le Monde* in 1978 that was meant to expose the party's shortcomings, the 'PCF could not accept criticism from inside its own ranks, and while the feminists were not actually thrown out of the party, their cards were not renewed' (Duchen 1987: 113).

Women's position in French culture and history should therefore be understood in terms of diversity and even contradiction, rather than mono-lithic uniformity. Moreover, the same principle may be applied to French feminism itself insofar as there is no *one* movement, theoretical trend or institution that could unproblematically receive this label. Even a limited selection of representative voices such as the ones cited in the opening segment of this *Introduction* instantly indicates that French feminist theory is a multifaceted cultural phenomenon, varyingly implicated with both philoso-phical speculation and political activity. One of this book's main objectives is precisely to highlight the variety of feminist positions in France through a focus on both frictions and interactions between distinct trends, their pre-mises, their aims and their interventions. French feminism's diversity is documented with reference to two main sites of contention: the debate between the advocates of equality and the advocates of difference; the dissen-sion between materialist, or social, positions and linguistic, or psychoanalytic, ones.

The book proposes that French feminism continually cultivates a thought-provoking dialogue between notions of *equality and difference*. Equality is the aspiration of several theorists who are intent on rectifying women's exclusion from dominant structures and relations of power by supplying them with civil rights and cultural credentials identical to those traditionally enjoyed by men. The critics that promote the principle of difference, conversely, alert us to the dangers inherent in the pursuit of equality: primarily, the reduction of feminism to the advocacy of women's admission to normative and normal-izing patriarchal systems. Of pivotal importance, in this respect, is the idea that the pursuit of equality, despite its long-standing popularity, may have to concede ground to a productive fostering of difference as the prerequisite of an understanding of parity-in-disparity and of a balanced relationship between the sexes ultimately consisting of *equivalence* rather than *sameness*. It may then become feasible to move beyond the concept of man-as-enemy and towards a deconstruction of patriarchal and phallocratic structures them-selves. Some theorists have described this deconstructive move as *post-feminist*. Although many critics are unsympathetic to the difference-based model and even more so to the idea of "postfeminism", it is nonetheless imperative to examine the potentially positive repercussions of both, not as inimical to the agendas of radical feminism but as an extension of women's struggle: an endeavour, hopefully, to achieve something rather more life-enhancing than merely tolerant acceptance into, and by, what already *is*.

Concurrently, the book emphasizes throughout the distinctiveness of two principal strands of French feminist theory in thematic and methodological terms, and the importance of acknowledging crucial divergences within and between them: not only, as suggested above, over issues of equality and difference but also over the meaning of feminism itself, as a movement from which some theorists have sought to disassociate themselves due to its potential proclivity to perpetuate patriarchal/binary structures of thought. At the same time, the book seeks to document the two trends' critical complementarity. It accordingly argues that while *materialist feminism* focuses on the fashioning of notions of gender and sexuality by patriarchal social institutions, *linguistic feminism* concentrates on the impact of symbolic representations of gender and sexuality on the psyche. However, the book also endeavours to show that both trends are ultimately committed to the demystification of biologism and to the exposure of ongoing processes of cultural construction and inscription. Even when the *body*'s functions and rhythms are posited as central, these are not unproblematically reduced to physiology and anatomy, nor are they shackled to economic determinants, for the body is inevitably a *text*: a function of semiotic and narrative encodings. Thus, although some French feminists are more concerned with material economic conditions and others with psychological and affective structures, their preoccupations often coalesce in attempts to identify and interrogate both obvious and latent connections between the social domain and the psyche, social change and individual transformation. Moreover, in different ways, both varieties stress that signifiers such as *femininity* and *masculinity* only gain meaning in the context of specific epistemological and economic formations as effects of performativity, and that identities which do not conform to dominant matrices of intelligibility (e.g. heterosexual ones) are automatically stigmatized as Other.

THE BOOK AT A GLANCE

The book's sections may be read sequentially and, where appropriate, links and cross-references between chapters are highlighted. However, the book also lends itself to a non-linear approach, insofar as each chapter has been conceived of so as to constitute a free-standing unit or *block*.

Chapter 1, French Feminist Theory: Backgrounds and Contexts provides a historical overview that examines protofeminist perspectives spanning the Middle Ages to the Enlightenment and the 1789 Revolution, the legacy of nineteenth-century feminism and the fight for female enfranchisement culminating in the suffrage reform of 1944. This aspect of the discussion establishes the book's historical dimension by drawing attention to developments and repositionings in the field of French feminism with reference to changing cultural and political scenarios. It then considers the relationship between the notional political power supposedly granted by those historical developments and the actual personal power of individuals, with close reference to the doctrine of Existentialism, Jean-Paul Sartre's notion of *engagement* and the philosophy of Simone de Beauvoir. Issues of political and personal power are further evaluated with reference to group manifestations of feminist theory and practice. Emphasis is laid on the impact of *les événements* of 1968 upon the emergence of the *Mouvement de Libération des Femmes* (MLF) and its plural groupings and positions. Moving on to examine the intellectual contexts developing in the post-1968 years, the chapter subsequently highlights points of contact between French feminist theory and structuralist, post-structuralist and psychoanalytic discourses proposing radical critiques of traditional approaches to concepts of meaning, consciousness, truth and the very significance of being human: primarily, the deconstructive approach to textuality; post-Freudian readings of subjectivity; post-Marxist models of power and ideology. Connections are thereby set up between the range of theories grouped under the heading 'Structuralism, Poststructuralism and Psychoanalysis' and the issues of political action and intellectual engagement discussed earlier. The opening chapter then proceeds to consider developments in French feminism from the 1970s to the present, drawing attention to its bifurcation into the *materialist/social* trend and the *linguistic/psychoanalytic* trend. French feminist theory's relation to the controversial concept of *post-feminism* is addressed in the closing part of this chapter.

Chapter 2, Sexual and Gendered Identities concentrates on the multifarious strategies through which gender, sexuality and related roles and positions are regulated and through which they may be quizzed and diversified. In the first segment of the chapter, traditional approaches to *sex* as an embodied being's putatively natural essence, in contrast with *gender* as the socialized manifestation of biological difference, are assessed and questioned. This is done in the light of deconstructive and denaturalizing interventions pointing to the constructedness of *all* levels of gendered and sexual identity. The inscription of varyingly asymmetrical, oppressive and exploitative power relations in the sex/gender map is investigated further in the following segments of the chapter with reference to materialist and psychoanalytic positions, and with illustrations from economic, medical, legal and anthropological discourses.

Chapter 3, Language and the Subject examines the specifically symbolic dimensions of sexual and gendered identities by investigating the relationship between linguistic structures and subjectivity: that is to say, the strategies through which language fashions and encultures individuals and collectivities and thereby maintains a culture's codes and conventions. The chapter engages with both feminist agendas that aim at exposing the sexist bias of patriarchal language from a sociological viewpoint, and psychoanalytic theories that seek to expose the limitations of patriarchal language and open up spaces for imaginative linguistic experimentation and transgression.

Chapter 4, Patriarchal Institutions explores the ways in which the encoding of gendered and sexual roles relies on specific discursive formations for their self-perpetuation and for the disciplining of the socialized subject. The institutions examined in this context encompass both microcosmic and macro-cosmic forms of organization: the family, the market, the legal system, the realm of rituals, the world of education. All these forms are seen to contribute crucially to the shaping of subjectivity in the name of crystallized patriarchal norms, and of related conceptions of acceptability and deviance.

Chapter 5, Writing and the Body develops some of the positions outlined in *Chapter 3* by focusing, specifically, on the relationship between textuality and corporeality. The chapter asks whether it is desirable or indeed viable to associate certain forms of textual productivity with particular genders and sexes. Concurrently, it emphasizes the need to move beyond deterministic connections between an author's gender and sexual preferences and her/his text in order to grapple with the sexuality/sexualities of the text itself. In assessing the relationship between subjectivity and creativity, this chapter also consistently explores the controversial concept of *écriture féminine*, or feminine writing, as one of the most famous theorizations within French feminist thought of the relationship between writing and the body.

Chapter 6, Power, Race and the Stranger addresses the confluence of sexist ideologies geared towards the commodification of the gendered subject with definitions of racial and ethnic alterity and colonial agendas. Concurrently, it investigates the psychological connotations of foreignness as an internal condition producing differences not just *between* but also *within* subjects. Three main areas within which French feminists of diverse provenance and orientation have approached those issues are discussed: the sociological exploration of parallels in the genesis and practice of racism and sexism; the theorization of the affective dimension of cultural displacement; the elaboration of feminist perspectives on race and postcolonialism in non-metropolitan France, especially by Algerian writers.

The *Conclusion* provides a rounding-off overview of the principal perspectives and arguments explored in the main body of the book, moving from the historical contextualization of French feminism, through the latter's relationship with a range of philosophical positions, to specific themes and concerns discussed in *Chapters 2–6*. This section ends with a brief assessment of the reception of French feminist thought in anglophone circles. It is noted, in particular, that the psychoanalytic/linguistic strand has attracted English-speaking theorists more consistently and broadly than the materialist/social strand. Indeed, the work of materialist feminists since the early 1980s has been by and large neglected within anglophone debates due to a reductionist tendency to associate French feminism almost exclusively with the writings of Cixous, Irigaray and Kristeva. Although this receptive tendency may be ascribed to the psychoanalytic strand's more emphatically challenging thematic and stylistic traits, it is necessary to reconsider the Anglo-American world's reductivism.

Although it would be inane to embark on a detailed comparative analysis of French and Anglo-American feminist theories in the present context, the *Appendix* provided at the end of this volume seeks to highlight points of contact and collusion between French feminisms of both varieties and Anglo-American feminisms, through a schematic analysis of major themes in French theory that have also been dealt with, in diverse ways, in anglophone contexts.

CHAPTER I

French Feminist Theory: Backgrounds and Contexts

BEGINNINGS

a woman should realize that if she marries a rich man more readily than a poor one, and desires her husband more for his possessions than for herself, she is offering herself for sale. (Héloïse 1101–64; quoted in Radice 1974: 114)

Many different men – and learned men among them – have been and are ... inclined to express both in speaking and in their treatises and writings ... many wicked insults about women and their behaviour. ... it seems that they all speak from one and the same mouth. ... And the simple, noble ladies, following the example of suffering God commands, have cheerfully suffered the great attacks which ... have been wrongfully and sinfully perpetrated against women. ... Now it is time for their just cause to be taken from the Pharaoh's hands. (Christine de Pisan 1365–c.1430, quoted in Richards 1994)

suppose we believed that the Scriptures indeed order woman to submit to the authority of man because she cannot think as well as he can, see here the absurdity that would follow: women would be worthy of having been made in the likeness of the Creator, worthy of taking part in the holy Eucharist, of sharing the mysteries of the Redemption, Paradise, worthy of the vision, even possession, of God, but not of the status and privileges of men. Wouldn't we be saying that men are more precious and sacred than all these things, and wouldn't that be the most grievous blasphemy? (Marie de Gournay 1565–1645, quoted in *Sunshine for Women* 1999)

The protofeminist assertions of writers such as the ones quoted above bear witness to the existence of oppositional voices in France since at least the Middle Ages. Christine de Pisan's contribution to early feminist philosophy is especially remarkable, if assessed in the context of the virulently disparaging evaluations of femininity – disseminated by both the Church and the aristocracy – that pervaded medieval France no less than other European cultures of the time. The notion of woman as a close associate of the Devil and hence a certain gateway to perdition was, to some extent, opposed by the ethos of *l'amour courtois* (courtly love) that spread from Provence to numerous parts of Western Europe in the second half of the twelfth century. This ethos accorded woman, narrowly conceived of as an aristocratic lady of unparalleled charm, superiority over the male lover prepared to undertake endless trials for her sake. Interestingly, as Eileen Power observes in *Medieval Women*, 'the counter-doctrine of the superiority of women' enshrining the world-view of courtly circles developed in parallel with the idolatry of Christ's mother: 'The cult of the Virgin and the cult of chivalry grew together' (Power [1975] 2001: 13) and the association between the idealized female of polished society and Mary was asserted 'in the refrain of French ballads', namely, 'En ciel un dieu, en terre une déesse' (p. 15).

However, as Power also stresses, even though 'a theory which regarded the worship of the lady as next to that of God and conceived her as the mainspring of brave deeds ... must have done something to counteract the prevalent doctrine of woman's inferiority' (p. 19), the philosophy of life advocated by *l'amour courtois* 'played a greater part in literature than it ever did in life' (p. 20). Moreover, the literary trend inspired by courtly love enjoyed a relatively limited lifespan to be replaced, in a monumental backlash, by literary forms such as the *fabliaux* – where women feature primarily as nagging and unfaithful wives, pernicious hags and scheming wenches – as well as 'didactic poems detailing the vices of women, *blastanges des fames, epystles des fames, blasones des fames*, which are apt to resolve themselves into a somewhat jejune game of mud-slinging' (p. 22). Furthermore, when approached from the perspective of contemporary psychoanalytic theory of a Lacanian orientation, the conception and practice of *l'amour courtois* does not valorize women at the expense of men but actually celebrates men's superiority in a circuitous fashion. Indeed, one of the main axioms of courtly love consists of the idea that the idealized lady is precious because she is unattainable and that the male lover should be inspired precisely by her unavailability. Rendering the lady accessible would devalue both her and the nature of the tasks to which the knight submits himself in compliance with her more or less capricious demands. Hence, if it is the case, as Lacanian theory argues, that all subjects, both male and female ones, are locked in a destiny of unfulfilment predicated on their inability to reach the true object of their desire, and that this makes both men and women inevitably vulnerable and lacking, courtly love could be said to offer male subjects a consolatory fantasy: if they cannot obtain the desired lady, this is not because of a deficiency on men's part but because they will *only* value that object *as long as* she is unattainable. Unfulfilment is glorified as an achievement intrinsic to the rules of the game, not merely tolerated as a failing.

De Pisan praised certain aspects of *l'amour courtois* as far more appreciative of feminine qualities than either the Church or the gentry or indeed increasingly popular literary forms cherished by the blossoming bourgeoisie. At the same time, she also engaged in a critique of religious assumptions often indistinguishable from blind superstition. Thus she was arguably the first woman to take a leading role in the controversies surrounding medieval definitions of femininity, thereby paving the way for the efforts of subsequent generations. By the time Marie de Gournay was writing, at the turn of the seventeenth century, a literary tradition of defences of women's rights, frequently emphasizing women's lack of access to education, had been steadily developing. De Gournay's demand for recognition of the spurious basis of sexual inequality was echoed, about fifty years later, by the writings of François Poullain, possibly the first author in French to associate women's oppression with patriarchy, where it is argued that all areas of intellectual and professional activity, including political and juridical leadership, ought to be made open to women.

If the Renaissance was an era of fervid support for the advancement of women's causes in certain areas of social life, it is nonetheless vital to realize that problematic asymmetries remained rampant. As Claire Goldberg Moses observes:

> from the time of the Renaissance, among the aristocracy and the emerging middle class (both of whom had political and economic rights to preserve), inequality weighed heavily on women. ... With the simultaneous growth of the modern bureaucratic state and the capitalist economy came the need for well-trained secular personnel. Education came to be highly valued, and the centuries-old exclusion of women from the universities took on a new, more powerful significance. ... An increased number of years was deemed necessary to prepare boys for the expanded responsibilities of male adulthood. The same, however, was not true of girls. (Goldberg Moses 1984: 3)

The debate on the *querelle des femmes* (woman question) gained further momentum with the Enlightenment, some of its most prestigious representatives being more than willing to acknowledge the circumstantial, rather than constitutional or metaphysical, character of women's presumed inferiority. Goldberg Moses usefully summarizes this scenario:

Voltaire wrote that women's inferiority was contingent upon circumstances, not upon natural necessity. Montesquieu symbolized human
tyranny in the person of a young Persian girl falsely presumed to be happy
in her place in the king's harem. ... Diderot, in his treatise on public
education, pointed out that improved education for boys would be in vain
if effective reforms were not also carried out for the training of girls.
D'Alembert defended women's right to an education equal to men's. (p. 8)

One of the most ambivalent and controversial contributions to the *querelle*, as
attested to by feminist theorists as historically and geographically diverse as
Mary Wollstonecraft and Michèle Le Doeuff, lies in Jean-Jacques Rousseau's
positions. These may seem to militate in favour of women by commending
the latter's unique societal roles. However, these roles are firmly confined to
the private sphere of the family, to a woman's function as a nurturing mother
and obligations as a devoted companion. Moreover, Goldberg Moses
observes, 'women's maternal responsibilities ... required their exclusion
from the civil, political, and economic activities that Rousseau championed
for all men' (pp. 4–5).

The Revolution of 1789 affected significantly further developments in
French feminism. Whereas prior to 1789 female emancipation was connected
almost exclusively with the extension and amelioration of educational opportunities, the Revolution ushered in a far more comprehensive feminist
agenda, whose demands included the right to full participation in political
life and leadership and the advocacy of equality in both the family and the
world of work. It is at this time that women first began to organize themselves into societies and clubs and to circulate revolutionary pamphlets
promoting their causes. Yet, the 'memory of the Revolution and the Terror'
led several post-1789 governments to obstruct 'the right to free expression of
new ideas' and, in these contexts, 'it was truly dangerous to espouse feminist
views' (p. ix). With Louis Napoleon Bonaparte's rise to power (1799–1815),
repressive penal codes exacerbated women's predicament by dictating that
they be 'legally grouped amongst "children and mental patients"'; by
asserting that a '"husband owes protection to his wife; a wife owes obedience
to her husband"'; by curbing the 'right to equal inheritance'; and by forbidding women 'to sign contracts or undertake work without [the] husband's
permission' ('Comparing American and French Feminism' 1998). Despite
this pervasively reactionary climate, in 1808 Charles Fourier 'put the corner-
stone of ... feminist thought into place' by maintaining that the emancipation
of women was bound to play a vital part in the evolution of human life and
society: 'social progress and changes from one era to the next are brought
about in proportion to the progress of women toward freedom, and social

decline is brought about in proportion to the decrease in women's freedom' (Goldberg Moses 1984: 92).

Fourier is often held to have coined the term *féminisme* but, according to Karen Offen:

> its origins are still uncertain. It only began to be used widely in France in the early 1890s and then principally as a synonym for women's emancipation. The first self-proclaimed 'feminist' in France was the women's suffrage advocate Hubertine Auclert, who from at least 1882 on used the term in her periodical, *La Citoyenne*, to describe herself and her associates. The word gained currency following discussion in the French press of the first self-proclaimed 'feminist' congress in Paris, which was sponsored in May 1892 by Eugénie Potonie-Pierre and her colleagues in the women's group *Solidarité*, who shortly thereafter juxtaposed *féminisme* with *masculinisme*. (Offen 1988)

However, multiple trends soon emerged and further problematized the applicability of the term "feminism". Among them were 'familial feminists', 'integral feminists', 'Christian feminists', 'radical feminists', 'male feminists', 'socialist feminists' and 'bourgeois feminists' (ibid.). The diversity of the twentieth-century *Mouvement de Libération des Femmes*, examined later in this chapter, could be seen, to some extent, as an inheritance of this initial plurality of viewpoints.

Following the Napoleonic backlash, it was not until the 1830s that feminism began to re-emerge as an active component of French public life. Its principal proponents, at this juncture, advocated mainly a utopian socialist programme with pacifist and internationalist priorities. Especially influential, and indeed controversial, were the Saint-Simonians, the socialist group inspired by Claude Henri, Comte de Saint-Simon, and led by Barthélemy Prosper Enfantin. According to Goldberg Moses, 'although Saint-Simonian theory encouraged women to believe themselves equal to men, the reality did not uphold the ideology', for women were still assigned a 'subordinate role within a male-dominated social change movement that touted egalitarianism'. It was this contradiction that spurred several women to organize themselves into 'a separate and autonomous movement' (Goldberg Moses 1984: 54). One of the most important results of this move was the constitution, in 1832, of the newspaper *La Tribune des femmes*, whose policy it was to publish solely articles written by women and to use only the contributors' first names in a desire to reject patriarchal and patrilineal labels: 'this was likely the first female collective venture in history whose purpose was specifically and exclusively feminist' writes Goldberg Moses. 'It was certainly the first consciously separatist feminist venture' (p. 63). No less significant was Flora Tristan's project, whose pursuit of sexual equality ran parallel to the determination to link 'women's emancipation to an organized working-class movement' (p. 116).

French feminism benefited considerably, in the preliminary stages of the revolution of 1848, from the elimination of existing restrictions on the press and on the right to assemble, since this move enabled women to reorganize themselves and to divulge their positions. Particularly significant was the foundation of the first feminist daily paper, *Voix des femmes*. However, brutally repressive measures soon implemented by the government of the time occasioned yet another severe backlash: women 'were forbidden to participate in political clubs' (p. 145) and it 'would be almost twenty years before feminists would regroup' (p. 149). One of the principal obstacles to female emancipation was the rampant opposition to women's suffrage. The views of the historian Jules Michelet (1798–1874) were particularly influential, in this regard, in maintaining that women were peculiarly susceptible to clerical domination and that their enfranchisement, therefore, would augment the power of the Church. Alarmingly, anti-suffrage positions were as widespread among left-wing men as they were among the more conservative ranks. A notorious case in point is that of the libertarian socialist Pierre-Joseph Proudhon, whose opposition to the female vote had important repercussions. Indeed, as J. F. McMillan observes, Proudhon was 'to exercise a considerable ideological influence on the development of the labour movement in France' and it is hence hardly surprising that 'French women found it difficult to mobilize left-wing opinion in favour of the cause of women's suffrage' (McMillan, 'Opposition to Women's Suffrage'). In spite of the brutally repressive measures following the proletarian uprising of 1848, and rendered fiercer still by the election of Louis Napoleon as President, suffragists were not entirely silenced. Jeanne Deroin and Pauline Roland, most notably, bravely pursued the fight for women's civic and political rights in the face of increasingly reactionary forces that would eventually coerce the former into exile and consign the latter to a premature death in an Algerian prison camp.

From the late 1840s onwards, French feminists tended to place unprecedented emphasis on women's maternal responsibilities as an aspect of femininity that should no longer be used to justify woman's entrapment in familial and private duties but actually become the basis of her right to participate in the public domain: a mother may only adequately fulfil her function as an educator of the young if she herself is comprehensively educated and entitled to intervene in both civil and political activities. This development could be accused of fomenting reactionary positions by positing motherhood as a woman's uniquely distinguishing attribute and hence essentializing femininity with reference to restrictive categories of being. Moreover, the emphasis placed by that approach on family structures could be read as a corollary of a long-standing Catholic legacy frequently inimical to women's emancipation: 'France's Catholic heritage kept women in a dominated ... state. According to the Catholic view on marriage, the woman's primary responsibility is to her husband as both wife and mother.' The ongoing influence of Catholicism is borne out by the fact that in France, 'divorce is not an option until the nineteenth century' ('Comparing American and French Feminism' 1998).

Nevertheless, the reconceptualization of motherhood also constitutes an important element in the formulation of a distinctive approach to feminism which hinges, as Offen (1988) observes, on a fundamentally 'relational' model. Examined in the context of nineteenth-century France, this model proposed

> the primacy of a companionate, non-hierarchical, male-female couple as the basic unit of society, whereas individualist arguments posited the individual, irrespective of sex or gender, as the basic unit. Relational feminism emphasized women's rights *as women* (defined principally by their childbearing and/or nurturing capacities) in relation to men. It insisted on *women's* distinctive contributions in these roles to the broader society and made claims on the commonwealth on the basis of these contributions. By contrast, the individualist feminist tradition of argumentation emphasized more abstract concepts of individual human rights and celebrated the quest for personal independence. (ibid.)

Relational feminism could also be said to have paved the way for subsequent debates about the ideals of difference and equality (discussed later in this chapter) which still animate contemporary French theory. According to Offen, 'the key arguments of relational feminism culminated historically', in nineteenth-century French society, 'in the seemingly paradoxical doctrine of "equality in difference", or equity as distinct from equality'. Thus, while pursuing the ideal of non-hierarchical co-operation, relational feminism simultaneously underscores the existence of '*both* biological *and* cultural distinctions between the sexes', underlying their respective roles 'in the family and throughout society', which must be respected and fostered (ibid.).

According to Goldberg Moses, a major turning-point in the history of French feminism was the establishment of the Third Republic in 1870, for it was at this point that women became entitled to hold public meetings and lectures without government approval and to produce and circulate political publications: 'for the first time, feminist groups survived beyond their infancy to reach maturity' (Goldberg Moses 1984:197). However, we should not ignore the prospective burden of what still remained to be dismantled, even at a time of relative success for women: in particular, the harsh reality of their legal and civil marginalization. Indeed, though France had been so eager to acknowledge and glorify the *rights of man*, it was stubbornly reluctant to appreciate, let alone codify, those of woman: French female citizens did not obtain the right to vote, as we shall see, until April 1944. Furthermore, the Third Republic was by no means an unadulterated blessing for French women. An exhaustive account of its impact on the battle for female rights is supplied by Paul Smith, who documents women's paradoxical status as non-citizens in a culture proverbially devoted to the assertion of full citizenship for its male members (Smith 1996). According to McMillan, the Third Republic 'in no way favoured the cause of women's suffrage – rather the reverse. The contradiction between the Republican discourse on "liberty, equality and fraternity" and its hostility to votes for women remained as prevalent a feature of the Third Republic as it had been of the First and Second Republics' ('Opposition to Women's Suffrage'). The anticlerical argument promulgated by the likes of Michelet, combined with a renewed emphasis on the detriment to familial responsibilities likely to result from women's involvement in the public sphere, produced a pervasive anti-feminist sentiment. Between the closing years of the nineteenth century and the opening years of the twentieth century, politicians and satirists conspired to disseminate a stereotypical image of the average suffragist as quintessentially unwomanly, un-French and ultimately aberrant. Even the Socialist Party, despite its professed commitment to the advancement of the rights of women, saw their enfranchisement as a marginal issue, remaining principally interested in a reformation of the system of proportional representation that would benefit the male electorate.

In the 1870s, an especially charismatic female voice, that of Louise Michèle, emerged in the context of the Commune of Paris (18 March to 28 May 1871), the self-governing formation voted in by 300,000 French citizens eager to challenge the authority of the Versailles government and its largely conservative Assembly. After a series of varyingly violent skirmishes, the Communard rump was eventually trapped and 35,000 of its members were executed, leaving behind a legacy of bitter disappointment. Michèle, an inspired and inspiring anarchist, was Secretary for the Improvement of Working Women during the Commune and was steadfast in her conviction that female emancipation was conditional upon women's ability to remove the physical and emotional shackles that had for so long restricted both their public and private functions:

In the street she [woman] is merchandize. In the convents, where she hides as if in a tomb, ignorance binds her, and rules ... pulverize her heart and brain. In the world she bends under mortification. In her home, her burdens crush her. ... Men, ... although they appear to help us, were always content with just the appearance. (Flick, 'Louise Michèle')

It seemed likely that women would finally obtain the vote in 1919, when a suffrage bill was passed by the Chamber of Deputies with a significant majority. Yet, this was rejected by the Senate, after much procrastination, in 1922. Renewed concern with the issue of women's suffrage in the aftermath of the First World War was related to a recognition of the vital roles played by females during the conflict, in their assumption of key economic and morale-sustaining responsibilities. The Senate's decision taken in 1922, however, indicated that the war had not aided women's cause. It was peremptorily declared that any argument based on the right to a reward for services given to the country was a spurious claim, for patriotism can only be genuine and praiseworthy if it is independent of any ulterior motives.

The Chamber of Deputies passed further bills in 1925 and 1927, only to be blocked again by the Senate. Notoriously vociferous in his opposition to women's appropriation of civic duties was the senator Pierre Marraud: 'The woman of the Latin race,' he maintained, 'does not feel, has not developed, in the same way as the woman of the Anglo-Saxon or Germanic races. ... As a person, she is generally more absorbed in her Church, whose dogmatism she does not dispute. It is perfectly reasonable, then, that her legal status should be different' (quoted in McMillan, 'The Coming of Women's Suffrage'). In spite of the Chamber's repeated expressions of support for electoral reforms that would guarantee votes for women, the Senate's anti-enfranchisement stance remained unfaltering well into the 1930s. Nonetheless, as McMillan points out, the Senate's attitude is not the only factor to be held responsible for the ongoing resistance to women's assumption of political rights. In fact, it is also important to take into consideration certain ideological positions deeply ingrained in the very nature of the Third Republic: 'a regime which prided itself on its commitment to democratic values' but was not willing, as noted above, to extend this commitment to the issue of universal suffrage and, in fact, saw it as 'a threat to the Republic itself'. In this respect, it could be argued that women were the principal casualties of fossilized political agendas uncritically devoted 'to defending the status quo' and of 'the sexism that permeated the Republican political tradition from its inception' (ibid.). According to Steven C. Hause, women's unprivileged position under the Third Republic is attested to by the 'long list of *revendications*' put forward by feminists. These included:

the opening of all schools and careers to women, with equal pay for equal work; the abolition of paternal authority within marriage and the family in favour of equal rights (for example, the right to be a guardian); drastic revisions of the Civil Code to end the treatment of adult women as minors and to permit them full civil rights (for exampe, the right to serve on juries). (Hause 1987: 98)

French women eventually won the vote on 21 April 1944 as a result of deliberations conducted in Algiers, where General Charles de Gaulle had established his headquarters following the Allied landings in North Africa of 1942, by a Consultative Assembly responsible for planning the constitutional reforms to be implemented after France's liberation from the Germans. According to some historians, female enfranchisement should be seen as a reward for the crucial contribution made by women to the anti-Nazi Resistance. Others consider it a gift dispensed personally by de Gaulle as a means of securing the foundation of a genuinely *new* Republic. Both hypotheses remain open to scrutiny, since no incontrovertible evidence for the correctness of either is, to date, available. However, as Siân Reynolds stresses, it is undeniable that de Gaulle was at least partly responding to 'international pressure ... for France to prove its democratic credentials. Since the pressure came from Britain and the United States, where women's suffrage was not in doubt, the non-enfranchisement of women would almost certainly be seen as a black mark.' As for women's participation in the Resistance, indubitable as its significance is, it cannot be unproblematically assumed that it affected profoundly the suffragist cause. 'The small number of women formally honoured by male colleagues for Resistance work,' writes Reynolds, 'sits uneasily with the readiness of the same men to explain the granting of the vote entirely in terms of this argument' (Reynolds 1996).

According to Hause, it remains important to assess French women's enfranchisement against a protracted and convoluted historical trajectory, rather than as an isolated phenomenon, and to resist the temptation to view it as an unproblematic triumph:

When women's suffrage in France was proclaimed by Charles de Gaulle in 1944, the myth that modern wars emancipated women received another boost. But the history of French women exposes the myth for what it is. The liberation of French women has taken place only over *la longue durée*. The First World War was certainly an important episode in that evolution, but not a climacteric for women, the gift of Mars. The ancient argument of attributing change *tam Marte quam Minerva* must be inverted: changes over *la longue durée* owe more to the accumulated wisdom of Minerva and the hard work of those who applied it. (Hause 1987: 113)

The paltry number of women elected to parliamentary seats for several years after their obtaining the vote should be taken as a further warning against the supposition that access to patriarchal institutions is sufficient unto itself to guarantee an equitable distribution of power. As Reynolds suggests, 'By assuming that "granting the vote" solved all ills, ... the flaws originating in the man-made system have not been analyzed ... . The inner sanctum itself is not yet visibly the home of a double-sexed democracy' (Reynolds 1996).

EXISTENTIALISM AND SIMONE DE BEAUVOIR

An insight into certain key moments in the history of French feminism can help us understand its significance in terms of political action and praxis. It is also important, however, to identify the philosophical and theoretical underpinnings of French feminism. Politics and theory are at all times interconnected, and it is therefore vital to grasp the function of the political as both a practice directed at redefining power relations between the sexes and a theory, or rather a range of theories, implying particular ways of approaching patriarchal cultures and of envisaging possibilities of change. Especially influential, in the development of French feminist thought, has been the tradition of Existentialism: a *theoretical* position that is also eminently *political*, particularly in its articulation by Jean-Paul Sartre.

Sartre's conception of human existence can be summarized boldly by recourse to three fundamental premises:

1 *Existence precedes Essence*
2 *Man is nothing but what he makes of himself*
3 *Man exists and only afterwards defines himself*

Existentialism as formulated by Sartre posits as a basic assumption the idea that man is defined by what he does and by how he acts. Sartre is deeply suspicious of essentialist conceptions of human nature resting on the possibility of ideal conditions which transcend the limitations of existence. In fact, he argues that life consists, at all junctures, of concrete choices which we operate under conditions of finitude. We make decisions and these decisions constitute our nature: reality and existence are thus expressed by action and by engagement. It is worth pointing out that in French, the word *engagement* carries multiple connotations. For example, it can be defined as "commitment" or as "engagement, a taking on". In conjunction with *sans, engagement* is defined as "without obligation". The concept of *consciousness* is also central to the Existentialist world-view: consciousness is not a free-standing faculty independent of a person's material context but is, in fact, always *about* something in the world. In other words, human beings are not detached observers *of* the world, but actors *in* the world.

According to Walter Kaufman, Existentialism is characterized primarily by a 'refusal to belong to any school of thought, the repudiation of the adequacy of any body of beliefs whatever, and especially of systems, and a marked dissatisfaction with traditional philosophy as superficial, academic, and remote from life' (Kaufman 1975: 12). This position often results in the adoption, as pivotal elements of Existentialism's lexicon, of terms such as "the absurd", "dread", "nothingness", "nausea" and "anguish". Anguish, specifically, refers to the recognition that humans cannot unproblematically derive their values from *the world as it is*: situations and objects have the meanings and values we invest them with according to circumstances that inevitably alter from moment to moment, and are therefore themselves subject to continual change. The only aspects of our humanity that do not change lie with the knowledge of certain death and with the obligation to go on making moral decisions without any external guarantee of their validity. We are *condemned* to freedom and to responsibility without any recourse to attenuating alibis. Human beings, therefore, are ongoing projects perpetually engaged in reinventing their humanity. It is by this realization, in Alfred Cobban's assessment, that Sartre himself was led to Marxism and politics: 'each man is his own self-created and self-perpetuating hell. Merely to be is to deny life; to exist is to act, to choose freely; yet freedom of choice is what man cannot have – all he can do is to engage himself in the world, as Sartre himself did in left-wing politics' (Cobban 1965: 232).

The French feminist philosopher most overtly indebted to Existentialism is Simone de Beauvoir. The publication of her seminal text, *The Second Sex*, in 1949 is undeniably a major turning-point in the history of twentieth-century French feminist theory. However, as Toril Moi points out, when this work made its appearance, Beauvoir 'was convinced that the advent of socialism alone would put an end to the oppression of women and consequently considered herself a socialist, not a feminist' (Moi 1985: 91). It was not until 1972, when Beauvoir joined the *Mouvement de Libération des Femmes* and embraced what she deemed an unprecedently radical ethos, that she described herself as a feminist and proclaimed that 'we must fight for the situation of women, here and now, before our dreams of socialism come true' (Beauvoir 1984: 32).

The Second Sex offers a social constructivist depiction of gender, famously encapsulated by the assertion 'One is not born a woman; one becomes one' (Beauvoir 1973: 301). This perspective is based on the notion that human beings are transformed into specifically gendered entities as a result of patri-

archal requirements and that women, in particular, are categorized as deficient creatures incapable of matching the norm embodied by masculinity:
'humanity is male and man defines woman not in herself but as relative to
him; she is not regarded as an autonomous being. ... He is the Subject, he is
the Absolute – she is the Other' (Beauvoir 2000a: 8). Following G. W. F.
Hegel's theorization of the master-slave relationship, Beauvoir emphasizes,
however, that masculinity cannot convincingly assert itself as an absolute
norm as long as it defines itself *in relation* to an Other: 'the subject can be
posed only in being opposed – he sets himself up as the essential, as opposed
to the ... inessential' (p. 9). In other words, the master relies on the existence
of the slave as a means of perpetuating his own dominant status.

The philosophical underpinning of *The Second Sex* is Jean-Paul Sartre's
Existentialism:

> our perspective is that of existentialist ethics. Every subject plays his part
> as such specifically through exploits or projects that serve as a mode of
> transcendence; he achieves liberty only through a continual reaching out
> toward other liberties. There is no justification for present existence other
> than its expansion into an indefinitely open future. Every time transcen-
> dence falls back into immanence, stagnation, there is a degradation of exis-
> tence. (p. 18)

Adapting Sartre's conceptual framework to the condition of women, Beauvoir
argues in *The Second Sex* that 'patriarchal ideology presents woman as immanence, man as transcendence' (Moi 1985: 92). Deprived of the right to an
independent subjectivity, woman has been insistently objectified and, more
alarmingly still, led to internalize this disabling world-view and to exist in a
state of *bad faith*, as Sartre would term it. Women, that is, evade the freedom
which, as human beings, ought to be their supreme aspiration. Chris Marvin
corroborates Beauvoir's debt to Existentialism in maintaining that *The
Second Sex* draws on Sartre's 'conception of human beings as creatures who
are free. Freedom of choice ... is the criterion for morality and immorality in
one's acts' (Marvin 2000). Relegated to the status of nebulous items incapable
of transcending the sphere of brute matter, women are often responsible for
perpetuating their objectification and victimization by patriarchy: for
example, by introjecting stereotypical versions of femininity that reduce
them to capricious and frivolous playthings. Moreover, women are insistently
encouraged to look for a modicum of meaning in their relationships with
men, primarily those they marry and those they give birth to. In fact,
Beauvoir maintains, those relationships negate woman's significance: while
'Genuine love ought to be founded on the mutual recognition of two liber-

ties' (Beauvoir 2000b: 33), the woman who 'abandons herself to love to *save herself*' paradoxically '*denies herself* utterly in the end' by surrendering to the phantasmatic lure of an 'idolatrous' sentiment (p. 28). As for motherhood, Beauvoir questions radically the so-called naturalness of the maternal instinct: children are indubitably *obligations*, but there can be 'nothing *natural* in such an obligation: nature can never dictate a moral choice; this implies an engagement, a promise to be carried out' (Beauvoir 2000c: 23).

Le Doeuff poses the question of whether Beauvoir actually needed to resort to Existentialism to expose patriarchy's operations and whether the employment of this theoretical frame of reference might, in fact, have impeded her insights into the condition of women. It is possible, for instance, that Beauvoir's dependence on the Sartrean notion of bad faith as a means of accounting for women's willing subjection to the oppressor might have ignored other sociopolitical factors contributing to women's predicament. In questioning the validity of the Existentialist model, Le Doeuff concurrently criticizes what she perceives as a lack of 'positive role models for women' and of 'the idea of a collective women's movement' in *The Second Sex* (Le Doeuff 2000: 47). Indeed, Beauvoir repeatedly stresses women's helpless scattering among men: 'They live dispersed among the males, attached ... to certain men ... more firmly than they are to other women. If they belong to the bourgeoisie, they feel solidarity with men of that class, not with proletarian women; if they are white, their allegiance is to white men, not to Negro women' (Beauvoir 2000a: 11). According to Le Doeuff, Beauvoir's position stems directly from the Existentialist view, according to which 'to create is "to found the world anew", to do which one must "unequivocally assume the status of a being who has freedom". It is thus essential to tell oneself, "I am the first and only one to do this".' The feminist voices of subsequent generations, 'including those who paid tribute to her', depart from Beauvoir's perspective by taking the view that '"fortunately, I am not the only one, nor the first here; but I am certainly here, all the same"' (Le Doeuff 2000: 47).

It is noteworthy, however, as Mary McGreevy asserts, that while embracing Sartre's ethics Beauvoir simultaneously evaluates the concept of freedom with specific reference to 'the viewpoint of women, who, she feels, are situated in particular circumstances and have relationships with others that circumscribe their possible freedom'. In other words, women are limited by concrete situations that make their own freedom conceivable 'only in relation to the freedom of others' (McGreevy 1997). Thus, although it is important to acknowledge Beauvoir's indebtedness to Sartrean positions, it is also crucial to appreciate her independence, and indeed divergence, from the latter. Elaine Stavro-Pearce emphasizes this point by proposing that Beauvoir's writings often evince closer affinities to the theories of another Existentialist philosopher, and fellow student of Beauvoir's at the Sorbonne – namely Maurice Merleau-Ponty – than they do to Sartre's output. This is borne out by Beauvoir's emphasis on the embodied and situated character of consciousness and subjectivity, whereby experience and perception are never wholly detachable from the membrane of flesh and blood in which human agency is embroiled, nor indeed from the material contexts in which they occur. According to Stavro-Pearce, 'her notion of the situated self, or body in situation, sees agency as embodied – culturally, socially and economically conditioned; consequently, free choice and freedom are enmeshed in relations with others and emerge out of these relations' (Stavro-Pearce 1999).

Sartre himself posits selfhood as a situated consciousness in maintaining that the subject does not exist prior to its recognition by others in specific circumstances. Nevertheless, he concomitantly marginalizes the corporeal realm by arguing that for the subject to be authentically free, it must be able to transcend 'the non-conscious material world, the social world and body' as 'sources of stagnation and immanence' (ibid.). 'The body', for Sartre, 'is ... the obstacle to be surpassed in order to be in the world' (Sartre 1978: 430). Beauvoir moves beyond Sartre's ethics by acknowledging the inherently gendered status of social and historical relations and by insisting that the constitution of woman as man's Other affects vitally any resulting notion of, and opportunity for, freedom. Whereas Sartre's universalized subject strives to transcend the corporeal domain, Beauvoir's gendered subject is inevitably caught in a web of material and culturally contingent structures and relations of power and has to recognize that freedom is not a context-independent, transhistorical achievement, since 'all acts of freedom occur in a situation or field that is not individually created and not all situations are alike' (Stavro-Pearce 1999). Ultimately, invoking a purely voluntarist philosophy encouraging women to *will* their emancipation would be naive and misleading: we must first address the question of whether a subject is *capable* of willing anything at all within conditional parameters.

1968 AND BEYOND: THE MLF AND ITS DISCONTENTS

The Sartrean notion of *engagement* underpins the political positioning of subsequent generations of French feminists, as evinced by the genesis of the feminist movement, or *Mouvement de Libération des Femmes*, in the context of the momentous events (*les événements*) of May 1968. Indeed, the movement endeavoured, in a variety of ways, to translate the aims of feminism as a philosophy devoted to the promulgation of women's rights into a concrete intervention in the revolutionary politics of the time. As Moi points out, 1968 produced 'an exuberant political optimism among left-wing intellectuals in France' and it is in 'this politicized intellectual climate, dominated by various shades of Marxism ... that the first French feminist groups were formed' (Moi 1985: 95). Kelly Oliver likewise comments on the emergence of the movement in an atmosphere of revolutionary fervour and faith in the possibility of radical social transformation: 'In the early 1970s the women's movement in France coalesced ... into the *Mouvement de Libération des Femmes*' (MLF), largely as a result of 'a sense of optimism about the possibility and necessity of change' that pervaded the 'monumental protests, riots, and strikes on college campuses' of May 1968. The movement's actual name 'was first used by the media reporting on a group of women who were arrested for putting a wreath on the Tomb of the Unknown Soldier at the Arc de Triomphe and dedicating it to a person more unknown than him, his wife' (Oliver 2000: viii–ix).

Right from the movement's inception, it was clear that the MLF did not constitute a homogeneous political formation but rather a galaxy of varyingly related or divergent groups. Three main issues have been causes for disagreement within the MLF practically since its emergence: (1) the relationship between the advocacy of women's rights and the programmes and missions of the political left, leading to tensions between those who promote the coalescence of feminism and socialism and those who view existing parties as inimical to the advancement of feminist causes; (2) diverging perspectives on the very meaning of "feminism" as either emancipatory or restrictive; (3) the conflict between the contrasting ideals of equality and difference. Let us consider each issue in more detail.

1. A number of women who joined the MLF in the wake of 1968 had belonged to left-wing political groups. However, many of them rapidly began to sense that male revolutionaries were insensitive to the specificity of women's conditions and that this was mirrored by their treatment of their female associates in 'traditional and patronizing ways' (Duchen 1987: 111). According to Duchen, the men in question tended to regard capitalism as the ultimate evil to be eradicated if a fairer society was to be achieved, whereas increasingly disaffected women felt that they had to assess their position 'not only in relation to capitalism', as the *Elles Voient Rouge* collective stresses, 'but also in relation to sexism (including the sexism of our comrades in the party)' (p. 116). It became more and more obvious that women had to face the effects of multifarious forms of exploitation perpetrated in tandem by capitalism and patriarchy, in order to move beyond abstract principles of equality and towards a critical recognition of their

specific demands. Concurrently, the patriarchal strain inherent in the attitudes of male socialists towards the issue of women's emancipation became a pressing concern. According to Eliane Viennot, the persistence of gender asymmetries in the context of party politics is borne out by the harrowing transition from 'the era of "capable women", or the dream of high office' – where a limited number of women are allowed access to power, thereby sealing the relegation of *other* women to the status of 'an anonymous, massive, shapeless, transparent group' (Viennot 1987: 125) – to the suspicion that 'women leaders ... merely serve to hide the oppression of other women' (p. 126) and, relatedly, a backlash based on the conviction that 'all [feminists] ever do is criticize', that 'all they want is power' (p. 129).

2. Diverging attitudes to the use of "feminism" as a viable denomination have, in some cases, resulted in its downright rejection. *Psych et Po*, for instance, 'declared itself against "feminism"' (Fallaize 1993: 9), largely due to the 'desire to break with a bourgeois past – with the inadequacies and fixed categories of humanistic thought' (Marks and Courtivron 1980: x). This group sought to establish a close connection between politics and psychoanalysis by developing a practice that would be consonant with a corresponding theory. This marriage of practice and theory hinged on the contention that women's principal enemy was their own internalized phallocentrism. Hélène Cixous, for a time associated with *Psych et Po*, has disassociated herself from feminism in the belief that this ultimately amounts to 'power-seeking for women who want full integration into a male, masculine world. Feminism therefore denies women's difference and accepts the misogyny of patriarchy' (Duchen 1987: 15). Moi corroborates this reading by pointing out that Cixous's

> refusal of the label 'feminism' is first and foremost based on a definition of 'feminism' as a bourgeois, egalitarian demand for women to obtain power in the present patriarchal system. ... Cixous does not reject what she prefers to call the women's *movement* ... and between 1976 and 1982 published all her work with *des femmes* [the press financed by *Psych et Po*] to demonstrate her political commitment to the anti-patriarchal struggle. (Moi 1985: 103)

In declaring 'I am not a feminist', Cixous seeks to oppose women who aspire to 'a place in the system, respect, social legitimation' within male-dominated domains (Cixous 1977: 482). By contrast, she endeavours to affirm sexual *difference*. Like Cixous, Julia Kristeva has been reluctant to identify wholeheartedly with feminist agendas, while at the same time valuing her situation as a woman as vital to her theoretical enterprise: 'It was necessary perhaps to be a woman to attempt to take up that exorbitant wager of carrying the rational project to the outer borders of the signifying ventures of men' (Kristeva 1980: x).

3. The dispute about equality and difference has animated ongoing debates in French feminism since at least the nineteenth century. For some critics, the assertion of difference amounts to women's acceptance of their second-rate status. They equate difference to what patriarchy considers anomalous in women: namely, their lamentable digression from a male norm. For others, difference is the indispensable precondition for a genuine under-standing of irreducible diversities between men and women, and hence for an advancement of the specific rights and abilities of both categories. Colette Guillaumin and Christine Delphy, among others, embrace the former view by highlighting the historical function of difference as an oppressive weapon. Luce Irigaray, conversely, commends the acknowl-edgement and integration in the legal system of the principle of difference as instrumental to social change. Relatedly, some celebrate equality as the basis of a just society, unhampered by asymmetrical distributions of power. Others, as already suggested, condemn the ideal of equality as women's ultimate aim by stressing that when women seek to be equal to men, they merely perpetuate patriarchal structures by begging admission to them, and that access to a male-dominated world will only, in any case, benefit a limited number of female subjects. It is yet to be proven that a woman rejecting marriage, motherhood and other familial responsibilities in a com-mitment to high-level professional positions and to their behavioural and sartorial adjuncts, for example, has actually achieved a form of equality between the sexes, or that, even assuming she has, her achievement is to be universally gainful for femininity at large.

An important moment in the history of the French feminist movement was the establishment, in 1977, of *Questions féministes*, a journal devoted to 'pursuing feminist studies from a materialist framework' (Hansen 2000a: 2). Its founding collective included Simone de Beauvoir as *Directrice de publica-tion*, Christine Delphy, Colette Guillaumin, Nicole-Claude Mathieu and Monique Plaza. Monique Wittig joined them in 1978. The journal's first editorial announced its intention to explore 'the connections between sexist mentality, institutions, laws, and the socio-economic structures that support them' with reference to the 'overall power of men over women, the psycholo-gical devaluation of women (beyond their material exploitation), the sexual and physical violence against women' (quoted in Marks and Courtivron 1980: 217). The publication came to an end as a result of a controversy surrounding the issue of lesbian separatism and this led, in 1981, to the foundation of *Nouvelles Questions féministes*, with Beauvoir as *Directrice* once again. The split that occasioned the demise of the original journal originated in the dispute sparked off by two key articles published by *Questions féministes* in February 1980: Monique Wittig's 'The Straight Mind' and Emmanuelle de Lesseps's 'Heterosexuality and Feminism'. The former 'attacks heterosexuality as the normative and oppressive structure underlying all institutions and all thinking', whereas the latter 'argues against political lesbianism ... saying that no one kind of feminism is the best' and 'defends heterosexuality as being subject to as much normative control as homosexuality' (Duchen 1987: 78-9).

The tension produced by these two articles does not constitute an isolated occurrence but actually throws into relief a major point of disagreement within the MLF. This is testified by numerous conflicting voices advocating the values of either homosexuality or heterosexuality. The editorial of the first issue of *Nouvelles Questions féministes*, published in March 1981, opposes the lesbian radicalism promoted by Wittig, claiming that it contradicts the objectives of the original journal and of feminism itself:

> According to this [radical lesbian] position, if women and men constitute two antagonistic classes, it follows that all contact between the classes is 'class collaboration', and for those of the oppressed class this is a betrayal of themselves. ... We felt it was incompatible with the principles of feminism and with the theoretical and political orientation of the journal. We believed the conclusion contradicted the premises of radical feminism: i.e. the recognition that women, all women, constitute an oppressed class; that we are all oppressed by men as a class; and that feminism is the struggle against this *common* oppression. (Quoted in Duchen 1987: 81)

At the opposite end of the spectrum, a 'Letter to the feminist movement', also penned in March 1981, by lesbian radical feminists who had divorced themselves from the *Questions féministes* collective, states: 'A woman who loves her oppressor is oppressed. A "Feminist" who loves her oppressor is a collaborator. In the war of the sexes, hetero-feminism is class collaboration' (quoted in Duchen 1987: 87). In this context, heterosexuality is regarded as patriarchy's main means of domination, and heterosexual women as inevitably complicitous with tyrannical patriarchs. Lesbianism, therefore, is the only viable form of productive resistance: 'The lesbian choice is *mobilization* .... Far from wanting to carve out spaces for ourselves in a hetero-patriarchal society ... we want to fight the mechanisms of its power' (quoted in ibid. 89).

It is ultimately undeniable that heterogeneity is a prominent trait of French feminism. It should also be stressed that this situation lends itself to both positive and negative readings. It cannot be conclusively established, for example, whether the MLF's diversity should be regarded as a healthy sign of pluralism or as a disabling marker of disunity. On the one hand, the movement exhibits an inveterate aversion to labels; on the other, many of its acolytes emphasize the need for women to identify with a recognizable ensemble.

According to Oliver, splits and disputes in the MLF have increased in direct proportion to its numerical growth:

> As more women and groups of women became part of the feminist movement in France, more disagreements and factions arose within the movement. Affiliation with the MLF became especially problematic when, in 1979, Antoinette Fouque registered the name *Mouvement de Libération des Femmes* as the trademark, and MLF as the logo, of the organization she led, *Psych et Po* (short for *Psychoanalyse et Politique*, or psychoanalysis and politics). (Oliver 2000: ix)

This was 'a source of great controversy among feminists in France' (p. ix). Particularly disturbing, for many, was the fact that *Psych et Po* was definitely *not* deemed to reflect a majority agenda within the movement: in fact, it had alienated numerous women by interrogating the validity of the term "feminism" in the first place. Thus, as Claire Duchen observes:

> when it was discovered that the group had registered the name MLF as a commercial company title, even those feminists who had previously extended goodwill were understandably alarmed and angry. It was feared that as the 'official' MLF, *Psych et Po* would manage to impose its own views as the MLF 'line' on questions, when there was never actually one MLF line on anything. (Duchen 1987: 20)

Fouque herself offers the following explanation for her contentious action: 'we believed that there was a need, an urgent need, to give a minimum of anchoring, of stability, to our movement. ... You can't live in a perpetual state of negating institutions. ... There was the threat that the MLF would be effaced'. Fouque also emphasizes the enduring flexibility of the concept of 'movement' in contrast with that of 'party' or 'organization' (Fouque 1987: 53). This explanation is variously quizzed or corroborated by several other critics aware of both the advantages and the disadvantages of the MLF's plurality. Let us consider a selection of representative voices.

According to Françoise Picq, the MLF 'shared May 68's overwhelming desire to change the world, to liberate speech' but it 'only really appeared after the May Movement ... as women realized that their hopes would not be fulfilled in the May Movement and that the anti-hierarchy discourse of the men was contradicted by their political practice'. It became clear to women that 'far-left groups perpetuated women's oppression through the power struggles inside the groups, the way that men monopolized discussions' (Picq 1987: 24). The most radically original trait of the MLF was that it established itself as 'a women-only movement' as a means of enabling female subjects to attain to 'individual and collective autonomy'. No less vital, stresses Picq, was its accommodation of 'different opinions' (p. 25). This plurality of perspectives has had undeniably positive connotations in reflecting the movement's 'rejection of organization' and 'glorification of spontaneity'. Yet, that very 'lack of formality' has simultaneously proved deleterious: it 'has paralysed the movement, has turned it into a closed world in which rival factions confront each other' (p. 30). Picq is especially unhappy about the role played by *Psych et Po*, which she views precisely as a result of the MLF's 'structurelessness' and concomitant openness to the danger of 'anti-democratic' appropriations (p. 31).

Delphy likewise maintains that the proliferation of relatively autonomous groupings within the MLF is 'positive', yet responsible for the 'difficulty ... of making the movement's voice, or rather the voice of radicalism, be heard and singled out, when it is mixed into a chorus of voices, louder and louder, more and more generalized, talking about women' (Delphy 1987: 35). For Delphy, the only way forward consists of fully grasping 'the ravages caused by patriarchy's annihilation and distortion of [women's] history' (p. 37) and hence of re-evaluating the distinctiveness of feminist battles and achievements in order to 'write' them 'into history' anew (p. 39).

Le Doeuff is also concerned with highlighting the advantages and disadvantages of the MLF's diversity: 'With hindsight we can see that in the women's movement of the 1970s women had extreme difficulty in identifying who they were in what they were doing, and indeed in precisely describing the theoretical or practical basis of the action they were taking' (Le Doeuff 2000: 47). However, she also states: 'This is my most vivid and precious memory from those years: having gradually learned, with other women, to put a name to what was hurting me, through the discovery that I was not the only one being hurt' (p. 48). A sense of commonality, therefore, could be gleaned even from the MLF's unclearly defined character. Indeed, Le Doeuff commends the fact that the movement 'never delineated its edges in any way' and proposes that if it had 'any particular effects it was due to its diffuse nature' (p. 49). In this account, polymorphousness, polyphony, boundlessness and a refusal to see the "woman's question" as the concern of experts are held to have been the MLF's most salient attributes. No less crucial was the movement's gradual elaboration of 'a language that did not respect the usual rhetoric of political demands', as attested to by slogans that employed defamiliarizing techniques: for example, "Amnesiacs of the world, forget us", "A woman without a man is like a fish without a bicycle" and "I'm a woman, why aren't you?" (p. 50).

STRUCTURALISM, POSTSTRUCTURALISM AND PSYCHOANALYSIS

While the notion of political, ethical and intellectual *engagement* promoted by Existentialism has doubtless influenced the development of French feminist theory, it is also vital to recognize the latter's collusion with major developments in the fields of anthropology, literary theory, philosophy of language and psychoanalysis, which found their inception in structuralism and proceeded to inform the intellectual climate associated with poststructuralism. The theories here under consideration grew out of the same cultural context that witnessed the political fervour described in the preceding segment, informing some of the liveliest debates of the late 1960s and of the 1970s and going on to affect deeply the intellectual history of the decades to follow. These perspectives signal a radical departure from Sartrean Existentialism. In spite of its apparently pervasive nihilism, Existentialism retained a humanist dimension based on its faith in the sacrosanct value of the individual. Neither structuralism nor poststructuralism shares such a faith. This dissension is exemplified by a severe controversy that arose in the late 1960s between Jean-Paul Sartre and Michel Foucault on the question of "man". In the closing paragraph of *The Order of Things* (1994), Foucault proclaimed the *Death of Man*, comparing the latter to a figure drawn on sand and soon to be washed away by a sea symbolizing language. Sartre answered with a strong defence of humanism as the foundation of Existentialism, and criticized Foucault for being unable to take into account the reality of man as a free actor in history.

Broadly speaking, structuralism and poststructuralism have proved worthy of serious consideration by French feminist philosophers insofar as they have supplied them with means of redefining and expanding their fields of thought and action. Specifically, they have indicated that the study of the patriarchal structures of society and the positions which men and women occupy therein requires not only a theory that can describe forms of social organization and the cultural meanings attached to them but also a theory that can relate issues of social organization and cultural value to the ubiquitous functionings of language, to power and subjectivity, to both collective and individual consciousnesses, and to the incessant dialogue between theory and practice in the sphere of politics.

Listed below are some of the discourses and concepts derived from structuralism, poststructuralism and psychoanalysis that are most directly relevant to French feminist theory. Each is subsequently discussed in some detail.

1 *Structural linguistics and binary oppositions (Saussure)*
2 *Power, knowledge and sexuality (Foucault)*
3 *Ideology and misrecognition (Althusser)*
4 *Deconstruction and différance (Derrida)*
5 *The psyche and language (Lacan)*
6 *Desire and the body (Deleuze and Guattari)*

1. *Structural linguistics and binary oppositions (Saussure)*. Structuralism's fundamental assumption resides with the notion that all aspects of our cultural existence, such as narratives, myths, kinship systems, food and fashion, function analogously to language insofar as they are all based on signs. Inspired by the theories of the Swiss linguist Ferdinand de Saussure, structuralism maintains that words do not name a pre-existing reality but actually shape it in ways that vary greatly from one culture to another. Relatedly, language does not reflect the world but rather produces it, by segmenting and categorizing an otherwise undifferentiated and hence undefinable environment. The recognition that, although the signs used by different cultures vary, all people organize reality semiotically makes language a universal phenomenon. Its most salient feature across time and space lies in the fact that the links which human beings establish between the sounds or images of words (signifiers) and the meanings or concepts they evoke (signifieds) is utterly arbitrary. Saussure's insights are relevant to feminist theory because they emphasize that there are no fixed meanings in either nature or culture and that signifiers such as "woman", "man", "feminine", "masculine", "female" and "male" are themselves variable, questionable and prone to slippage.

Structuralism also aims at identifying universal patterns of signs in the belief that the most disparate societies organize their contents into structures that are fundamentally similar. Structuralism looked for reality in the relationships among things rather than in individual entities, thus seeking to define and quantify given systems to which particular items could be connected: a system of literature embracing individual works with common characteristics and an anthropological system based on universal principles giving rise to various laws, rituals and prohibitions, for example. A central strategy deployed by structuralism in the erection of its systems consists of the sustained use of binary oppositions: pairs of contrasting signs which suggest that things are primarily definable in relation to what they are not. The first term of a binary opposition is generally privileged as a positive concept, while the second is marginalized as negative.

French feminist criticism has usefully appropriated this idea to show that binary oppositions have been used throughout history to assert men's superiority over women. Cixous, in particular, has shown that in the binary oppositions promoted by patriarchal ideology, femininity is always associated with powerlessness:

Activity/Passivity
Sun/Moon
Culture/Nature
Day/Night
Father/Mother
Head/Emotions
Intelligible/Sensitive
Logos/Pathos
(Cixous and Clément 1987: 63).

Irigaray, analogously, has emphasized throughout her output that binary oppositions have enabled men to occupy privileged positions at women's expense. As Jennifer Hansen observes in her evaluation of Irigaray's writings:

The opposites *man* and *woman* are not symmetrical, but clearly hierarchical. ... Man *alone* is the paradigmatic metaphysical concept of human beings, and women are merely inferior instances of this concept. The operation of binary oppositions in culture works insidiously to shape our psyches so that we learn that *man* is the Universal, while *woman* is contingent, particular, and deficient. (Hansen 2000b: 201)

Many feminists have challenged binary thought by arguing that there is nothing natural, let alone metaphysical, about the encoding of masculinity as privileged and positive, and of femininity as subordinate and negative. Binary thought is a cultural construction produced by patriarchal language, whose main function is to establish masculinity as the norm and so frame femininity in contrast with that norm: as lacking, inept and inadequate. However, it is possible to subvert this oppressive model by demonstrating that if meaning is inevitably the product of relations and oppositions, then the sign "man" itself would not carry any meaning independently of "woman". In binary oppositions, each of the two terms needs the other if it is to signify anything at all, the relationship between the two ultimately amounting to a form of interdependence, or complementarity, rather than adversarial dualism.

Structuralism has played a vital part in undermining traditional approaches to language, by asserting that the signifying chain is not a given but rather a cultural construct and thus encouraging a critical interrogation of the processes whereby meanings are socially produced. However, structuralism was unable to relinquish totally the universalistic aspirations beloved of mainstream Western thought since at least the classical age, its lodestar remaining the conviction that unchangeable deep structures may be discovered beneath the surface structures of reality. In the mid-1970s, a number of critics and philosophers started questioning these positions, following the premise that the linguistic model is never unproblematically dependable insofar as what it offers is not a universal structure but rather a web of clues and traces which stubbornly elude the possibility of conclusive interpretation. Poststructuralism has challenged radically the idea of a universal system sustained by binary oppositions, maintaining that the latter underpin a repressive strategy committed to the blockage of the endless play of language: an ongoing process in which one single sign can evoke multiple meanings and in which one single meaning can be evoked by legion signs. Language is incapable of representing a stable order, the meaning of a sign being inexorably contextual, and this flexibility makes it open to constant challenge and redefinition.

2. *Power, knowledge and sexuality (Foucault).* Poststructuralism has complicated and expanded the notion that social organizations, structures of power, systems of knowledge and cultural values are fashioned by the common factor of language, by advocating that institutions such as the legal and educational systems, the church, the family, political governments and the media can all be conceived of as *discourses*: ways of mediating between language, power and knowledge to give meaning to the world according to specific ideologies. This notion plays a key role in the writings of Foucault, who argues that in any one culture, power and knowledge are inextricably interconnected, and that the dominant beliefs of a society are articulated through discourses, or discursive practices, which mould and discipline human beings in various fashions. Cultures foster insistently prevailing encodings of normality, criminality and insanity, for example, in

order to control individuals by rendering their bodies compliant and useful. For Foucault, as for other poststructuralist philosophers, subjectivity is not innate but rather the effect of discourses that constantly determine people's identities, by enforcing matrices of visibility and expression that dictate what we are able (or made) to see and say, and how we negotiate the invisible and the unsaid therein. Thus, discourses systematically emplace cultural partitions between the legitimate and the illegitimate, the desirable and the undesirable.

Foucault's writings supply feminism with theoretical tools for analysing the ways in which power structures come into being and for understanding how particular cultures and ideologies have repressed women by disciplining their bodies. Especially relevant to feminist thought and practice are Foucault's reflections on the relationship between discourse, power and sexuality. Power relies heavily on sexuality to assert and strengthen itself and indeed exploits it as a vital means of constructing its subjects and of controlling them by constantly monitoring their bodies. According to Foucault, there is no such thing as a natural sexuality any more than there is any such thing as a natural body, since both only acquire meaning from the specific discursive formations of which they are a part. In *The History of Sexuality*, Volume I: An Introduction, he describes sexuality as

> an especially dense transfer point for relations of power: between men and women, young people and old people, parents and offspring, teachers and students, priests and laity, an administration and a population. Sexuality is not the most intractable element in power relations, but rather one of those endowed with the greatest instrumentality: useful for the greatest number of manoeuvres and capable of serving as a point of support, as a linchpin, for the most varied strategies. (Foucault 1978: 103)

Foucault argues that female sexuality, in particular, has been politically and culturally organized according to invasive strategies that began to gain scientific momentum in the nineteenth century. In *The History of Sexuality*, the 'hysterization of women's bodies' is described as the principal of those strategies of control. Insofar as women were regarded as excessively sexual, measures were taken in order to marshal their pathological eroticism, and their bodies accordingly became objects of study for the medical sciences, passive entities to be penetrated by the male doctor's gaze. At the same time, female sexuality was firmly inscribed in the sphere of social and domestic obligations: women were seen as responsible for guaranteeing the reproduction of the species, for holding together the family space, for relieving the husband's body and soul from the ruthless pressures of the public world, and for rearing and educating their children. The idea of an unruly and excessive female sexuality was thus kept at bay, and the female subject exhibiting any signs of dissatisfaction with this state of affairs would automatically be relegated to the stereotypical categories of the nervous woman, the neurotic, the hysteric. Related disciplining strategies include: the 'pedagogization of children's sex', namely the regimentation of preadult desire; the 'socialization of procreative behaviour', or the regulation of heterosexual intercourse in relation to reproductive and demographic priorities; the 'psychiatrization of perverse pleasure', that is, the systematic classification of pathological and hence unacceptable, as opposed to healthy and hence commendable, manifestations of the sexual drive (pp. 104–5). Although several feminist critics have objected to Foucault's analysis by arguing that he does not pay sufficient attention to issues relating to sexual and gender difference, thus obfuscating the structural inequalities between male and female subjects insistently erected by Western cultures, it is undeniable that Foucault has made groundbreaking interventions into the study of dominant discourses on sexuality and desire. According to Joseph Bristow, *The History of Sexuality*, in particular, 'made a distinct advance on earlier theories of desire' by indicating 'how explanatory categories such as sexuality itself had the devastating effect of naturalizing types of appropriate and inappropriate eroticism' (Bristow 1997: 197).

3. *Ideology and misrecognition (Althusser)*. By examining the cultural processes through which human beings are constructed and controlled, poststructuralism challenges drastically certain traditional notions of identity, particularly liberal humanist ones. Where liberal humanism saw the subject as permanent and autonomous, poststructuralism sees it as split and unstable. In the area of political philosophy, the subject has been decentred by the assertion that identity is an effect of *misrecognition*. Louis Althusser, in particular, has argued that ideology wants us to perceive ourselves as free agents, in control of our choices and actions, when in fact we are not (Althusser 1972). The notion of a conscious and unified self is imaginary: this position is closely related to the idea that although we tend to think we are in control of words and meanings, language actually shapes us at all times or, as some poststructuralists would put it, *speaks us*. Althusser's work is relevant to contemporary feminism because it stresses that there are no given identities and that there is therefore nothing sacred or immutable about patriarchal definitions of woman.

4. *Deconstruction and différance (Derrida)*. The relationship between language and subjectivity is also central to the area of poststructuralist theory gen-

erally termed *deconstruction*, and associated primarily with the work of
Jacques Derrida. Like the other thinkers already mentioned, Derrida stresses that subjectivity is fluid and that it is fashioned by language systems
which are likewise unstable. Furthermore, he maintains that *there is nothing
outside the text*, thus intimating that *everything is a text*, namely something
open and mobile. Texts, moreover, are always questionable because they
only ever offer prejudiced and partial versions of reality and because they
are inevitably disrupted by internal contradictions. Derrida maintains that
a linguistic articulation meant to demonstrate a certain truth invariably
contains elements that undermine its main argument, and thus dismantles
itself through its own inconsistencies, paradoxes, aporias, gaps and silences. Deconstructing a text means being able to recognize these internal
contradictions, to expose the trace of otherness in what may appear self-
identical and the trace of displacement in what may appear firmly
anchored. What Derrida's work offers to feminism is the understanding
that the values attached to gender roles, sexualities, patriarchal ideology
and female subordination can never be definitively fixed. Indeed, the
meanings associated with gender difference and the relations of power
based upon it are floating signifiers for language's efforts to moor reality,
which by definition are, bound to fail. All meaning is relative and fleeting,
for it slides incessantly through the mechanism of *différance*: a linguistic
principle combining "difference" and "deferral", which assumes that words
only mean something by virtue of their difference from other words, and
that when one tries to establish the meaning of a sign, one is inevitably led
to more and more signs. Feminism can appropriate this idea by showing
that the definition of gender difference is also a matter of constant deferral:
it is impossible to emplace it so unquestionably that it will be universally
applicable to all cultures, places and times (Derrida 1976, 1981).

5. *The psyche and language (Lacan).* The reassessment of Freudian psychoanalysis initiated by Jacques Lacan makes language central to psychosexual development, thereby reaching the conclusion that the ego is
oppressed and depleted by its subjection to signs that elude linkage to
conclusive meanings more than by its imbrication with biological drives.
The Oedipus complex is reassessed in relation to language acquisition:
what the child must give up is not a literal, physical mother figure but
rather the sense of fullness that characterizes life before the entry into language, namely before culture forces us to adopt signs that can never
express properly our emotions and desires. The child is torn away from
the early state of fullness by a law that Lacan calls the *Name of the Father*.
The word "Name" indicates the child's subjection to language and its

institutions, while the word "Father" symbolizes the patriarchal structures of Western culture.

The order of early childhood is termed by Lacan the *Imaginary*. This coincides with the pre-Oedipal stage and is characterized by the principle of undifferentiation: there is as yet no awareness of any separation between self and other, infant and Mother, inside and outside, male and female. A crucial moment in the Imaginary is the *mirror phase*: between six and eighteen months, the infant sees its reflection in the mirror and identifies with it. Although the infant is still, at this stage, physically uncoordinated and dependent on others for support and sustenance, the reflection with which it identifies offers the gratifying illusion of an autonomous and unified body-image. The budding subject consequently derives intense pleasure from its identification with an ostensibly whole and coherent entity. The order of adult language, laws and institutions, on the other hand, is called the *Symbolic*. This marks the advent of difference and an increasing consciousness of the individual subject's separateness from other people and objects. The unity of self and other (infant and Mother) is broken up by the appearance of a third figure (the Father). The terms "Mother" and "Father" do not refer to parental figures in a literal way: the former refers to the figure to whom the infant is physically and emotionally closest in the early phases of its development, whereas the latter indicates the social and cultural forces that the child must learn to acknowledge and adjust to if it is to develop into an adult subject. Beyond both the Imaginary and the Symbolic lies the *Real*, namely what neither language nor culture are capable of naming.

In both the Imaginary and the Symbolic, human identity is split: it is based on mechanisms of alienation, fiction and misrecognition. The first split occurs in the mirror phase, as the division between the "I" that watches and the "I" that is being watched. At this stage, the subject constructs an image of itself that is based on alienation, on the subject's identification with something other than itself: that is to say, with its reflection in a mirror or in another person's mirroring gaze. The image is also fictional: it does not consist of a flesh-and-bone body but of a fleeting apparition. Finally, it is a product of misrecognition: the subject is attracted to the reflection, finds it pleasing and adopts it as a genuine representation of itself insofar as it provides a unified configuration of the Self when, in fact, the infant's body still amounts to a jumble of disjointed impulses and activities. What the infant finds in the looking-glass is not itself but an illusory projection of its ego, a hallucinatory fantasy starkly at odds with its actual being: 'the total form of the body by which the subject anticipates in a mirage the maturation of his power is given him only as a *Gestalt*', a formation that 'fixes it ... in contrast with the turbulent movements that the subject feels are animating him' (Lacan 1977: 2–3).

The second split occurs when the subject enters the Symbolic order of language, as the division between the "I" that speaks and the "I" that is spoken about. The image of itself that the subject fashions at this juncture is also founded on alienation: namely, on the individual's subjection to an impersonal order of signs. The image is concurrently fictional since the subject's entry into the realm of language causes it to become akin to a fictional character in an ongoing story: that is, the endless narrative which language goes on telling without any regard for individual aspirations or desires. Symbolic subjectivity, like its mirror-phase predecessor, is also a result of misrecognition because the subject misperceives itself as the autonomous author of its utterances when, in fact, it is spoken by language. Thus, the phenomenon of displacement – experienced in the mirror stage as a result of the young child's identification with an unreal, albeit pleasing, appearance – 'prefigures' the ego's 'alienating destination', namely its subjection to the disembodied signs, or 'phantoms', of the Symbolic order. Anything we may call an "I" ultimately amounts to 'the armour of an alienating identity' (Lacan 1977: 4). Language, in seeming to give its subjects a means of asserting their identities and of voicing their unique demands, actually governs them despotically by engulfing individuality in the black hole of an impersonal order: 'I identify myself in language', Lacan states, 'but only by losing myself in it like an object' (p. 86). The entry into the Symbolic, accordingly, produces lack and hence desire. Just as meaning in language is constantly deferred, so is the satisfaction of desire, which becomes the motivating principle of human life and occasions the genesis of the *unconscious*, as the ensemble of longings, fantasies and fears which language cannot and will not allow us to articulate. Embracing an ethos analogous to the one proposed by Derrida, Lacan argues that the production of meaning is a forever deferred process, since any signifier will always require other signifiers to support its tentative claim to meaning in a limitless proliferation of possible links. So-called linguistic units, far from being unitary, are comparable to 'rings in a necklace that is a ring around another necklace made of rings' (p. 153).

According to Lacan, sexual difference is not biologically ingrained in the body from birth but is actually produced by the subject's entry into the Symbolic order since it is language that is responsible for placing individuals into particular cultural structures by designating them as "women" or "men". Moreover, sexual difference is conceived of as an arbitrary construction built around the *phallus*. Many feminists are very suspicious of the emphasis placed by Lacan on this concept, which they see as a way of strengthening patriarchal values. However, it is possible to argue that Lacan is not so much concerned with prescribing a model of gender relations as with describing a particular situation: that of a culture which attaches certain meanings to the presence or absence of designated attributes and, relatedly, invests them with distinctive ideological and mythological connotations. These meanings and connotations are not fixed by biology: indeed, the phallus operates as a symbol, not as a physical organ. While Sigmund Freud saw the material penis as the marker of sexual difference, Lacan argues that gender positions are produced by an abstract concept of power. The phallus, more specifically, is supposed to structure gender relations by positing a distinction between *having* and *being*, the corollary of which might appear to be that masculinity "has" the phallus, whereas femininity can "be" the phallus. In other words, male subjects are expected – by the patriarchal system governed by masculine discourse – to own that attribute as the ultimate signifier of paternal authority, while female subjects, deemed incapable of such ownership, are expected to embody that signifier for the benefit of others, to incarnate the ultimate symbol of erotic gratification. According to Lacan, this dialectic of desire rests on a mendacious imposture: it endeavours to efface the male subject's own constitutive lack, a universal concomitant of everybody's absorption into the Symbolic, while simultaneously concealing the female subject's self-dispossession: the fact that when woman is cast in a phallic role, she is not valued for herself but as a specious construct, a character in a 'masquerade' (p. 290). Finally, although men have the penis and women do not, nobody, whether male or female, can either *possess* the phallus, since this denotes proprietorship of an absolute power which the Symbolic simply denies, or *embody* it, since no human being is in a position to fulfil totally another's desire.

6. *Desire and the body (Deleuze and Guattari).* The relationship between desire and lack, as theorized by Lacan, is questioned radically in the writings of Gilles Deleuze and Félix Guattari, where it is argued that desire is a *productive* mechanism, and that this is borne out by its boundless propensity to produce objects capable of satisfying wish-fulfilling fantasies. Psychoanalysis errs, according to Deleuze and Guattari, in positing a subject from which desire emanates as lack. In fact, what is lacking is the subject itself: 'Desire does not lack anything, it does not lack its object. It is, rather, the *subject* that is missing in desire' (Deleuze and Guattari 1984: 26). The term "subject", in this context, alludes to the more or less stable locus of consciousness tirelessly glorified by Western humanism. By contrast, *Anti-Oedipus* conceives of human beings in radically anti-humanistic terms as 'desiring-machines' through which desire unrelentingly flows, the

flux being occasionally interrupted by the agency of a phenomenon termed the 'body-without-organs', whose aim is to stem or impede the movement of desire by absorbing its energies and thus produce stasis. Despite their drastic departure from Freudian and post-Freudian perspectives, Deleuze and Guattari fully embrace poststructuralist notions of limitlessness and dislocation in their approach to signification, enculturement and embodiment. Their main contribution to feminist theory, specifically, could be said to reside precisely in their application of a poststructuralist model of endless play to the body itself. In reconceptualizing the relationship between people and desires by undermining the validity of the subject, Deleuze and Guattari could be said to subscribe to a feminist agenda devoted to a meticulous reassessment of corporeality. Elizabeth Grosz has underscored this point:

> Deleuze and Guattari's notion of the body as a discontinuous, non-totalized series of processes, organs, flows, energies, corporeal substances and incorporeal events, intensities, and durations may be of great relevance to those feminists attempting to reconceive bodies, especially women's bodies, outside of the binary polarizations imposed on the body by the mind/body, nature/culture, subject/object, and interior/exterior oppositions. (Grosz 1994: 193-4)

At the same time, however, Grosz alerts us to the dangers inherent in a model which, by prioritizing diffusion, may reduce femininity to a state of dispersed and amorphous *becoming*, which could obscure and neglect the specificity and materiality of feminist endeavours.

As will be argued in greater depth in subsequent chapters, in interrogating the humanist idea of identity as a unique correlative of some core individuality, French feminist theory has contributed vitally to the development of a poststructuralist understanding of identity as a social construct designed and implemented by cultural systems and institutions, and hence to the deconstruction of the very concept of selfhood. Indeed, in exploring the cultural construction of gendered and sexual identities, various strands of feminist theory have increasingly moved away from the word *self* and adopted the term *subject* instead: while "self" conventionally evokes the notion of identity as a private possession and a view of the individual as stable and autonomous, "subject" ambiguously combines connotations of activity and passivity. For example, the subject of a sentence may denote both the agent performing the action described by the sentence and the patient upon whom the action is performed. Connotations of passivity are

also borne out by a phrase such as "the Queen's subjects" and by the idea of
the subject as medical patient. Above all, the term "subject" aptly mirrors
the recognition that human beings are shaped by the processes whereby they
become the *subjects of language* and that their identities, concomitantly, are
provisional effects of strings of signifiers. In tandem with poststructuralism
and Lacanian psychoanalysis, therefore, various developments in feminist
philosophy have emphasized that the subject is not a self-contained
consciousness or stable essence but rather a product of multifarious
discourses, and that subjectivity, as a corollary, can only be comprehended
by examining the ways in which people and events are *emplotted*: inscribed in
the narrative tapestries that societies unrelentingly weave so as to fashion
themselves.

CONTEMPORARY FRENCH FEMINISM: TRENDS AND DEBATES

Speculations about the genesis of subjectivity in the context of both individual experiences and cultural formations animate the debates brought to the
fore by the two main strands of contemporary French feminist theory into
which the MLF's projects have bifurcated: namely, the materialist, or social,
trend and the psychoanalytic, or linguistic, trend.

The former is primarily concerned with the exploration of 'patriarchal
social institutions and material and economic conditions' (Oliver 2000: vii).
This is conducted with sustained reference to a problematization of the sex/
gender binary opposition: sex, it is argued, is no less a social construct than
gender is, despite its presumed association with biology and anatomy; relatedly, the basis of social existence does not consist of natural imperatives but
of cultural fabrications. The phrase 'materialist feminism', specifically, was
coined in the 1970s by Delphy 'to describe a feminist analysis of women's
oppression that derives from the Marxist analysis of capitalism'. This theory
was elaborated 'in response to the radical left's subordination of women's
issues to the class struggle' (Alphonso 2000: 59). Indeed, one of the materialist strand's principal objectives consists of challenging the orthodox
Marxist assumption that the material oppression of women can be understood purely by recourse to an analysis of capitalism, and of demonstrating
that women's labour is also commodified and appropriated through non-capi-
talist strategies. Indeed, if economic relations are viewed solely in terms of
the opposition between capital and labour, their specifically *gendered* dimension is likely to be neglected. Processes of production and consumption, in
fact, are always embedded in gendered and sexual relations and in material

conflicts between dominant definitions and embodiments of masculinity and femininity. Believing that traditional Marxism cannot account for forms of exploitation that victimize women *qua* women, Delphy and her followers have posited 'two interlocking but independent class systems: capitalism and patriarchy', and 'two independent modes of production: the capitalist mode ... and the domestic mode' (p. 60). Both exploit women, but it is vital to recognize the distinctiveness of the forms of appropriation of female labour deployed within the family rather than subsume them to the general economy.

The psychoanalytic/linguistic trend, for its part, is concerned primarily with 'psychic structures and patriarchal colonization of the imaginary and of culture' (Oliver 2000: vii–viii). In this respect, it is intimately connected with the theoretical positions promoted by *Psych et Po* in the 1970s and 1980s and further developed by Kristeva, Irigaray and Cixous. It is noteworthy, however, that psychoanalytic concepts also play an important part in the writings of theorists not associated with Antoinette Fouque's movement, such as Sarah Kofman and Michèle Le Doeuff. The most prominent representatives of the psychoanalytic/linguistic strand of French feminist theory are largely inspired by Lacanian thought and, in particular, by its contention that ideas of *woman* and *femininity* are fundamentally at odds with the Symbolic order dominated by the Law of the Father and hence by patriarchal authority. What should be opposed, in this context, is not masculinity *per se* but rather, in Duchen's words, 'the masculinity in women's heads', the internalization of patriarchal values that has led women to repress or turn away from their 'woman-ness', in order to re-invent radically 'the way we think, the concepts we use, the language we use. We need a Revolution of the Symbolic' (Duchen 1987: 48).

Both strands of French feminist theory, ultimately, share the determination to move beyond conventional naturalistic approaches and towards a thorough evaluation of notions of sex, sexuality, desire and gendered subjectivity as culturally fabricated. Moreover, virtually all the theorists discussed in this book are devoted to the investigation of the multiple relationships that obtain between society and the psyche, collective change and individual change, external and internal worlds. It is precisely this 'negotiation between social theory and psychoanalytic theory', according to Oliver, that 'speaks to one of the most promising tensions in recent feminist theory in the English-speaking world' (Oliver 2000: viii).

Of pivotal importance to the materialist trend is the constructivist approach ushered in by Beauvoir's assertion, cited earlier, that 'One is not born a woman; one becomes one' (Beauvoir 1973: 301). This ethos, discussed in some detail earlier in this chapter in relation to Beauvoir's philosophy,

emphasizes the fashioning of gender roles and positions by societal structures. Although human beings are born with bodies and anatomical characteristics, they are not actually born as either men or women but only become
gendered creatures as a result of external pressures and demands. The
psychoanalytic trend takes this position further by arguing that 'woman has
never existed'. This allegation ensues from the acknowledgement of woman's
persistent silencing and engulfment by patriarchal values and institutions:
'From the moment that she [a woman] begins to speak ... she has to face
problems which are all masculine and this is what puts her in mortal danger
– if she doesn't use them, she doesn't exist, if she does use them, she kills
herself with them' (Fouque 1987: 48). Beauvoir, though implying that certain
beings are compelled to become women, retains scope for an element of
choice. Indeed, she does not overtly state that "one *is made to* become a
woman" and we cannot therefore automatically assume that the process of
becoming is merely *forced* upon prospective females. It may well be a case of
a person *choosing* to become a woman. According to Judith Butler, 'implied
in her formulation is an agent, a *cogito*, who somehow takes on or appropri-
ates that gender and could, in principle, take on some other gender'. This
makes the adoption of a gender role somewhat 'volitional', and cultural
construction 'a form of choice' (Butler 1990: 15). The psychoanalytic trend's
view, conversely, could be said to elide the Existentialist notions of agency
and free will. However, this does not incontrovertibly amount to a bleakly
deterministic move, for the possibility of transgression is consistently
stressed in the overarching project of deconstruction of the Symbolic. Where
Beauvoir posits woman as an entity that *exists*, albeit as an artificial rather
than a natural being, psychoanalytic feminism questions the very concept of
existence by envisioning "woman" as a shifting signifier, a trace in a boundless
chain of signification. In this respect, it could be said to promote a shift from
"feminism" to "postfeminism".

The concept of postfeminism is here invoked in *one* of its current
meanings, of which there are many: namely, as indicative of a heightened
recognition, within feminist theory, of the need not only to expose the
cultural constructedness of masculinity and femininity but also to differ-
entiate between gendered individuals and the societal structures to which
they are subsumed, and to allow room for the expression of plural feminist
viewpoints. Before looking in more detail at this acceptation of "postfeminism", however, it must be stressed that the term has proved highly
controversial. Several critics have rejected it on the grounds that it connotes
a backlash against feminism's fight for equality by dismissing feminism as
somehow outdated. Embracing the notion of postfeminism, according to
these critics, amounts to assuming that feminism is dead: either because its

projects have not led to any substantial gains and it is therefore pointless to continue pursuing them, or because it has achieved everything it could and it is now time to move on. Both positions can be disputed on the basis that the objectives of traditional feminism have neither fizzled out nor triumphed conclusively. Nevertheless, a number of critics have proposed a more positive version of postfeminism as a repositioning of feminism itself intended to confront the reality of entrenched patriarchy from multiple and diversified perspectives. In this scenario, the ideal of equality is radically questioned: if women presume to achieve parity in terms of civic and economic rights by gaining access to patriarchal institutions and indeed power within them, they merely aspire to become honorary men and hence to ameliorate their individual circumstances in ways that leave the conditions of other women unlike them quite unaltered. Fouque advocates this view by encouraging a shift from the fight for equality to a critique of the Symbolic at large, entailing an understanding not of the male subject himself as the oppressor but of cultural and linguistic structures as disadvantageous to women: 'post-feminists' are women whose 'enemy isn't man but phallocracy; that is, the imperialism of the phallus'. Feminism has too often amounted to challenging empowered men with the message 'up you get so I can take your place, in your phallocratic society without changing it' (Fouque 1987: 52). What if, as Viennot argues, 'women leaders' ultimately 'serve to hide the oppression of other women? And women realize that it isn't enough to decree that men and women are equal for reality to change' (Viennot 1987: 126)?

Beside quizzing the equality-based ethos, several theorists wholly or partly sympathetic to postfeminism have emphasized its implication in a broader critique of universalism and foundationalism, conducive to the expansion of feminism both as a philosophy and as a movement. In this perspective, plurality and diversity are conceived of as correctives of the tendency to protect the concept of a monolithic *feminist self* that is generally, and ominously, ideated as white, middle-class and heterosexual. Postfeminism so understood would have the advantage of challenging earlier feminist epistemologies hinging on the notion that patriarchal and imperialist forms of oppression are universally imposed and experienced, thus diversifying the spectrum of gendered, sexual and racial identity-constructs with which feminist theory has to engage. As Ann Brooks argues, postfeminism may then be capable of intersecting with other 'anti-foundationalist movements including postmodernism, poststructuralism and postcolonialism', the 'post' implying, in all cases, 'a process of ongoing transformation and change' (Brooks 1997: 1). The *post*-ing of feminism may therefore refer, as Michael Archer suggests, not to 'supercession through loss of validity' (Archer 1994: 5) but to the process of reorientating a theoretical discourse into uncharted territory.

An understanding of postfeminism that does not merely lead to facile assumptions about either the achievements or the failures of feminism ought to take into account important attempts to redefine two principal discourses: history and ethics. According to Cixous, contemporary reorientations in philosophy of gender must grapple with the idea that 'history is always in several places at once, there are always several histories underway; this is a high point in the history of women' (Cixous and Clément 1987: 160). The diversity and unrelenting proliferation of histories/stories/herstories, of so-called *facts* and of their chronicling, of the angles from which events are experienced, remembered and misconstrued, necessitates a move away from the traditional dependence on the presumed authority of a monolithic subject/text towards an examination of any one subject's or text's imbrication with countless *other* narratives. As for ethics, an analogous imperative to negotiate the relationship between dominant and peripheral subjectivities is stressed by Kristeva, whose views on the topic Oliver summarizes as follows:

Before we can discuss ethics or formulate our possible obligations to others we need to renegotiate how we conceive of the relation between subject and other; we need to conceive of the relation between subject and other as a relation of difference. Some traditional ethical theories postulate an autonomous agent whose obligations to the other come from his realization that the other must be the same as himself. The autonomous subject of these traditional ethical theories does not have a relation to any other; rather this subject always and only has a relationship to the self-same. Until we reconceive of a true relation between subject and other, we cannot reconceive of ethics. We cannot conceive of obligations to others. (Oliver 1993: 1)

An effective reassessment of ethics requires us to challenge what Kristeva terms '*identificatory thinking*' (Kristeva 1996a: 259), namely the philosophical tradition which identifies humanity with *consciousness* and maintains that we are human to the extent that we are capable of using reason to make sense of ourselves, others and our environments. Kristeva deems this model dangerously reductive and welcomes postmodernism as fostering an approach which, by contrast, is eminently anti-identificatory, which does not reduce humanity to the single reality of consciousness but rather emphasizes all that is discordant, heterogeneous and polysemous in the subject and the other alike.

In addressing the postfeminist condition, Kristeva is especially concerned with highlighting the specificity of the afflictions besetting the contemporary subject. Women, specifically, are presented as still facing considerable difficulties despite their wider access to educational and professional opportunities. Many women's identities are actually divided as a result of their having to perform a balancing act between public and professional commitments, on the one hand, and maternal and familial responsibilities, on the other. Kristeva states: 'Women's sexual and material independence has helped them by creating an image of autonomy, performance, and social value that gives them a certain amount of pleasure.' Yet, she also observes

> a very striking split in the discourse of postfeminist women. We see a joyful liberation ('our life is our own', 'our body is our own'), but at the same time we hear women express deep feelings of pain. ... The media talk a great deal about staying home, but this home often seems empty once the husband and the children are gone. Regardless of any professional or other attractions that society may offer a woman ... we must acknowledge that women are suffering. Perhaps the pain is greater today because they are more acutely aware of the dichotomy between phallic aspirations and certain narcissistic gratifications. (Kristeva 1996b: 71)

This situation is closely connected with what Kristeva terms '*new maladies of the soul*', the nexus of syndromes characteristic of a society wherein 'people have a hard time representing their emotions', largely as a result of the fact that 'modern men and women often appear to be impaired by two sorts of problems, the first having to do with the body and the second with a relentless desire for social and financial success' (Kristeva 1996c: 86).

The feminist and postfeminist positions just outlined ultimately constitute attempts to formulate theoretical models capable of negotiating a pervasive sense of cultural *crisis*. While this term refers to the possibility of productive changes in the spheres of both intellectual speculation and political activity, it concurrently points to a painful awareness of the ravaging uncertainties that inevitably accompany all moments of transition and metamorphosis. Most troubling, in this respect, are intimations of psychological and physical fragmentation which, though potentially ushering in promises of imaginative self-dissemination, also connive with the threat of utter disintegration. These ambiguous feelings are emblematically encapsulated by a fictional text directly concerned with the state of French culture in the closing part of the twentieth century and opening part of the twenty-first century: Michel Houellebecq's *Atomised* (2001). In reflecting on the breakdown of myriad values and on the emergence of increasingly dehumanized subjects and sexualities, the book supplies a dispassionate, postapocalyptic depiction of a society not merely *in* crisis but also *of* crisis, of the kind with which several French feminist theorists have endeavoured to grapple.

Atomised consistently relates the disaffected status of singular subjects to the unfeeling proclivities encouraged by the social and historical frameworks within which they hesitantly move, weaving their ways in and out of more or less mechanical, reified and routinized sex acts: 'the latter half of the twentieth century,' writes Houellebecq, 'was miserable and troubled. ... Feelings such as love, tenderness and human fellowship had, for the most part, disappeared' (p. 3), to be replaced by 'a weary, exhausted humanity, filled with self-doubt and uncertain of its history' (p. 354). At the same time, the novel tantalizingly situates the sense of loss experienced by both individuals and groups in a colossal vista of cosmological unanchoring: 'There had been no unique, wondrous act of creation; no chosen people; no chosen species or planet, simply an endless series of tentative essays, flawed for the most part, scattered across the universe'; ultimately, 'the very notion of particles having intrinsic properties in the absence of observation had to be abandoned. The latter opened up a deep ontological void' (pp. 144–5). Like Houellebecq, many of the theorists discussed in the following chapters urge us to wonder what both individuals and collectivities might conceivably conjure out of, or into, such a *void*.

CHAPTER 2

Sexual and Gendered Identities

. . . I scrawled a sentence. Woman without her man is nothing. . . . This here is the equation of the sexes, right in this line, the embodiment of gender-consciousness. . . . This is what a man reads in that sentence. Woman, without her man, is nothing. This is what a woman reads. Woman: without her, man is nothing. (Collins 2000: 249)

SEX AND GENDER: SOME DEFINITIONS

According to *The New Oxford Dictionary of English* (1998), *sex* refers to 'either of the two main categories (male and female) into which humans and most other living things are divided on the basis of their reproductive functions', whereas *gender* indicates 'the state of being male or female (typically used with reference to social and cultural differences rather than biological ones)'. *The Cambridge Encyclopaedia*, fourth edition (2000), likewise, defines *gender* as the 'social expression of the basic physiological differences between men and women – social behaviour which is deemed to be appropriate to "masculine" or "feminine" roles and which is learned through primary and secondary socialization. Thus, while sex is biological, gender is socially determined.' These definitions suggest that while the term *sex* has traditionally referred to the difference between males and females with regard to biology and, by extension, to activity leading to reproduction, the term *gender* surpasses reductionist accounts of femininity and masculinity as coterminous with an individual's biological sex, by stressing their sociopolitical determination. Therefore, *gender* plays a pivotal role in multifarious processes of cultural classification and organization. Indeed, the categories *masculinity* and *femininity* are the primary societal formations around which relationships between men and women develop and practices of domination and subordination unfold. These function objectively in material power relations, such as the assignation of cultural roles and the division of labour, as well as subjectively, depending on how male and female subjects perceive themselves and internalize sets of symbols and standards of conduct. The distinction between the biological and the social dimensions of a person's sexuality is assumed in French culture as it is in the anglophone world, even though one single word, *sexe*, is used in French to designate both "sex" and "gender".

French feminist theory of both varieties refutes the concept of gender as a concomitant of an anatomical essence intrinsic to the nature of sexual difference. Although theorists are divided, as seen in *Chapter 1*, over the issues of equality versus difference and heterosexuality versus lesbianism, they varyingly stress that the distinction between femininity and masculinity is central to the generation of a wide range of discursive technologies and that its exploration accordingly calls for an interdisciplinary approach. Hence, without wishing to deny important differences between the materialist/social trend and the psychoanalytic/linguistic trend, or indeed the diversity of disciplines underlying their projects, it is useful to acknowledge the two strands' collusion in viewing gender as an open question rather than a given. If materialist feminism sometimes appears to emphasize the constructedness of gender, via sociological and economic analysis, more explicitly than the psychoanalytic strand, where priority is often accorded to affective and symbolic phenomena, it could nonetheless be argued that the ultimate objective of both trends is denaturalization. After all, psychoanalysis, even in its most universalistic Freudian guises, aims at foregrounding the Self's ongoing instability and the status of both femininity and masculinity as elements of identities that are never fully and conclusively acquired. Therefore, the appropriation of a gender role will inevitably result from cultural practices that fashion our identities in merely tentative and provisional ways. Although certain individuals may appear more firmly anchored than others to *one* gender role, and hence to possess a more stable identity, *all* people are potentially capable of adopting, modifying, displacing and experimenting with plural roles and hence engaging in what is colloquially referred to as *gender fuck*.

Many of the theorists discussed in this chapter maintain that sex and sexuality are no less constructed than gender. The principal problem they face is that it has commonly proved more arduous to expose the constructedness of sex and sexuality than that of gender. According to Mary Klages, this is 'in part because of the way our culture has always taught us to think about sexuality. While gender may be a matter of style or dress, sexuality seems to be about biology, about how bodies operate on a basic level.' However, this conventional distinction flounders once we acknowledge the shortcomings of mainstream representations of sexuality. On the one hand, its association with 'animal instincts' is inadequate since

human sexuality doesn't work like animal sexuality. ... We are ... the only species that can copulate more or less at will, without regard to fertility or

hormonal cycles .... We also have an enormous repertoire of sexual beha-
viours and activities, only some of which are linked to reproduction .... .
And – most importantly – human sexuality is about pleasure, and about
pleasure mediated by all kinds of cultural categories. (Klages 1997)

On the other hand, the connection between sexuality and 'moral and ethical
choices' is problematic insofar as the variable (historical and geographical)
character of 'statements about what forms of sexuality are right, or good, or
moral' indicates that 'definitions of sexuality are not "essential" or timeless or
innate' (ibid.). The representative voices discussed in the pages that follow
indicate that the key contribution to debates on gender and sexuality made
by French feminist theory lies in the latter's claim that practically *all* definitions of sexuality are fabricated. Before proceeding to examine specific
authors and texts, it is worth outlining some general positions that can help
us situate French feminist theory in a broader cultural and critical scenario.

The etymology of the word *sex*, namely the Latin verb *secare* (= "to
separate"), may come as something of a surprise if assessed against the
conventional assumption that sex enables intersubjective collusion and
fusion. However, the concept of separation plays a prominent role in any
critical evaluation of sexuality insofar as the latter is concurrently implicated
with life-affirming and life-threatening drives, with bliss and violence, with
prospects of liberation and of repression. Moreover, as Joseph Bristow
emphasizes, sexuality embodies the principle of separation because it may
connote simultaneously 'sexual desire' and 'one's sexed being' and therefore
'points to both internal and external phenomena, to both the realm of the
psyche and the material world'. As a result, it 'occupies a place where sexed
bodies (in all their shapes and sizes) and sexual desires (in all their multifar-
iousness) intersect only to separate' (Bristow 1997: 1). Furthermore, the
linguistic origins of *sex* will not come across as inordinately unexpected if one
considers that the ideological and political uses to which sex and sexuality
have been repeatedly put serve precisely to classify and hence divide people
and their practices from one another, by recourse to disciplines as diverse as
sexology, anthropology, sociology, medical science, criminology and psychoanalysis, and thus produce 'a gap between the experience of eroticism and
the category used to contain that experience' (p. 5).

The classifying urge is borne out by the objectives of sexual morality,
namely the subfield of ethical philosophy concerned with establishing the
principles of moral behaviour in sexual matters, and with clarifying the
means by which the observance of such principles may be secured, by enforcing neatly compartmentalized definitions of normality and deviance: certain
forms of sexuality are commended, or even imposed, as dominant and lawful,

while others are marginalized or demonized as perverse and illicit. However, there is no universal agreement across disparate ideologies as to the ideal form sexuality should take; likewise, there is no consensus among feminists as to how the sexual field should be explored to women's advantage. Radical feminists, including certain voices within the materialist strand of French feminist theory, have often condemned heterosexuality for supporting patriarchal institutions and for subjecting women to defenceless exploitation by male power. In this perspective, to put it bluntly, heterosexuality spells out violence. Critics who find these positions reductive, or even simplistic, argue that sexuality, particularly heterosexuality, cannot be regarded as monolithically oppressive and constraining for women. Various kinds of sexuality, they maintain, can supply women with means of exploring their own desires and experiences of pleasure, both physical and intellectual, and of challenging the coercive strategies fostered by patriarchy.

In recent years, increasing emphasis has been placed on the need to conceive of gendered and sexual identities in the *plural*: there are many genders and many sexualities, resulting from multiple and changing roles which subjects are expected, or elect, to perform in both private and public contexts. Moreover, it is vital to recognize that sexual pleasure is not a fixed category. The tendency to define sexual pleasure in terms of the binary opposition heterosexuality/homosexuality, evinced by both patriarchy and certain forms of radical feminism, is limiting because it does not adequately take into account a more comprehensive spectrum of *other* sexualities taking shape within both homosexual and heterosexual zones. Indeed, homosexuality and heterosexuality encompass diverse practices: not all heterosexuals live their heterosexuality in the same way and, analogously, talking about homosexuality as though it constituted a uniform category is spurious. According to Cherry Smyth, this is borne out by the sheer diversity of 'queer' sexualities: 'there are straight queers, biqueers, tranny queers, lez queers, fag queers, SM queers, fisting queers' (Smyth 1992: 17). Most crucially, not all individuals are univocally homosexual or heterosexual, nor indeed exclusively feminine or masculine.

The tendency to interrogate monolithic notions of femininity and masculinity is prominent in much French feminist theory and entails the possibility of enhancing the range of sexualities, in terms of both preferences and activities, of which human beings may be capable. This has also been the primary objective of Queer Theory, an approach significantly influenced, as we shall see shortly, by Michel Foucault's writings. It must be emphasized that this approach is here introduced not in order to set up exact historical correspondences between French and Anglo-American feminisms, or indeed the formation of gay and lesbian movements, but rather to suggest an *analogy* between various forms of sexual and gender diversification in different cultures. Queer Theory has played a particularly significant role in dissolving conventional sexual and gendered identities and thereby encouraging a recognition of pleasures not previously acknowledged. According to Klages (1997):

> [it] emerges from gay/lesbian studies' attention to the social construction of categories of normative and deviant sexual behaviour. But while gay/ lesbian studies, as the name implies, focused largely on questions of homosexuality, queer theory expands its realm of investigation. Queer theory looks at, and studies, and has a political critique of, anything that falls into normative and deviant categories, particularly sexual activities and identities. The word 'queer', as it appears in the dictionary, has a primary meaning of 'odd', 'peculiar', 'out of the ordinary'. Queer theory concerns itself with any and all forms of sexuality that are 'queer' in this sense [and] insists that all sexual behaviours, all concepts linking sexual behaviours to sexual identities, and all categories of normative and deviant sexualities, are social constructs, sets of signifiers which create certain types of social meaning.

Thus, this body of ideas provides scope for a greater proliferation of gender and sexual roles and positions, of their cultural interpretations and of their private and public enactment than earlier mappings of sexual conduct and identity could presume to afford.

Queer Theory is indubitably related to Foucault's theorizing of the discursive construction of eroticism and pleasure and of the oppressive homo/ hetero duality. In expanding the range of available sexualities and gender roles, this approach has also indicated, in a Foucauldian vein, that apparently dissident relationships are ostracized not so much because of the sex acts they involve as because of their potential for creating 'as yet unforeseen kinds of relations that many people cannot tolerate' (Foucault 1989: 332). Queer Theory, brought to public attention in 1990 by the group Queer Nation, has sought to widen the vocabulary employed to define various sexual and gender modalities, largely as a reaction against existing gay and lesbian groupings whose main concern was the establishment of distinctive identities, and whose politics tended, as a result, towards separatist and exclusionary strategies. As Warren Hedges observes, whereas the 'identity-based gay and lesbian criticism' prominent from the late 1970s to the late 1980s 'assumes that *representations are a function of sexual identities*' and that 'these identities preexist and define representations', Queer Theory 'assumes that *sexual identities are a function of representations*' and that such 'representations preexist and define, as well as complicate and disrupt, sexual identities' (Hedges

1997). The use of the term *queer*, as already intimated by Klages, is in itself thought-provoking: generally considered an abusive label for homosexuals, it is here positively appropriated and hence displaced to embrace multifold forms of sexual dissidence and, relatedly, to connote a controversial discourse through which normative attitudes to gender and sex may be contested. While appreciating the type of approach commended by Queer Theory, several commentators have emphasized that it must endeavour to more than merely replace crystallized orthodoxies with yet another system liable to become naturalized and institutionalized, by keeping invigorating options for diversification dynamically open.

The notion of *transgender* is especially important, in this respect. A trans-genderist is not unproblematically equatable to either a transvestite or a transsexual: s/he is not defined univocally by cross-dressing or by a literal change of sex effected by medical technology. Rather, s/he is someone who moves across conventional gender boundaries, even regardless of sexual proclivities, and enacts multiple parts through diverse identity narratives. According to a number of theorists, it is vital to conceive of transgender as a flexible notion that 'includes everything not covered by our culture's narrow terms "man" and "woman". A partial list of persons who might include themselves in such a definition includes transsexuals (pre, post, and no-op); transvestites; crossdressers; persons with ambiguous genitalia; persons who have chosen to perform ambiguous social genders; and persons who have chosen to perform no gender at all' (Stone, 'Transgender'). Reorientations in the analysis of sexual and gendered identities may thus usher in fresh oppor-tunities for a plurisexual individual who does not ultimately 'bother', as Kate Woolfe puts it, 'to figure the gender of the people [s/he is] attracted to' (Woolfe 1998: 90).

'GENDER PRECEDES SEX': MATERIALIST ANALYSES OF THE CONSTRUCTION OF SEXUAL DIFFERENCE

The debates on sex and gender that have animated materialist French feminism since the 1970s evince three main objectives: (1) demonstrating that sex, far from constituting the natural substratum of gender as a social phenomenon, is itself an artificial category that conceptually emanates from, rather than predates, the codification of gender positions; (2) highlighting the incidence of non-heterosexual identities and practices in various forms of both consolidation and transgression of the patriarchal status quo; (3) ques-tioning naturalized notions of masculinity and femininity that have tradition-ally facilitated patriarchy's appropriation and exploitation of the female body and of its functions and drives, on both the biological and the economic planes. Central to the pursuit of these aims is the assumption that sexual and gendered identities are inevitably inscribed in a material order and therefore embody specific ideological priorities which, in Marxist parlance, can be shown to correspond to the interests of the ruling classes.

Monique Wittig's writings have proved especially influential in advancing the argument that masculinity and femininity are artificial classes, naturalized by the patriarchal system in order to efface the real character of sexual difference as social conflict. 'The ideology of sexual difference,' Wittig states in 'The Category of Sex' (Wittig [1982] 1996: 24), 'functions as censorship in our culture by masking, on the ground of nature, the social opposition between men and women. Masculine/feminine, male/female are the categories that serve to conceal the fact that social differences always belong to an economic, political, ideological order.' Radically interrogating the presumption that while gender is socially determined, sex is biological and hence rooted in nature, Wittig subjects sex and gender alike to a thoroughgoing process of denaturalization and posits patriarchal domination as their artificer:

> there is no sex. There is but sex that is oppressed and sex that oppresses. It is oppression that creates sex and not the contrary. The contrary would be to say that sex creates oppression, or to say that the cause (origin) of oppression is to be found in sex itself, in a natural division of the sexes preexisting (or outside of) society. (p. 25)

In fact, *no* concept, *no* classification and *no* relationship situated within the patriarchal economy, or indeed any other political system erected by humans, can ever be presumed to transcend social determination. As Wittig suggests, the reason for which we are taught insistently that the 'sexes', their 'biological' and 'genetic' attributes, and the 'division of labour' they underpin precede 'all thinking, all society' is to present them as unquestionably 'belonging to the natural order' and therefore discourage any possible inclination to speak of them with reference to 'social relationships' (p. 26). In this context, the principal task of feminism consists precisely of carrying out a merciless exposure of 'the category of sex' as an eminently 'political category'.

Furthermore, Wittig urges women to recognize that the structures of dominance sustained by this category are predicated upon the valorization of heterosexuality as synonymous with normality, and as the justification for assigning to woman a reductive, reproductive role: 'women are "heterosexualized" … and submitted to a heterosexual economy … that imposes on women the rigid obligation of the reproduction of the "species", that is, the reproduction of heterosexual society' (p. 27). Patriarchy as a system can only be subverted if the heterosexual economy upon which it relies for its self-preservation is overthrown. This position accords lesbians a privileged political role: indeed, Wittig posits a *materialist lesbian feminism* as the only movement ultimately likely to erase the spurious sexual categories that function to perpetuate the myths of man and woman as metaphysical givens. Since women are supposed to exist merely in relation to men, lesbians cannot be considered women in that their existence does not depend on that of men. In 'The Straight Mind' (Wittig [1981] 2000a), on this basis, Wittig has declared that 'it would be incorrect to say that lesbians associate, make love, live with women, for "woman" has meaning only in heterosexual systems of thought and heterosexual economic systems. Lesbians are not women' (p. 143). Moreover, as Doris Mitterbacher points out, a 'lesbian society is a proof that those features that mark a woman are actually neutral. Only when seen in a heterosexual context do they acquire a certain meaning' (Mitterbacher, 'Monique Wittig').

In 'One Is Not Born a Woman' (Wittig [1981] 2000b), Wittig pursues further the theme of lesbianism as a political choice for feminists by maintaining that 'the designated subject (lesbian) is *not* a woman, either economically, or politically, or ideologically. For what makes a woman is a specific social relation to a man, ... a relation which lesbians escape by refusing to become, or to stay, heterosexual' (p. 135). In the same essay, Wittig opposes the celebration of matriarchy and of 'mother right' undertaken by certain strands of feminism on the grounds that it ultimately strengthens sexual inequality by leaving heterosexual partitions inviolate: 'Matriarchy is no less heterosexual than patriarchy: it is only the sex of the oppressor that changes. Furthermore, not only is this conception still imprisoned in the categories of sex (woman and man), but it holds onto the idea that the capacity to give birth (biology) is what defines a woman' (p. 129). The theoretical repudiation of conventional labels designed to preserve the existing hierarchy is mirrored, in Wittig's fictional practice, by the systematic avoidance of sex-based identities and tags. '[Wittig] maintains that the very concepts of "woman" and "man" are political constructs whose function is to keep women subordinate to men. Rejecting the categorization of people by sex is a necessary stage in eliminating the oppression of women; hence, her near-total suppression of the words "woman" and "man" in her fiction' (Crowder 1994: 526). (Wittig's fiction and use of language will be discussed in further detail in *Chapter 5: Writing and the Body*.)

In the anglophone world, Wittig's work has been especially influential in the fields of gay and lesbian studies, particularly where the issue of performativity is concerned. As will be shown in detail in the *Appendix*, this concept plays a vital part in the writings of Judith Butler, where heterosexuality, in a vein reminiscent of Wittig's work, is posited as 'that grid of cultural intelligibility through which bodies, genders, and desires are naturalized' (Butler 1990: 151).

Christine Delphy has endeavoured to denaturalize sex, sexuality and sexual difference by arguing, along lines analogous to those traced by Wittig, that gender precedes sex: that is to say, *constructedness*, not *nature*, constitutes the basis of social organization and of political and economic relationships. Hence, gender can be deemed primary to sex insofar as, by being more explicitly constructed than sex and more overtly employed as an enculturing tool, it exposes more emphatically the artificiality of the very foundations of human society. Biology itself, moreover, is conceived of within the parameters of specific cultural formations that are by and large determined by hierarchical relations between the sexes. In 'Rethinking Sex and Gender' (Delphy [1993] 1996), Delphy sums up her manifesto as follows: 'Up till now, most work on gender, including most feminist work on gender, has been based on an unexamined presupposition: that sex precedes gender. However, although this presupposition is historically explicable, it is theoretically unjustifiable, and its continued existence is holding back our thinking on gender.' In advocating the need for a drastic inversion of one of the most deeply ingrained dogmas underlying sociological, anthropological and philosophical speculations on the relationship between sex and gender, Delphy is concurrently endeavouring to create the context for an unbiased, open and adventurous approach involving a willingness 'to abandon our certainties and to accept the (temporary) pain of an increased uncertainty about the world' as well as 'the courage to confront the unknown' (p. 30).

Delphy's most memorable pronouncement, arguably, lies in the assertion that '*gender* precedes sex' and that 'sex itself simply marks a social division; that it serves to allow social recognition and identification of those who are dominant and those who are dominated' (p. 35). To substantiate this claim, she examines major developments in the study of sex and gender and draws attention, specifically, to the shift from the evaluation of 'sex roles', usually associated with the writings of Margaret Mead (Mead 1935) and their attribution of 'different reproductive roles' to men and women (Delphy 1996: 31); through the assessment of masculinity and femininity as socially determined functions by authors such as Mirra Komarovsky (Komarovsky 1950), Viola Klein, Alva Myrdal (Myrdal and Klein 1956) and Andrée Michel (Michel 1959); to the analysis of 'the concept of gender' as such (Delphy 1996: 32) brought into focus in the early 1970s by the work of Ann Oakley. The latter's *Sex, Gender and Society* is one of the first texts explicitly concerned with gender and with proposing that whereas 'sex' refers to 'biological differences' related to reproduction, 'gender ... is a matter of culture' (Oakley [1972] 1985: 16). Delphy commends Oakley's departure from 'biological determinism', yet remains dissatisfied with her omission of two fundamental factors: namely, the *'asymmetry'* and *'hierarchy'* that inevitably shape sexual and gender relations (Delphy 1996: 32).

Delphy, conversely, believes that 'values are *hierarchical* in general' (p. 38) and that a radical redefinition of gender from a materialist standpoint is only imaginable if the abolition of hierarchical systems is entertained as a primary aim. Seeking to engineer a situation in which femininity and masculinity harmoniously coexist is a misguided effort, unlikely to yield more that skin-deep effects, for 'masculine and feminine values' are always already fostered 'in, and by, hierarchy'. Autonomy for both men and women requires a 'non-hierarchical society' (p. 40) as the prerequisite of an existence wherein gender is released from structures of dominance and containment: 'we shall only really be able to think about gender on the day when we can imagine non-gender' (p. 41). Delphy is well aware that her project could be dismissed as fatuously idealistic but fends off this potential accusation by reminding her readers that 'having a Utopian vision is one of the indispensable staging-posts in the scientific process – in *all* scientific work' (p. 40). Indeed, the imaginary status of Utopia (from the Greek *ou* = "not" + *topos* = "place") decrees its non-existence in the *here-and-now* but does not automatically consign it to the *never-never*. If we are to believe, with Thomas Kuhn, that the 'paradigm shifts' that make drastic transformations possible are not dictated by logical and predictable criteria, we cannot dispense with a modicum of imaginative speculation (Kuhn 1962).

Working with a materialist model related to the one promoted by Wittig and Delphy, and at the same time drawing consistently on ethnographic and anthropological research, Nicole-Claude Mathieu corroborates the thesis that sex is no less artificial than gender and further argues that both sex and gender, in turn, contribute crucially to the cultural construction of discourses aimed at assigning particular roles and identities to women and men of diverse orientations. In 'Sexual, Sexed and Sex-Class Identities' (Mathieu [1989] 1996), specifically, she elucidates ways in which sex and gender operate in tandem to consolidate specific ideological formations not so much through mutual support as through programmed strategies of reciprocal transgression. Pivotal to Mathieu's approach within her essay is the notion that there are three modes of relationality between sex and gender:

- *Homologous mode*: this posits sex as the ultimate foundation of embodied and cultural existence and 'sex difference' as 'the basis of personal identity, the social order and the symbolic order' (p. 45). Sex constitutes a person's anatomical destiny and the gender identity conforming to that sex follows naturally from it; thus, to be born biologically male or female at the level of sex will automatically determine our femininity or masculinity at the level of gender. Gender translates sex: that is to say, the biological reality of sex is quite effortlessly transposed into the social reality of gender. This mode is favoured by the philosophy of *naturalism*.

- *Analogous mode*: this still accords importance to biology but prioritizes the communal expression of gender identities within particular cultural clusters: 'Here, people do not situate themselves only individually in relation to their biological sex; personal identity is also strongly linked to a form of *group consciousness*' and 'gender is experienced as a collective way of life' (p. 49). Gender symbolizes sex: that is to say, the forms of behaviour exhibited by the members of a group on the basis of their gender consciousness can be regarded as symbolic representations of their biological traits. The experiential dimension highlighted by this approach aligns it with *pragmatism*.

- *Heterogeneous mode*: this argues that the connection between sex and gender is a fundamentally '*socio-logical* and political' construct which, by and large, serves to sustain male domination, and must be radically interrogated through 'a materialist analysis of the social relations of sex'. There is nothing natural about gender bipartition since this is foreign to anatomical reality: it only comes to be invested with biological meanings as a result of the tendency to see sex and gender as coextensive. Sex does not constitute a natural substratum from which gender emanates as a cultural invention: in fact, sex is constructed by gender. This mode embraces the ethos of *anti-naturalism* in advocating the necessity of a shift of attention from 'the cultural construction of gender to the cultural construction of sex, and particularly of sexuality' (p. 59).

The tripartition just described gives rise to a further, related, taxonomy whereby men and women are supposed to be classifiable by recourse to three identity types:

- To the first mode corresponds the notion of '"*sexual*" *identity*', namely an identity 'based on an individualistic consciousness of sex' (p. 44). This rests on the assumption that 'personal psycho-social traits should fit with biological traits (and there are problems if they do not)' (p. 45). Within this logic, 'gender is normally adapted to sex' (p. 46). However, there is also scope for 'transgressions of gender by sex' that ultimately enable more complex forms of 'convergence' of sex and gender (p. 63). Mathieu offers, among other examples, that of Inuit transvestites as a case in point. She observes that the belief, among the Inuit, that 'one or more people re-live *in each individual*, and she or he receives their name from them' can give rise to a conundrum if the sex of the baby is different from that of the eponym. It is common, in such cases, to resort to '*transvestism*': 'a child is dressed and brought up in the gender that conforms to the sex of the eponym'. Thus, for example, a male child with a female eponym would be brought up as a girl. This practice represents a transgression of gender by sex: specifically, of the gender which, according to the naturalistic ethos, ought to conform to the child's sex by the sex of the name-giver. A further transgression occurs when, 'at puberty, the transvestite Inuit children ... take (and learn) the activities and the behaviour of their biological sex/gender, with a view to marriage and procreation'. In this case, we witness a transgression of the gender identity passed on by the name-giver to the child by the sex of the adolescent her/himself (p. 48).

- Mathieu associates the second mode with the concept of '"*sexed*" *identity*', namely an identity 'based on a sex group consciousness' (p. 44). While in the case of *sexual identity*, sex was held capable of crossing over into the realm of gender, in the present case we discover the possibility of 'transgressions of sex by gender' that occasion a 'divergence' of sex and gender (p. 63). These can be observed, for instance, in the context of 'homosexuality as a group culture' that asserts 'the predominance of *gender* over sex'. The presumed authority of anatomy is also flouted by homosexuals disinclined to identify unproblematically with members of their biological sex: not all gay men will wish to associate primarily or exclusively with males and not all lesbians will seek wholly female company. Mathieu cites the example of 'a man dressed as a woman and calling himself a "*lesbian* man"' who tried to get himself accepted by a group of lesbians and refused to join male homosexuals in gay demonstrations' (p. 51). (The novelist Poppy Z. Brite, incidentally, has frequently described herself as a gay man inhabiting a female body.) According to Mathieu, another case of transgression of sex by gender may be seen in the fact that the 'principal attributes of gender – the differentiation of tasks and social functions – are ... reproduced even within marriages between people of the same sex' (p. 54).

- The third mode gives rise to the principle of '"*sex-class*" *identity*', namely an identity 'based on a sex class consciousness' (p. 44). In this scenario, there are no compensatory attempts to resolve 'incongruencies between sex and gender' (p. 63) of the types found in the two previous categories. In fact, what is paramount in the case of *sex-class identity* is a focus on two principal 'aspects of the relationship between the biological and the social': namely, (1) 'how societies *use the ideology of the biological definition* of sex to construct a "hierarchy" of gender, which in turn is based on the oppression of one sex by the other'; (2) 'how societies *manipulate the biological reality* of sex to serve this social differentiation' (p. 59).

The writings of the two materialist critics discussed below, Colette Guillaumin and Paola Tabet, exemplify these concerns. The former concentrates on the appropriation and ideological materialization as *objects* of the female body and of female labour, on the basis of putatively natural sexual differences, as means of sustaining the distinctively hierarchical class system on which patriarchy thrives. The latter focuses specifically on the regimentation of reproductive faculties and on the management of reproductive conditions, demonstrating how these work not only to secure the continuation of the human species but also to domesticate female sexuality and sever woman's hormonal attributes from desire and pleasure.

In 'The Practice of Power and Belief in Nature' (Guillaumin [1978] 1996), specifically, Guillaumin maintains that gender politics inexorably entail the physical appropriation of women, *all* women, both at the macrocosmic level of general cultural structures and at the microcosmic level of individual relationships with men. Insofar as bodily ownership is gendered, it is inappropriate and misleading to conceive of labour and economic exploitation in disembodied terms, for this eclipses the specificity of the forms of oppression of which women *as a class* are notoriously the victims. Guillaumin stresses that the treatment of women as 'common property' (p. 72) consists simultaneously of a '*power relation*' and an '*ideological effect*': the former denotes 'the power play that is the appropriation of women by the class of men', while the latter refers to the deployment of 'the idea of "nature"' as a fundamental reality 'supposed to account for what women are supposed to be'. Ownership as a power relation revolves around the enacting of 'social relationships in which actors are reduced to the status of appropriated material units'; as an ideological effect, it relies on the authority of a 'mental construction' that 'turns these same actors into elements of nature – into "things"' (p. 74). The ideological reduction of female subjects to the status of natural objects has two principal repercussions.

On the one hand, it is conducive to the dehumanization of woman as sheer materiality, as an irrational, capricious, intuitive and merely visceral creature: '*intuition*', in particular, 'classes women as the expression of fluctuations of pure matter. According to this notion,' Guillaumin argues, 'women know what they know *without reasons*. Women do not have to understand, because they know. And what they know comes to them without their understanding it and without their using reason. In them, this knowledge is a direct property of the matter of which they are made' (p. 91). This stereotype has repeatedly been fuelled by the association of femininity with a mythical notion of 'Mother Nature' (p. 95): a feminized patriarchal ideation of all the inchoate *stuff* which masculine wisdom and expertise are expected to invest with form and meaning. Indeed, the appropriation of the female body and of female labour under patriarchy is consistently paralleled by the typically male fantasy of effecting what Guillaumin terms a pervasive 'transformation of nature' (p. 99) by recourse to man-made concepts of science, technology and philosophy as discourses from which females are proverbially excluded. On the other hand, 'direct physical appropriation in relations based on sex ... includes the pre-emption of labour power': what is effaced is not merely the status of housework *as work*, but also woman's ability to perform any activity worthy of that denomination. The term coined by Guillaumin to designate the power relation in which woman and her labour power are appropriated in one single movement is *'sexage'* (p. 75). As Linda Murgatroyd, the article's translator, points out, this derives from an amalgamation of the words *'esclavage* (slavery) and *servage* (serfdom)' (p. 104).

Both woman's reduction to the level of brute matter and her subjection to *sexage* proceed from the *naturalist* tendency to assume that 'the status of a human group, like the order of the world that has made it the way it is, *is programmed from within the living matter*'. Thus, femininity is regarded as the unquestionable outcome of 'an internally programmed "nature"' intrinsic not merely to women as a group but also to the very order of things (p. 92). This inveterate and pervasive penchant for naturalization and, relatedly, for utilizing genetic determinism as the justification for bodily and psychological appropriation, is precisely what the materialist feminism promoted by Guillaumin seeks to dismantle so as to allow the emergence of a *'class consciousness'* that opposes any 'spontaneous belief in [women] as a natural species' (p. 104).

Guillaumin is overtly unsympathetic to the concept of *difference* advocated by various representative voices in the psychoanalytic camp of French feminist theory. Indeed, she views it as univocally advantageous to men:

Being different is not like being curly-haired; it is being different FROM – different from something else. But, of course, you will say, women are different from men. We know perfectly well from whom women are different. Yet if women are different from men, men themselves are not different. If women are different from men, men themselves are men. (p. 95)

Guillaumin does not seem at all interested in exploring the poststructuralist perspective according to which, in any dual relationship based on difference, neither term can ultimately be regarded as superior, for each is dependent on the other – indeed on *its difference from the other* – in order to subsist. In fact, her argument hinges on an established materialist interpretation, which harks back to Simone de Beauvoir, of masculinity as the norm against which femininity is insistently constructed as the deficient or defective Other. Guillaumin's aversion to the principle of difference is elaborated further in 'The Question of Difference' (Guillaumin [1979] 2000a), where she asserts that women do not stand to gain anything from the celebration of that ideal and indeed of the right to be different. This view is based on Guillaumin's reading of social fragmentation and heterogeneity as lamentable conditions imposed upon women by patriarchal systems that want them to perceive themselves as split and hence powerless:

> The practices of the dominant class which fragment us [women] oblige us to consider ourselves comprised of heterogeneous pieces. In a sort of patchwork existence we are forced to live as things distinct and cut off from one another, to behave in a fragmented way. But our own existence ... is constantly being reborn in our corporeal unity and in our consciousness of that unity. (p. 116)

The atomized situation to which Guillaumin draws attention is, as shown in the closing part of *Chapter 1*, undoubtedly responsible for generating a ubiquitous sense of uncertainty and crisis. Yet, fragmentation and heterogeneity are not unequivocally in contrast with homogeneity, nor is the latter an obvious corrective of a culture of perplexity and doubt. In fact, there is ample evidence for processes of homogenization of both individuals and broad political trends based precisely on their atomized status, on the pervasiveness of disunity and self-division on both the personal and the collective planes. It is only fair to observe, however, that writing in the late 1970s, Guillaumin might not have had such evidence as readily available to her as might feasibly have been the case today, when the valorization of 'a life not divisible' (p. 117) no longer seems unproblematically appealing.

Tabet examines cultural dynamics of corporeal ownership analogous to those exposed by Guillaumin in 'Natural Fertility, Forced Reproduction' (Tabet [1985] 1996) with a specific focus on both ritualistic and technological strategies of appropriation of women's procreative faculties and, concomitantly, of domestication of feminine eroticism. 'Human reproduction and women's fertility,' Tabet writes, 'are often called upon in anthropology to explain, even to justify, the subordination of women and inequalities between the sexes. ... In the end, women's subordinate position is supposed to be due to the "natural, biological constraints" weighing them down.' However, procreation is not merely a 'biological event': if it has been insistently represented as such, this is because it has traditionally been in the interest of the dominant class and gender to obscure 'the historical and social character of relations of reproduction' (p. 109). What Tabet argues for, conversely, is a radical severing from biology of all aspects of the reproductive process, from copulation, through conception and pregnancy, to birth and lactation. This requires us to reject the concept of natural fertility by focusing on multifarious forms of 'intervention in biology' which, on the one hand, 'empirically *use* biological givens' and, on the other, '*transform* the biological givens themselves' (p. 112).

Concurrently, we must acknowledge the status of reproduction as exploited work and as a means of producing a female organism specialized for childbearing, whereby procreation is posited as the primordial signifier of femininity and as somehow irrelevant to, if not explicitly alien from, the substance of masculinity: 'Instead of ... being the result of a process which obviously needs two sexes, it has become the essence, the very nature, of "women"' (p. 111). This ploy does not only serve to efface man's responsibility in the reification of the female body: it also aids two further aims. Firstly, it facilitates the extrication of masculinity from nature and everything nature symbolizes in contrast with culture. Secondly, it enables the dissociation of procreation from social relations between the sexes by pretending that reproductive functions pertain just to *one* sex. The role played by numerous technologies of reproduction in the context of patriarchal institutions will be the object of a more detailed discussion in *Chapter 4*. Here, Tabet's analytic exposition of the complex mechanisms underpinning various forms of intervention in human biology will be examined in relation to illustrative instances drawn through the practice of comparative anthropology.

EQUALITY VERSUS DIFFERENCE: UNPICKING THE SYMBOLIC ORDER

An illuminating critique of the construction of female sexuality by numerous symbolic systems of representation and encoding is supplied by Michèle Le Doeuff's *The Philosophical Imaginary* ([1980] 1989). In her analysis of Pierre Roussel's *Système physique et moral de la femme* ([1777] 1820), specifically, she concentrates on the part played by pseudo-scientific discourses. Roussel argues that woman does not merely differ from man with regard to 'sexual functioning' (Le Doeuff 1989: 141), for 'the essence of sex is not confined to a single organ, but extends, through more or less perceptible nuances, into every part'. A rather harrowing analogy is then proposed: 'as with hunchbacks the curvature of the spine always induces a certain disorder of the other parts', so 'woman is not woman merely in virtue of one place, but rather is so in every aspect from which she is regarded' (Roussel 1820: 8). Although sexual difference cannot be reduced to a sexual attribute, the female sex is none the less 'assigned a directing role. By degrees it comes to inform all the other parts and functions of woman's body, as well as her "moral" and relational existence. The sex is a sort of causal nucleus' (Le Doeuff 1989: 142).

Roussel extrapolates a series of axioms defining women's perceptive, cognitive and creative limitations from the fanciful construct which he indiscriminately assumes to constitute their biological makeup. In this respect, his work epitomizes the tendency to categorize various facets of femininity according to more or less imaginary preconceptions, as exposed by materialist writers such as Guillaumin. Above all, the *fact* that woman's 'organs have more sensibility than consistency' is presumed to result in an unreflective, impressionistic and fickle disposition towards the images and objects they perceive, which binds their attention wholly to 'immediate causes', thus making them unsuitable for engagement in any form of truly imaginative, philosophical, scientific or political activity. For Roussel, argues Le Doeuff, woman 'masters nothing, has no gift for the Fine Arts, and is incapable of creativity; ... general notions of politics and the great principles of morals escape her grasp ... . Her imagination is too mobile for her to devote her study to the abstract sciences' (p. 143).

One might expect a project that genitalizes the female body and psyche so thoroughly and unflinchingly as to render them virtually interchangeable to pay some respect, at least, to certain physiological characteristics that are specifically and uniquely feminine. This is not the case: the construction of female *nature* undertaken by the likes of Roussel actually aims at implicitly *denaturalizing* woman's biology. Thus, processes exclusive to women are crudely explained away as instinctive responses to the demands of brute matter: 'whereas Roussel has attributed every other possible feminine quality to a genital cause, he is at pains to show that periods have nothing to do with procreation or fertility'. In fact, they are deemed concomitant with the phenomenon of overindulgence associated with advanced culinary habits and gustatory expectations. Having pointed out that 'Brazilian women', arguably a metonym for non-Western femininity in its entirety, and 'females of other mammal species have no period' (p. 146), Roussel reaches the conclusion that 'this incommodious exaction' (Roussel 1820: 121) results from the fashion, rampant within more sophisticated societies, 'of exceeding strict alimentary needs and consuming dishes prepared with the perfidious refinements of art. ... Nature sought for a means to re-establish metabolic balance through compensating bodily evacuations' (Le Doeuff 1989: 147).

Le Doeuff is not merely 'exhuming' something of a 'baroque relic suitable for a museum of scientific horrors' (p. 138) in her critique of Roussel's seminal text. This is unlikely to be taken as seriously now as it was in the eighteenth and nineteenth centuries, when it actually enjoyed sensational levels of popularity; yet, it can hardly be denied that pseudo-medical accounts of the genesis of sexual and gendered identities are still accorded validity among various components of Western society and still underpin unquestioned forms of so-called *wisdom* on which the Symbolic order largely depends. Le Doeuff's reading demonstrates that theories which claim scientific validity in positing sex as a natural substratum, upon which culturally defined differences subsequently grow, are ultimately deconstructive. They can be shown to contradict their own premises and to fall by their own criteria since, in declaring the naturalness of sex, they paradoxically construct it according to utterly arbitrary and Byzantinely artificial strategies. In Roussel's *Système*, this is patently borne out by the aporetic desexualization of woman's biology *in the very process* of presenting the feminine as a product of genital determinism. Arguably, this inconsistency results from an age-old proclivity to conceive of woman as a being saturated with sexuality, and indeed rendered dangerous, primarily to man, by her insatiable appetite. On the one hand, patriarchal discourses need to perpetuate this stereotypical notion as one of their fundamental beliefs; on the other, they aim at curtailing woman's supposedly deleterious powers by effacing the significance of her sexual functions.

Sarah Kofman adopts a deconstructive approach akin to Le Doeuff's in her exploration of dominant definitions of femininity, especially those provided by Freudian psychoanalysis. At the same time, *her own* texts could be described as self-deconstructive to the extent that she deliberately undermines the very concepts she appears to endorse by turning them against themselves. In *The Enigma of Woman* (1985) and *The Childhood of Art* (1988a), specifically, Kofman invokes the notion of castration to show that, while ostensibly sustaining what Sigmund Freud poses as the fundamental *truth* about femininity, they actually call into question the existence of any truth in the realm of the psyche. Freud, for Kofman, typifies the male philosopher committed to the deciphering of secrets, to the unmasking of the supposedly original meanings lying behind the manifest content of psychic productions. Kofman, by contrast, emphasizes 'the absence of originary meaning' (Kofman 1988b: 39). However, she also argues that in endeavouring to unveil a foundational signified, Freud ultimately exposes the lack of any such anchoring point in spite of himself. Thus, beside the Freud eager to believe in an ultimate truth there for the analyst to retrieve, there is the Freud who recognizes that meanings are not immutable givens intrinsic to objects and situations but rather ephemeral consequences of retrospective speculation. As Penelope Deutscher observes, the composite Freud examined and problematized by Kofman does not rely unequivocally on biological determinism, for he 'also wants to say that there is no brute anatomical difference to "discover", but only the retroactive effects of interpretation and construction, which are overdetermined by the influence of cultural forces and conventions. ... For this Freud,' suggests Deutscher, there is no original significance as "castration" of the discovery of woman's sex' (Deutscher 1999: 171).

On the one hand, Freud posits the castration complex as a fundamental point of reference, the presence or absence of the penis utterly determining the sexual and gendered identity of a person. On the other hand, he shows that meanings are established through the mechanism of *deferred action*: namely, that they are not grounded in the material world but actually depend upon varyingly distorted representations produced in hindsight. As far as definitions of femininity are concerned, this double-bind perspective leads to a further contradiction. If the lack or possession of the penis is taken as the basis upon which incontrovertible truths about femininity and masculinity can be erected, then the female body's "castrated" status will inevitably configure the *truth* about woman as a state of deficiency and aberration. If, conversely, the lack or possession of the penis is not considered a *fact* invested with some irrevocable significance but rather a state to which meaning is attached arbitrarily and retroactively, then it can be argued that woman's non-ownership of the penis makes her different from, yet not automatically inferior to, man. The latter possibility grants woman an autonomous existence as a sexual being in her own right, thus inaugurating a scenario quite incompatible with the one depicted by Freud's normative economy.

The deconstructive approach is also used by Kofman in order to alert us to insidious forms of patriarchal domination that work to demonize femininity even as they appear to value it. She draws attention, in particular, to the ambivalent function played by the notion and practice of *respect* as one such ploy. Turning to Immanuel Kant's assessment of this concept, Kofman examines its utilization as a means of distancing and protecting men from women, and indeed of pathologizing femininity within a markedly ungenerous sexual hierarchy. Kofman uses the metaphor of the *'parapluie'* ("umbrella") to describe respect in the Kantian sense as a man-made device designed to insulate masculinity from femininity (Kofman 1982a: 16). What is presented as regard for women is actually a way of exerting control over them, 'an operation of mastery' (Kofman 1982b: 385–6): in saying to a female *I respect you*, patriarchal man is implicitly saying *I am distancing myself from you in order to dominate you.* Furthermore, women will be held in respect only as long as they preserve appropriate standards of modesty: they must make themselves worthy of respect and, having done so, must submit to relations that do not afford any authentic consideration for their rights but rather confirm their disenfranchised status. Modesty, moreover, is idealized by Kant as the quality that 'prevents man from having ... disgust for the sex of woman, to which the full and entire satisfaction of man's inclinations inevitably leads him' (p. 388). Man may only endure the existence of the female sex, then, as long as this is veiled by decorum. In turn, woman is supposed to benefit from the assumption of a humble and reserved attitude as a means of protecting herself *from herself*: from potentially unruly passions for which her nature is notorious. Why exactly man should find the female sex so repulsive remains a moot point in Kant's ethics. It would not be preposterous to surmise, however, that it is the perception of woman's sexually rapacious tendencies that renders the adoption of domesticating measures so vital. As Natalie Alexander comments, 'in order not to become an object of disgust, woman must become not a rational object but an object of propriety .... She must hold herself under this umbrella of respect in order to mask her nature, in order to protect both herself and men from women's power' (Alexander 1999: 157). This, according to Kofman, is the "woman" upon whom patriarchy dispenses its spurious esteem: an invariably enigmatic, and by and large undependable, *stranger* to be kept at arm's length.

The exposure of the marginalization of woman, as both a flesh-and-bone entity and as a concept, by phallocentric cultures is also one of Luce Irigaray's central concerns and means of decoding the Symbolic order. While focusing on the construction of woman as Other, Irigaray consistently returns to two further themes: the strategies of visual objectification deployed to consolidate woman's peripheral status; the irreducibility of sexual difference as the basis of human society. Let us consider each of these three issues in turn.

In Irigaray's work, 'femininity is theorized as an effect of the organization of female desire in a female libido' (Weedon 1987: 63). This has been insistently repressed by patriarchal phallocentrism as incompatible with the male sexual economy and, as a result, women have lost touch with their own sexuality, their bodies and their penchant for heterogeneous and plural forms of pleasure. Regaining contact with these submerged dimensions entails two related practices: a recognition of the multiplicity of female sexuality and the elaboration of an analogously plural feminine language. In *This Sex Which Is Not One* (Irigaray [1977] 2000d), Irigaray argues that just as female 'pleasure does not have to choose between clitoral activity and vaginal passivity' and 'woman has sex organs just about everywhere', so female language is diffuse

and diverse, meaning being 'constantly in the process of weaving itself'
(quoted in Marks and Courtivron 1980: 102–3). As Claire Goldstein
observes, the 'title of Irigaray's book' is itself worthy of notice insofar as it

> makes use of the polyvalence of the French word, 'sexe'. As in English, in
> French 'sexe' denotes both sexual category and sexual activity. Irigaray
> plays on yet a third French meaning for the word – the sexual organ,
> usually the penis. By a strange coincidence, the noun with its definite
> article, 'le sexe' may be used to designate either 'the fair sex' or 'the penis'.
> With such a title, Irigaray is pointing to the slippage between the real, the
> imaginary and the symbolic which she plays off in her resistant re-reading
> of Freud and the construction of the feminine. (Goldstein 1997)

Moreover, Irigaray emphasizes that woman's 'multiple, diffuse, tactile sexuality is eclipsed in the predominant phallic scopophilia of western eroticism.
Female desire is repressed from the cultural imaginary much as her physical
body, seen in relation to the male sexual organ, is perceived as a passive
negative space' (ibid.). (Irigaray's views on the relationship between
embodied subjectivity and language are discussed further in *Chapter 3* and
Chapter 5.)

The term "sex" is not the only highly charged signifier calling for redefinition. As Toril Moi stresses, there is an urgent need to problematize a whole
cluster of words related to women, their gender, their sexuality and their
politics. It is therefore vital to 'distinguish between "feminism" as a political
position, "femaleness" as a matter of biology and "femininity" as a set of
culturally defined characteristics' (Moi 1997: 246). Concurrently, it is vital to
recognize that patriarchy has insistently tended to collapse femaleness and
femininity together in order to sustain the ethos of essentialism, primarily by
appealing to putatively "feminine" characteristics (sweetness, modesty,
subservience, humility, etc.)' (p. 247).

Some commentators have criticized Irigaray for linking female libido and
biological femaleness so tightly as to seem to promote a return to an essentialist agenda. However, Irigaray has endeavoured to avoid essentialism by
refuting the possibility of defining woman and by stressing that both the
creation of a fixed concept of femininity and the emulation of men in the
quest for equality would be profoundly detrimental to the advancement of
women's rights. In *This Sex*, specifically, she warns us against the construction of a *logic* of femininity that would ineluctably pander to patriarchy's
own passion for logical categories, logos itself, reason and order. Julia
Kristeva echoes this view: 'To believe that one "is a woman" is almost as
absurd and obscurantist as to believe that one "is a man"' (Kristeva 1974: 20;

my translation). 'I therefore understand by "woman"', Kristeva later adds, 'that which cannot be represented, that which is not spoken, that which remains outside naming and ideologies' (p. 21). Woman, then, denotes a subject position that must always retain elements of fluidity and liminality if it is to escape a fate of reductive stereotyping analogous to the one imposed upon women by patriarchy through the binary representation of femininity as coterminous with *either* 'Lilith or the Whore of Babylon' *or* 'Virgins and Mothers of God' (Moi 1985: 167). Hélène Cixous embraces a germane position in 'The Laugh of the Medusa' (Cixous [1976] 2000a) where she argues that 'there is ... no general woman, no one typical woman. ... you can't talk about *a* female sexuality, uniform, homogeneous, classifiable into codes'. Relatedly, femininity is associated with the possession of an 'inexhaustible' unconscious through which a virtually limitless 'stream of phantasms' flows as in 'music, painting, writing' (p. 258). Le Doeuff likewise promotes a critical programme of diversification in proclaiming that 'trying to produce and impose a model of woman, however "new", prevents one from getting to know and understand the plurality of the womanhood of real women' (Le Doeuff 2000: 54).

As intimated by Goldstein, the marginalization of femininity under patriarchy is, to a considerable extent, a corollary of the discourse of visuality that posits man as the owner and woman as the object of the *gaze*. Irigaray seeks to rectify this hierarchical codification of visuality: 'Perception should not become a means of appropriating the other, of abstracting the body, but should be cultivated for itself, without being reduced to a passivity or to an activity of the senses' (Irigaray 2000b: 43). Moreover, she points out that

> investment in the look is not as privileged in women as in men. More than other senses, the eye objectifies and masters. It sets at a distance, and maintains a distance. In our culture the predominance of the look over smell, taste, touch and hearing has brought about an impoverishment of bodily relations. The moment the look dominates, the body loses its materiality. (Irigaray 1978: 5)

Female eroticism, by contrast, prioritizes the tactile over the scopic. The discourse of the gaze as a patriarchal form of domination has been primarily promulgated by the 'Freudian theory of sexual difference' as 'based on the *visibility* of difference', namely on 'the basic fact that the male has an obvious sex organ, the penis, and the female has not; when he looks at the woman, Freud apparently sees nothing' (Moi 1985: 132). As Irigaray argues in *Speculum of the Other Woman* (Irigaray 1985), this pushes femininity outside the realm of representation into forbidden interstices between signs and between meanings. In patriarchy, woman is only conceptualizable in terms of negativity and absence, as man's subordinate Other. "Speculum" is in itself a term that deserves some consideration due to its multiaccentual status. It refers to the medical, and primarily gynaecological, instrument of penetration that enables the subjection of the female body to the male gaze; to the mirror of the world (*speculum mundi*) fabricated by patriarchy to project its particular world-view and meant to reflect back the image of "Man" as master of the cosmos; to resulting *speculations* about human nature; and to the notion of woman as the *specular* image of man, a mirror reflecting and confirming his virility as long as she herself is seen to lack what he possesses, or to merely offer a disfigured variation on the dominant theme of masculinity.

The recognition that the image of the mirror is replete with metaphorical connotations varyingly conveying women's repression should encourage a careful questioning of its currency. However, we ought not to yield to the facile assumption that mirrors can simply be annihilated. Indeed, as Lacanian theory shows, they are instrumental to the genesis of subjectivity. Moreover, mirror images, deceptive and distorting as they may be, do not contradict but actually typify the intrinsic character of our worlds, for whatever we may indeed call "reality" is not the domain of some transparent and self-evident truth but rather a hazy realm riddled with hidden passage-ways, secret chambers, murky cellars and spectre-infested closets. In the chapter of *This Sex* entitled 'The Looking Glass, From the Other Side', Irigaray supplies a sort of parable demonstrating that attempts to reject the specular dimension in a world where meanings are inseparable from more or less illusory representations is an ill-advised move. Here, Alice is paralysed by an existence wherein her reflections in the mirror function exclusively *for others*. In penetrating the screen and eluding surveying gazes, she may appear to win a modicum of freedom. In fact, Irigaray argues, this is not the case, for there are ultimately no selves, names or properties beyond represen-tation in a system that posits identity itself as an effect of images.

Irigaray is one of the most enthusiastic advocators of sexual difference, as opposed to equality. In *The Forgetting of Air*, for example, she stresses the irreducibility of difference by claiming that women and men constitute 'horizons and bodies that cannot inter-belong to one another in the sameness of the one' (Irigaray [1983] 1999: 135). As Margaret Whitford observes, Irigaray frequently resorts to spatial and architectural metaphors to fore-ground the distinctiveness of masculinity and femininity. Thus, while man is often ideated as a 'closed house', woman is compared to a 'threshold': 'because of the rhythms of male sexuality, men can establish limits, bound-aries, punctuation in time. But woman as threshold knows nothing of temporal boundaries' (Whitford 1991: 159). Furthermore, man 'sets himself forth, and sets forth the whole, by surrounding himself, by surrounding it, with borders' (Irigaray 1999: 47), whereas woman 'remains neither intact and safe in herself nor a gaping opening' (p. 105) and is therefore 'indefinitely open and closed' (p. 106). It would be erroneous to assume that Irigaray is here naively *accusing* masculinity of being overprotective of its dominion. In fact, while stressing man's dependence on the clear demarcation of zones and limits, she also draws attention to the fate of dispossession that inevitably ensues from self-confinement:

[man is] so localized within his territory that he speaks with himself alone – or at most with his brothers and fellow men, who share the same tone . . . . The proprietor, certainly, but one who is shut up in his house. Cordoned in a knotwork that protects his place but that in the end deprives him of free space. (p. 131).

In *Democracy Begins Between Two* (Irigaray [1994] 2000a), Irigaray develops further her theorization of sexual difference with reference to the concept of the Other. Reluctant to simply indict the conventional association of femininity with alterity, she fosters the elaboration of more adequate definitions of the Other than those promulgated by Western philosophy. The liberal objective pursued by Beauvoir and her followers, namely women's achievement of equality with men, is rejected in favour of an assertion of specifically female traits, rights and demands, in the belief that so-called equality is merely a ploy designed to induce women to emulate men. Irigaray maintains that in taking 'a singular subject' as its fundamental premise, Western philosophy has signally failed to conceive that 'man and woman might be different subjects' (p. 121). Accordingly, she seeks to undermine the approach that posits a 'solitary and historically masculine' subjective exemplar as the ruling referent (p. 122). In her earlier work *I Love To You*, she does so by showing that the West has traditionally entertained a reductive notion of alterity, where 'the other is not defined in his actual reality' but as 'another me': in this framework, 'there is not really any other, but rather only the same: smaller, greater, equal to me' (Irigaray [1992] 1996: 61). In *Democracy*, Irigaray pursues this line of enquiry and asserts that she wants woman 'to be recognized as really an other, irreducible to the masculine subject' (Irigaray 2000a: 125) and maintains that this will only become possible when we move away from the 'model of the one . . . on to the *two*'. Sexual difference encapsulates Irigaray's own paradigm insofar as 'it implies two subjects who should not be situated in either a hierarchical or a genealogical relationship, and that these two subjects have the duty of preserving the human species and of developing its culture, while respecting their differences' (p. 129). Two main objectives govern the project undertaken by Irigaray: the fostering of an ability to practise 'respect for the other as other' (p. 137); the attribution to women *qua* women of 'a language, images and representations' (p. 131) that do justice to their specific proclivities and rights in ways which economic and legal measures alone could never achieve. Clearly, the kind of *respect* commended by Irigaray is utterly unlike the version of male regard for women theorized by Kant and deconstructed in Kofman's writings.

The commonplace notion that sexual relationships are conducive to fusion and possession are drastically challenged in the already mentioned *I Love To You*, where the transformation of "to love" into an intransitive verb serves precisely to emphasize the concepts of difference and distance. Commenting on this work in the later *To Be Two*, she observes: 'Far from wanting to possess you in linking myself to you, I preserve a "to" .... . This "to" safe-guards a place of transcendence between us, a place of respect which is both obligated and desired, a place of possible alliance' (Irigaray [1994] 2000b: 19). This theme is developed further by arguing that far from constituting a curse, the distance between the sexes and its frank acknowledgement are the preconditions of a genuinely intersubjective relationship based on mutual recognition: 'I am sensible to you, leaving you to be you. I am sensible with you, each of us remaining ourselves. ... But is my existence not protected by your irreducibility? Is the total other that you are not my guardian?' (p. 9). Difference is what allows identity to be retained rather than engulfed and suffocated. Drastically reversing the conventional notion that the distance between two people decreases in proportion to the intensity of their love for each other, Irigaray contends that 'we need to love much to be capable of such a dialectic', that is, to be able to love the life of another person 'without giving him one's own' (p. 12) and to shield the other's alterity without seeking either to incorporate it or to be absorbed by it. From this radical inversion, a comprehensive reassessment of sexual relationality, as tradition-ally conceived of and indeed mythologized by the West, follows: 'Where we are constrained to fusion, to discover a gap. Where language unites us fictitiously, to return to our difference. Where others assimilate us, to safe-guard our autonomy. Where some desire to consume us, to preserve a distance' (p. 15).

In 'Rootprints' (Cixous [1994] 2000b), Cixous echoes Irigaray in presenting sexual difference as an exchange between two irreducibly diverse parties: a move which would indubitably seem pointless were it not for the fact that it is triggered by a prodigious curiosity comparable to the sentiment that draws artists towards creation. Moreover, sexual difference should not be regarded as a concomitant of a *single* point of departure or discordance, for it is actually 'innumerable, obviously never reducible to a sex or gender or a familial or social role. It is a wonderful myriad of differential qualities. It passes. It surpasses us. It is our incalculable interior richness' (p. 294). It is the acceptance of separation, paradoxically, that enables a dialogue to take place between beings whose radical diversity may only appear conducive to mutual alienation. The sense of gradual and tantalizing *discovery* which Cixous aims at describing is stylistically epitomized by the following passage:

> In that instant where we hold together, in this point where we would give everything to exchange ourselves and the exchange does not happen, the inexchangeable makes its strange and invisible presence felt. How we want to 'explain' ourselves: to say: to translate: to show: to paint: to add the one to the other, the one in the other, there, precisely, in that unparalleled experience, precisely that experience where desire and impossibility have never been so acute. So acute that a sort of paradoxical miracle is produced: right where the exchange is impossible, an exchange happens, right where we are unable to share, we share this non-sharing ... we stand separaunited, tasting separately-together. (p. 295)

For both Irigaray and Cixous, then, a relationship based on authentic affection and trust requires the preservation and loving cultivation of a space *in between* which belongs to neither party and to which, more importantly, neither will lay claim following the ancestral call of proprietorial instincts. It is by protecting this liminal territory that we may develop an ability to live in harmony with the loved one without *becoming* him or her, and to remain open to the possibility of novel forms of both physical and mental *jouissance* continually emerging from both the words and the silences we share with our partners.

Like Irigaray, Cixous is committed to the celebration of woman's plural sexuality, yet is wary of anchoring female libido to a biological substratum. Her principal concern lies with the exposure of the mechanisms through which sexual and gendered identities are regulated by recourse to binary oppositions, such as male/female and activity/passivity, that serve to hierarchize meaning and subordinate femininity to a phallogocentric order. As Moi observes, 'against any binary scheme of thought, Cixous sets multiple, heterogeneous *difference*' (Moi 1985: 105). Even the terms "masculine" and "feminine" are suspect for they trap both thought and praxis in an adversarial logic concordant with the 'classical vision of sexual opposition between men and women' (Conley 1984: 129). Cixous's analysis of sexual difference revolves around four main themes: the distinctiveness of female libido; the association of femininity with darkness; the domination of the Symbolic order by the principle of the "Selfsame"; the problematization of bisexuality. These themes play a particularly prominent part in the section of *The Newly Born Woman* (Cixous and Clément [1975] 1987) entitled 'Sorties: Out and Out: Attacks/Ways Out/Forays', to which the ensuing paragraphs are devoted.

Pursuing theoretical objectives analogous to Irigaray's, Cixous endeavours to assess the impact on Western culture of Freud's approach to the feminine and to female libido. This, she argues, hinges on three fundamental premises: (1) 'The "fate" of the feminine situation is an effect of an anatomical "defect".' (2) 'There is only one libido and it is male in essence ... .' (3) 'Since the first object of love, for both sexes, is the mother, it is only in the boy that the love of the opposite sex is "natural"' (p. 81). Cixous contends that while sexual difference has undeniable psychological repercussions, the directives stipulated by Freud are reductive, for they are wholly reliant on a perceived *'anatomical* difference between the sexes' and, concomitantly, on the subject's 'fantasized relation to anatomy'. Above all, the supposed primacy of phallic sexuality, insofar as it is based on the valorization of a unitary symbol of power, serves to negate the existence of an eroticism of *'jouissance'*, namely a heady mix of orgasmic bliss, ecstasy and disorientation, that respects neither unity nor boundaries (p. 82). This kind of eroticism is associated by Cixous with femininity and, as will be shown in some detail in *Chapter 5*, with a specifically feminine practice of writing.

The metaphorical link between woman and dark, impenetrable territories has traditionally been invoked both to encode symbolically the troubling mystery of femininity and hence render it tolerable, and to exploit woman's alterity as the ultimate justification for patriarchal strategies of oppression without which phallic conceptions of power and hierarchy would crumble:

> Night to his day – that has forever been the fantasy. Black to his white. Shut out of his system's space, she is the repressed that ensures the system's functioning. Kept at a distance so that he can enjoy the ambiguous advantages of the distance, so that she ... will keep alive the enigma, the dangerous delight of seduction. (pp. 67–8)

However, woman is not only posited as a remote Other so as to allow man to detach himself from her menacing darkness, on the one hand, and to indulge in fantasies of conquest by seeking to bridge the gap between her and himself, on the other. In fact, in constructing femininity as a "dark continent", patriarchy has also engendered a situation in which woman can be 'kept at a distance from herself' and 'made to see (= not see) woman on the basis of what man wants to see of her, which is to say almost nothing' (p. 68).

In describing the power structures underpinning the Symbolic, Cixous observes: 'We are still living under the Empire of the Selfsame. The same masters dominate history from the beginning, inscribing on it the marks of their appropriating economy: history, as a story of phallocentrism, hasn't moved except to repeat itself' (p. 79). The French word used by Cixous to designate the concept of the "Selfsame" is *Propre*, a multiaccentual term which, as Betsy Wing stresses in her Glossary for *The Newly Born Woman*, 'has overtones of property and appropriation' while also meaning ' "proper", "appropriate" and "clean" '. Femininity's relation to the *Propre* is markedly ambivalent: 'Since woman must care for bodily needs and instil the cultural values of cleanliness and propriety, she is deeply involved in what is *propre*, yet she is always somewhat suspect, never quite *propre* herself' (p. 167). The stereotypical demonization of the female genitalia as objects of abhorrence has indubitably fuelled the suspicion that woman's both sanitary and moral decorum is little more than skin deep. Masculinity, conversely, is unproblematically associated with the logic of the "Selfsame" as synonymous with the patriarchal valorization of norms and laws, or what must be considered *proper*, as well as with sexual politics that hinge on *property*, *appropriation* and the dread of *expropriation*. Closely connected with the ethos of the *propre* is that of the *gift*. This refers to traditional masculine responses to the reception of a present, especially one invested with social and ritual connotations. Men find this experience endangering, conducive to a potentially debilitating openness to others, and hence strive to return the gift by means of an offering, often exceeding the value of the original present, in order to restore their sense of control.

Giving and receiving, in the context of patriarchal dispensations, are invariably implicated with the imperatives of self-assertion and self-advancement: 'what *he* wants, whether on the level of cultural or of personal exchanges, ... is that he gain more masculinity: plus-value of virility, authority, power, money, or pleasure, all of which reinforce his phallocentric narcissism at the same time'. According to Cixous, women are capable of transcending this acquisitive mentality. Although this conclusion may come across as rather an arbitrary idealization of female generosity, it follows quite logically from the exclusion of the feminine from the realm of the *propre*: 'She [woman] too gives *for* ... pleasure, happiness, increased value, enhanced self-image. But she doesn't try to "recover her expenses". She is able not to return to herself .... If there is a self proper to woman, paradoxically it is her capacity to de-propriate herself without self-interest' (p. 87).

Exhibiting affinities to the stance proposed by Queer Theory, Cixous's writings argue that the pluralization of erotic desire requires a radical reassessment of the concept of bisexuality. Conventionally, this has been taken to denote the state of 'a complete being, which replaces the fear of castration', thus keeping at bay the ominous phantom of female otherness. Such a creature embodies 'a fantasy of unity', a myth summoned out of an ancestral longing to erase the inevitable marks of sexual difference and the antagonistic relations that this is expected to generate. Cixous radically opposes these traditional approaches intent on using bisexuality as a means of obliterating plurality, and aims, conversely, at asserting difference as a means of undercutting monosexual phallocentrism. Accordingly, she introduces an *'other bisexuality'* (p. 84) keen on facilitating the diffusion of multifarious forms of pleasure: a sexuality that is 'multiple, variable and ever-changing' (Moi 1985: 109) and that thrives on differences and their proliferation. The scenario depicted by Cixous is one wherein

> every subject, who is not shut up within the spurious Phallocentric Performing Theatre, sets up his or her erotic universe. Bisexuality – that is to say the location within oneself of the presence of both sexes, evident and insistent in different ways according to the individual, the nonexclusion of difference or of a sex, and starting with this 'permission' one gives oneself, the multiplication of the effects of desire's inscription on every part of the body and the other body. (Cixous and Clément 1987: 85)

A genuine commitment to the diversification of sexual and gendered identities, and hence of the forms of pleasure and desire available to both men and women, requires us to adopt a critical attitude not only towards the homogenizing programmes indefatigably fostered by Western phallocentrism, whose primary aim is the representation of femininity as a uniformly dubious category of being, but also towards feminist idealizations of womanhood which may ultimately amount to equally grandiose, and therefore no less misleading, generalizations. This idea is expounded by Kristeva in 'Women's Time' (Kristeva [1981] 2000a), where the history of modern Western feminism is subjected to a systematic analysis that demonstrates the shortcomings of both pre- and post-1968 agendas devoted to the emplacement of woman as something of a religious ideal. The quest for equality in which feminists, mainly suffrage advocates and socialists, engaged in the pre-1968 phase ultimately amounted, according to Kristeva, to an effort to guarantee women's participation in male institutions and in a distinctively masculine conception of history. Post-1968 feminists, especially those influenced by psychoanalysis, have, by and large, resisted this assimilative trend. Yet, in celebrating the uniqueness of the feminine, they have often indirectly sustained the patriarchal tendency to relegate woman to the periphery of the Symbolic. This critique of post-1968 feminist theory echoes Guillaumin's reservations about the valorizing of difference. Kristeva, however, does embrace the principle of difference: indeed, she is eager to extend its significance and impact and show that *each person* is irreducibly different and that, as a corollary, there are as many sexual and gendered identities as there are human beings. I will return to this proposition after a more detailed examination of 'Women's Time'.

The essay's central argument proceeds from the assumption that the West knows two main approaches to time: the 'linear', namely historical and chronological, and the 'monumental', namely repetitive and cyclical (p. 183). The latter is frequently associated with femininity on the basis of its affinity with women's biological rhythms. Nevertheless, it is not incompatible with masculine values insofar as it fosters notions of timelessness, continuity and foreseeable recurrence which are traditionally treasured by male-dominated versions of humanist philosophy. To the bipartition of temporality correspond two prevailing ways of classifying human beings as either national units or transnational groups (for example, women, men, the young, etc.). Pre-1968 feminism, suggests Kristeva, embodied the former modality insofar as its principal proponents aimed at situating women and the advocacy of their rights within a linear understanding of history and their programmes were 'deeply rooted in the sociopolitical life of nations' (p. 186). Post-1968 feminist theory, conversely, has sought to emphasize the distinctiveness of femininity as a category not directly tied to national contexts and to rehabilitate a female language and a female history which patriarchy has insistently 'silenced' (p. 187).

Kristeva proposes a third possible model, the premises of which are grounded in Lacanian psychoanalytic theory. She draws attention, in particular, to Jacques Lacan's redefinition of Sigmund Freud's interpretation of the fear of castration as a sociosymbolic phenomenon: that is, a dread of the demise of totality and presence occasioned by the entry into language and by the budding subject's severance from nature. 'Castration, then,' states Kristeva, 'would be the advent of sign and of syntax, that is, of language, as a *separation* from a fusion state of pleasure' (p. 189). Hence, it does not refer to a physical act or experience of mutilation but rather to the 'loss of wholeness and completeness' which inevitably accompanies socialization and the figurative 'ensemble of "cuts" that are indispensable to the advent of the symbolic'. Kristeva contends that although this fate of separation and loss befalls women and men alike, it has different psychological and cultural implications for female and male subjects. Women are commonly assigned an inferior standing in the Symbolic order and considered merely capable of perpetuating a social obligation to the enculturement of the young, and to the assistance of their partners and of their charges: their 'role', accordingly, consists of 'maintaining, developing, and preserving this sociosymbolic contract as mothers, wives, nurses, doctors, teachers' (p. 190). It would be pointless to aim at subverting this time-honoured establishment by merely pursuing the utopia of a 'countersociety' (p. 192), for little is to be gained and much to be imperilled when power changes hands without altering its fundamental nature. Like Wittig, Kristeva argues that the idealization of motherhood, for instance, easily deteriorates into yet another form of mythologization, a refusal to grapple with the reality, or rather the legion *realities*, of femininity in the name of the unifying icon of woman-as-procreator.

Kristeva's concurrently theoretical and pragmatic alternative consists of examining and foregrounding not the difference between men and women as such but the sociosymbolic internalization of difference as the basis of identity. Psychoanalysis can aid this difficult process by showing precisely that the key events in our psychosexual development, as argued in relation to castration anxiety, are always already invested with multiple layers of sociosymbolic significance. Moreover, Kristeva contends, psychoanalytic theory emphasizes the divided status of human subjectivity, the idea that every person is simultaneously 'the same *and* the other, identical *and* foreign', and can therefore help us both recognize and allow scope for the expression of the multiplicity and diversity of each being's potential selves: 'I simply have to analyze incessantly the fundamental separation of my own untenable identity' (p. 198). The acknowledgement of the distinctiveness *of* each subject and of diversity *within* each subject leads Kristeva to propose a shift from a feminism of difference that encourages us to 'think only of two', namely men and women as distinct entities, towards an ethos of 'singularity' that hinges on the recognition of 'the irreducibility of individuals – whether they be men or women' (Kristeva 1996d: 43). This position may seem incongruous with Irigaray's determination to extol *the two*. However, Kristeva, like Irigaray, views the recognition of unassimilable difference as the precondition of any relationship based on mutual respect, and respect, in turn, as both a concept and a practice to be continually negotiated. Thus, the bonds we form with others require choices that are made 'temporarily and forever' (Kristeva 1996a: 72): choices that are contingent upon circumstances and always susceptible to redefinition, yet constant in their unremitting demand that this process of reassessment *must go on*.

In expounding her views on sexual difference and subjective uniqueness, moreover, Kristeva posits love as 'the space of freedom for the individual' (Kristeva 1996e: 121). She is not, through this assertion, advocating the reinscription of femininity and masculinity in a network of signs wherein love is deployed as a stabilizing factor or as a cultural regulator of intersubjectivity. In fact, she is proposing a discourse of love which may form the basis of an ethics capable of defying the concurrently atomizing and homogenizing agendas of the Symbolic order and hence usher in novel ways of addressing the emergence of sexual and gendered identities. As already argued at the end of *Chapter 1*, Kristeva's positions on sexual politics are inseparable from her evaluation of both the personal anxieties and the collective sense of crisis of contemporary culture, and this is characteristically epitomized by her ethics of love:

What I emphasized through the theme of love, of sexual difference and of the role of women, was the singularity of individuals, which seems to me to be the only interesting struggle, especially in relation to this society that stifles, that uniformizes, represented by the spectacle of the stock market. I do not imply by this a romantic cult of love, or a feminist cult of woman as the only solution. It is an insistence on difference ... an insistence on love in its specificity in the context of a society governed by professional demands ... it carries a voice of irony and defiance of the consensus. (Kristeva 1996f: 222–3)

CHAPTER 3

Language and the Subject

if we hold ... that *all* meaning is contextual, it follows that isolated words or general syntactical structures have no meaning until we provide a context for them. How then can they be defined as either sexist or non-sexist *per se*? ... If it is the case ... that similar speech by men and by women tends to be interpreted quite differently, then there is surely nothing inherent in any given word or phrase that can always and forever be constructed as sexist. The crudely conspiratorial theory of language as 'man-made', or as a male plot against women, posits an *origin* (man's plotting) to language, a kind of non-linguistic transcendental signifier for which it is impossible to find any kind of theoretical support. (Moi 1985: 157)

the words rush out of the cornucopia of my brain to course over the surface of the world, tickling reality like fingers on piano keys. Caressing, nudging. They're an invisible army on a peacekeeping mission, a peaceable horde. ... Only – here's the rub – when they find too much perfection, when the surface is already buffed smooth, ... then my little army rebels, breaks into the stores. ... My words begin plucking at threads nervously .... It's an itch at first. Inconsequential. But the itch is soon a torrent behind a straining dam. Noah's flood. (Lethem 2000: 1–2)

the body is our medium for having a world in the first place. We perceive the world only through the body, and when the world reacts to our body in a more or less ideologically oppressive way, we react to the world. Our subjectivity is constituted through such ongoing, open-ended interaction between ourselves and the world. We constantly make something of what the world makes of us. ... It [the body] is perhaps the fundamental ingredient in the make-up of our subjectivity. Yet subjectivity can never be reduced to some bodily feature or other. (Moi 1999: 391)

As shown in *Chapter 1*, debates about the status of language as an ensemble of multifarious symbolic systems have played a pivotal role in developments

in critical and cultural theory since at least the 1970s, with important repercussions in the study of gender and sexuality. As argued in *Chapter 2*,
moreover, sexual and gendered identities are eminently cultural constructs,
practically meaningless independently of the codes and conventions
governing their production. In this chapter, these propositions are expanded
to show that debates about language and debates about the construction of
sexual and gendered identities come together in the recognition that language
itself is instrumental to the fashioning of subjectivity. The relationship
between language and the subject is here examined with reference to three
areas of enquiry: the inscription of sexist ideologies in linguistic structures
and semantic customs; the role played by language in the constitution of
subjectivity as an open-ended process; the exposure of the limitations of
patriarchal discourse, especially in its deployment by mainstream Western
philosophy. Throughout the three segments of the discussion devoted to
these topics, two main issues are foregrounded: (1) French feminist theory's
positions on the possibility or viability of undermining patriarchal forms of
signification; (2) the notion that no assessment of subjectivity can dispense
with an evaluation of language insofar as the latter plays a vital part in engendering, and indeed *speaking*, the subject. Finally, it must also be stressed that
Chapter 3 is closely linked up with *Chapter 5*, as they both address issues of
language. However, the present chapter focuses primarily on the status of
language as the underpinning of the Symbolic order, through which socialized subjectivities are moulded. The later chapter, while stressing that the
Symbolic cannot be conclusively eluded, highlights aspects of language that
retain a connection with the phenomena of corporeality and embodiment.

SIGNS IN QUESTION: ADDRESSING LINGUISTIC STEREOTYPES

In the social/materialist camp, considerable emphasis is placed on the need to
denaturalize a vast body of assumptions about femininity by exposing their
discursive character and their frequently stereotyping proclivities. Colette
Guillaumin, for instance, has stressed the reductivism of the linguistic
conventions on which male-dominated structures of signification, and hence
of power, insistently rely. 'The appropriation of women,' she writes, 'is
explicit in the very banal semantic habit of referring to female social actors
by their sex as a matter of priority (as "women")'. Thus, while male subjects
are designated by recourse to social, political and professional appellations
without any overt reference to their sex, women are invariably defined on the
sole basis of their femaleness. Guillaumin offers the following examples:

A *pupil* has been punished with compulsory detention for a month; A *girl* has been reprimanded (report of disciplinary action at the École Polytechnique); A company director, a lathe-operator, a croupier and a woman ... (about a group meeting to give their opinion on some matter); They killed tens of thousands of workers, students and women (Castro on the subject of the Batista regime). (Guillaumin 1996: 73)

It is simply taken for granted, in such phrases, that all subjects not explicitly referred to as female are, by definition, male. The practice of expunging all allusions to a woman's role speaks volumes, by virtue of its very silence, about the relationship between language and gendered subjectivity: 'What is said, and said only about female human beings, is their effective position in class relations: that of being primarily and fundamentally women. This is their social existence; the rest is additional and – we are made to understand – does not count' (p. 73).

Like Guillaumin, Monique Wittig is acutely aware of the linguistic manoeuvres carried out by patriarchal forms of signification so as to delimit woman's social status. At the same time, she seeks to highlight the dangers implicit in some feminists' endeavour to counteract the operations of masculinist language by glorifying a quintessentially female, primordial discourse associated with an idealized notion of matriarchy. Indeed, such a programme merely spawns yet another progeny of reductive slogans. As Doris Mitterbacher observes, Wittig invites women to beware of the 'myth of motherright', the ideal of a matriarchal society being itself 'based on heterosexuality' as the norm, and of slogans along the lines of 'Woman is wonderful' because these 'reinforce the trap of the myth of woman ... created by men in the first place' (Mitterbacher, 'Monique Wittig'). What Wittig is concerned with, conversely, is the elaboration of an alternative model that underscores the fundamental instability of all linguistic identities. Faithful to the idea, discussed in *Chapter 2*, that lesbianism constitutes the only radically political means of subverting patriarchy by refuting its heterosexual priorities, Wittig extends the aims of materialist lesbian feminism to her exploration of the relationship between language and subjectivity, and contends that a truly innovative discourse requires the abolition of the terms "man" and "woman" themselves. Wittig uses the neologism *to lesbianize* to describe the transgression of patriarchal heterosexism by a discourse that releases identity from the constraints of man-made codes: an identity constantly involved in processes of readjustment and reconfiguration and hence irreducible to *he* and/or *she* and best rendered by the neutral *one*. (Wittig's practical application of these ideas in her fictional work will be addressed in *Chapter 5*.)

Language is so thoroughly permeated by patriarchal tenets that even apparently innocent signs, even words as anonymous as "the", can ultimately be shown to sustain patriarchy's universalizing strategies: namely, the conversion of contingently produced 'concepts into general laws which claim to hold true for all societies, all epochs, all individuals. Thus one speaks of *the* exchange of women, *the* difference between the sexes, *the* symbolic order, *the* Unconscious' (Wittig 2000a: 140). If it is proverbially arduous to interrogate and transcend these generalizing metanarratives, this is because they saturate social existence at all levels, since the signifying systems through which they are invoked are themselves ubiquitous and often impenetrable due to their very pervasiveness. As Carolyn Guertin observes, in Wittig's interpretation of the relationship between language and the subject, 'the entire world' is conceived of as

> a great register where the most diverse languages come to have themselves recorded, such as the language of the Unconscious, the language of fashion, the language of the exchange of women where human beings are literally the signs which are used to communicate. These languages, or rather these discourses, fit into one another, interpenetrate one another, support one another, reinforce one another, auto-engender, and engender one another. Linguistics engenders semiology and structural linguistics, structural linguistics engenders structuralism, which engenders the Structural Unconscious. The ensemble of these discourses produces a confusing status for the oppressed, which makes them lose sight of the material cause of their oppression and plunges them into a kind of ahistoric vacuum. (Guertin, 'Critical Stings')

Wittig's critique of the Symbolic includes a drastic questioning of the role played by binary oppositions in Western thought. In 'Homo Sum', in particular, she inspects

> the first table of opposites which history has handed down to us, as it has been recorded by Aristotle (*Metaphysics*, Book I, 5, 6):

Limited	Unlimited
Odd	Even
One	Many
Right	Left
Male	Female
Rest	Motion
Straight	Curved
Light	Dark

Good	Bad
Square	Oblong

We may observe that

right	left
male	female
light	dark
good	bad

are terms of judgment and evaluation, ethical concepts, that are foreign to the series from which I extracted them. The first series is a technical, instrumental series corresponding to a division needed by the tool for which it was created ... The second series is heterogeneous to the first one. So it happens that as soon as the precious conceptual tools resting on division (variations, comparisons, differences) were created, they were immediately ... turned into a means of creating metaphysical and moral differentiation in Being. (Wittig [1990] 2000c: 146–7)

In this respect, Wittig's work bears affinities to the project undertaken by Hélène Cixous. As shown in *Chapter 1*, in the context of a delineation of poststructuralist philosophies, one of Cixous's principal concerns consists of highlighting the part played by binary oppositions in demonizing femininity and of exposing their specious status: in attempting to privilege one term over another, they ultimately reveal the two terms' interdependence. Wittig, as we have seen, also emphasizes the sinister tendency to link up femaleness with negative concepts. However, there are crucial divergences in the two critics' political objectives: while Cixous encourages men and women to embrace the principle of sexual difference as the prerequisite of a productive appreciation of their irreducible distinctiveness, Wittig is committed to dismantling that principle by transcending the very categories of masculinity and femininity. Furthermore, she contends that difference has been insistently deployed by patriarchy as a means of marginalizing women by becoming synonymous with moral deficiency and sprawling multiplicity: 'Everything that was "good" belonged to the series of the One (as Being). Everything that was "many" (*different*) belonged to the series of the "bad", assimilated to nonbeing, to unrest, to everything that questions what is good' (p. 47; emphasis added). Wittig is clearly unwilling to contemplate a deconstructive scenario of the type envisaged by Cixous. Binary oppositions, in her critique, nakedly encode conflicts and are not, therefore, appropriable as a means of demonstrating the lacunae of phallogocentric discourse.

Christine Delphy is comparably unsympathetic to poststructuralist interpretations of difference and binary thought. In commenting on the proposition that 'things can only be distinguished by opposition to other things', which she ascribes to 'Derrida and his clones' (Delphy 1996: 34) – although, strictly speaking, it strikes its roots in structuralist philosophy – Delphy accuses Derrida of reinforcing narrowly hierarchical conceptions of difference:

> We may agree things are only known by distinction and hence differentiation, but these differentiations can be, and often are, multiple. Alongside cabbages and carrots, which are not 'opposites' of each other, there are courgettes, melons, and potatoes. Moreover, distinctions are not necessarily hierarchical; vegetables are not placed on a scale of value. Indeed, they are often used as a warning against any attempt at hierarchization: we are told not to compare (or try to add) cabbages and carrots. They are incommensurable. ... Those who adhere to Derrida's thesis thus fail to distinguish between the differences on which language is based. (p. 35)

Delphy's reading of Derrida, however, is somewhat unilateral and hence potentially misleading. Derrida *has* indeed emphasized the notion that differences are always already plural and proliferating and, as a corollary, ill-disposed to accommodation within a rigid and durable hierarchy. Moreover, he has consistently maintained that if meaning in language is a product of differential oppositions, it is also, inevitably, transient and prone to *play*. The slippage of meaning is epitomized by the concept of *différance*. This designates the principle of "difference" – namely the mechanism whereby, as proposed by Ferdinand de Saussure, a sign derives meaning from its phonemic difference from another sign within a minimal pair – while concurrently referring to the idea of "deferral". In trying to establish the meaning of a sign on the basis of difference, argues Derrida, we cannot limit ourselves to minimal pairs, for a sign leads not to *one* other sign but rather to legion other signs ("dog" is not "log", but also not "fog", "jog", "don", "dot", and so on). The mendacious character of Western philosophy ultimately lies with its endeavour to arrest the displacement of meaning by subordinating the unpredictable detours of language to overarching ideas, or transcendental signifieds, such as "reality", "truth", "self", "presence", "man" and "god", on the basis of which hierarchical relations may be founded.

Arguably, Wittig's and Delphy's approaches bear witness not merely to the radical materialist aversion to a feminism of difference but also, more broadly, to a poststructuralism committed to the sustained exploration of difference in both the linguistic and the psychoanalytic fields. The following segment of this chapter is devoted to the elaboration of a feminist approach to the relationship between language and subjectivity, both of which, conversely, embrace poststructuralism. Wittig and Delphy are deeply suspicious of theories of language that foreground the notion of difference because they regard the latter as a principle inimical to the advancement of feminist causes. Julia Kristeva, whose writings are examined next, adopts quite a contrasting stance, seeking to integrate a range of poststructuralist positions with a novel approach to the relationship between language and the subject's psychosexual development.

SUBJECTS-IN-PROCESS: JULIA KRISTEVA'S PHILOSOPHY OF LANGUAGE

According to Kristeva, the subject is fundamentally a product of language. Redefining Jacques Lacan's distinction between the Imaginary and the Symbolic in the light of both her early research as a semiotician and a linguist and her subsequent involvement with psychoanalytic theory and practice, Kristeva has been concerned throughout her career with the processes through which the subject is brought into the discursive domain. As Diane Prosser MacDonald points out, one of the most intriguing aspects of Kristeva's conception of language is its definition as 'a heterogeneous process within which the "speaking subject" is constituted'. As such, it does not represent 'a fixed structure' but rather 'a complex and ever changing "signifying process"' (Prosser MacDonald 1995: 89). A related leading thread throughout Kristeva's work is the idea that subjectivity is precarious:

> all identities are unstable: the identity of linguistic signs, the identity of meaning and, as a result, the identity of the speaker. And in order to take account of this destabilization of meaning and of the subject I thought the term 'subject in process' would be appropriate. Process in the sense of process but also in the sense of a legal proceeding where the subject is committed to trial, because our identities in life are constantly called into question, brought to trial, over-ruled. (Kristeva 1989a: 19)

Kristeva's theories have developed through three main phases whose principal concerns can be summarized as follows. In her writings of the 1960s, Kristeva focuses on *semiotics*, namely the science of signs, and on *poetic language* and promotes the idea that experimental writing and art are capable of subverting the conventions of everyday language by defying logic and by evoking alternative meanings, patterns and rhythms of expression. In the 1970s, Kristeva's pivotal preoccupation resides with the exploration of the relationship between linguistics and psychoanalytic theory. It is at this juncture that she formulates the concepts of the *semiotic* and the *symbolic* to describe contrasting modalities of signification which coincide with different stages of human development. In the 1980s and 1990s, Kristeva's emphasis shifts to the elaboration of theoretical models capable of accounting for the complex and mutable relations between language and the *body*. Especially important, in this context, is the notion of the *abject* as the epitome of the defiling and ambiguous states which challenge the subject's bodily and mental boundaries. Developing an interest which can be traced back to the 1970s, in this phase Kristeva also tackles the issue of *foreignness*, as a condition of estrangement and alienation *internal* to the Self. Kristeva's positions on the relationship between language and the body will be discussed in *Chapter 5* and her views on the foreigner in *Chapter 6*. The present chapter is specifically concerned with elucidating the perspectives formulated in the first two phases.

In an interview with Serge Gavronsky, Kristeva has described the objectives pursued in the initial stage of her career thus: 'I wanted to propose models that would most convincingly take into account the polyphonic elements in works of twentieth-century avant-garde writers .... . In order to read a text, I think you've got to get into the precise details of signification, rhythm, syntax' (Kristeva 1996g: 205). As indicated by the title of one of Kristeva's earliest works, *Séméiotiké: Studies Towards a Semanalysis* (first published 1969), her initial focus is on semiotics. (Many of the essays included in *Séméiotiké* have been translated into English as *Desire in Language: A Semiotic Approach to Literature and Art*, 1980.) Semiotics argues that the signs through which human beings attempt to express themselves and to communicate with others include not merely words and visual images but also gestures, postures, clothes, food, music, art, advertising and legion other structures of symbolization, thus expanding substantially conventional notions of language and of textuality to encompass virtually any form of exchange of signals in time and space. Kristeva uses semiotics to show that the idea of a stable sign is a myth promoted by certain strata of society at particular times in the interests of ideological stability, and therefore stresses the necessity of developing theoretical tools that will enable us to identify the aporias and lacunae in language where meaning falls apart and sign systems no longer function as a guarantee of order. Kristeva also maintains that a science of signs can never be universal, general and objective in the way a natural science may aspire to be. In a sense, it can never be truly *scientific*. Moreover, all general principles can ultimately be shown to assume a rationality which, in the West, has invariably been the product of specific cultural conditions rather than a timeless truth.

In *Séméiotiké*, Kristeva proposes a shift from the analysis of meaning to the analysis of the signifying process: she is not so much concerned with what texts mean as with the creative and interpretative acts which give them meaning. *Signifiance* is the term used to describe the process of production of meaning, while *semanalysis* designates the critical method designed to explore this process. In this early work, Kristeva argues that language produces not only meanings but also human subjects, in both psychological and physical terms, and that the body, though traditionally marginalized by linguistics, actually plays a vital part in the signifying process and should become a central object of study. Furthermore, human minds and bodies alike can be regarded as products of ever-proliferating stories that we unremittingly tell to others about ourselves and which we also, in a sense, tell to ourselves in order to consolidate our self-images. Concurrently, we are constantly narrating other people in much the same way as we are narrating ourselves. In this perspective, anything one might call 'personal development' will consist of modifications in 'the leading questions that one addresses to the tale of one's life and the lives of important others' (Schafer 1983: 219). Most importantly, identity is not established by a personalized life script, for subjectivity moves backwards and forwards among several narratives. Kristeva uses the term *intertextuality* to describe both texts and human subjects as points of intersection of multiple voices, as multi-layered and plural entities.

One further keyword introduced by Kristeva in *Séméiotiké* is *ideologeme*, by which she means a textual formation produced within specific cultural and historical circumstances. Epic, myth and the folktale, for instance, are said to be based on the ideologeme of the *symbol* insofar as they are closed and static, and the ideas and characters they present are supposed to be decodable according to a fixed repertoire of symbols. The modern novel, by contrast, is associated with the ideologeme of the *sign*: it is open and dynamic because there is no officially sanctioned way of reading and decoding its linguistic chains. From this it follows that certain textual formations are more likely to be supportive of the status quo than others. The *monological* text, namely a text committed to promoting a single ideology, aims at conveying a stable reality, whereas the *dialogical* text, namely a text which celebrates polyphony, transgresses the symbolic law and suggests that any definition of reality is inexorably rescindable.

The type of language that overtly subverts mainstream conventions is *poetic language*: a discourse that refuses to reduce the available systems of signs to communicational vehicles by suspending the rules of logic, truth, consciousness and identity, and where meaning is never localizable to the extent that it is nowhere and everywhere at once. Poetic language is not exclusively peculiar to poetry, for it can also be found in prose. Indeed, it can be found wherever language challenges and reorders the principles of everyday communication and the structures of grammar and syntax, and whenever an artist chooses to experiment, more or less disrespectfully or flamboyantly, with sounds and images in a fashion reminiscent of oneiric representation. The 'poetic word' is 'polyvalent and multidetermined, adheres to a logic ... exceeding that of codified discourse and fully comes into being only in the margins of recognized culture' (Kristeva 1980: 65) by promoting the coexistence of 'nonexclusive opposites' (p. 71). The subversive moves enacted by poetic language cannot be regarded merely as an effect of individual idiosyncrasies, since they frequently reflect broad cultural preoccupations by encoding the apprehension of crisis as an anxious search for novel forms of expression and speculation. Thus, although poetic language indubitably undermines dominant structures of discursive exchange, it does not incontrovertibly transcend them, or indeed seek to do so. As Prosser MacDonald observes, 'poetic language can be transgressive because it is neither outside of the reigning social/symbolic order nor inside it, but at its limit' (Prosser MacDonald 1995: 94). Furthermore, while the Symbolic may be defied and punctured by means of an imaginative reactivation of the instinctual drives which adult language notoriously silences, it cannot be conclusively abandoned. Indeed, its relinquishment would be conducive to a psychotic condition marked by a total lack of reference: that is to say, by the loss of any ability to relate to the world and articulate it semiotically.

In the 1970s, Kristeva develops her ideas on *poetic language* by focusing on a selection of experimental writers in order to investigate the relationship between literature and the social dimension of language. The principal text of this period is *Revolution in Poetic Language* (Kristeva [1974] 1984), the central assumption of which is that culture represses certain forms of language and that this repression is both psychological and political. Both fascism and xenophobia, for example, assert the validity of their statements by ostracizing any oppositional voices. Fascism is an effect of the transformation of repressed fantasies into despotic political regimes. Xenophobia, for its part, is an effect of the transformation of repressed desires into a fear of otherness. Kristeva argues that to prevent social structures from becoming tyrannical, we must embrace an *ethics of dissolution* and hence become capable of questioning all values before they crystallize to the point that they degenerate into totalitarianism. This requires a grasp of the multidimensionality of all discourses. Specifically, we need to recognize that there are always at least two interplaying levels of textuality. On the one hand, we experience the *pheno-text*: a term related to the Greek *phenomenon*, namely "appearance", and hence to sets of words we actually see and conventionally connect with certain meanings. On the other, we interact with a *geno-text*, a term related to *genesis*, that is, "origin", "process", "production", and, by extension, to aspects of the text which we do not immediately see and must retrace by inspecting the ways in which meaning is engendered. As long as we are wholly reliant on the apparent meaning of a text, we have no way of mapping out the process of its construction. We just take it for granted as a neatly bundled package of meaning and are unable to question its political affiliations. Conversely, once we concentrate on the processes through which the text has been produced, we may be able to understand its relation to myriad ideologies.

One aspect of the project delineated above which is immediately relevant to feminist theory consists of its determination to expose various reductive approaches to the relationship between discourse and gender fostered by the Symbolic. It is especially vital, for Kristeva, to acknowledge that what culture designates as *feminine* language is not, in a literal sense, the language used by women but rather the kind of language which disrupts the rigid rules of the Symbolic and, by implication, of patriarchy. In modernist poetry and poetic prose, for example, this feminine language manifests itself in fluid structures and musical sequences which bring into play unconscious drives and bodily affects. However, such texts are not necessarily produced by women: in fact, three of the main writers discussed by Kristeva are Joyce, Mallarmé and Lautréamont. Our attention, argues Kristeva, should shift from the *gender of the author* to the *gender of the text*. Concurrently, the text capable of challenging and fragmenting conventional syntax and logic may be considered revolutionary even if its content is not overtly feminist or indeed political. A text's political significance often lies with its unorthodox structure and use of language, imagery and rhythm rather than its themes. Virginia Woolf's fiction is a case in point. Several feminist writers, most notably Kate Millett and Elaine Showalter, have accused Woolf's novels of being apolitical: they cannot be regarded as feminist because they do not tackle openly ideological problems pertaining to women's oppression, and because Woolf's ideal of the *androgynous mind* as an amalgamation of feminine and masculine elements constitutes an escape from conflict and struggle in favour of a desensualized and depoliticized world-view. Yet, as Toril Moi has suggested (Moi 1985), in a Kristevan frame of reference Woolf's novels could be seen as political, for in highlighting the fragmentation of subjectivity and the fluctuations of the mind between consciousness and the unconscious, rationality and dream, past and present, they undermine the logic of symbolic discourse.

Most importantly, Kristeva invites us to interrogate the assumption, endemic in Western thought, that language, as an abstract system, is able to produce unified and rational subjects and that syntax, in particular, serves to stabilize language by subjecting expression to relatively inflexible rules: in other words, that an orderly language secures an orderly mind. In order to challenge this assumption, Kristeva posits an ongoing tension between two conflicting linguistic modalities: the *semiotic* and the *symbolic*:

> What I call 'the semiotic' takes us back to the pre-linguistic states of childhood where the child babbles the sounds s/he hears, or where s/he articulates rhythms, alliterations, or stresses, trying to imitate his/her surroundings. In this state the child doesn't yet possess the necessary linguistic signs and thus there is no meaning in the strict sense of the term. It is only after the mirror phase or the experience of castration in the Oedipus complex that the individual becomes subjectively capable of taking on the signs of language, of articulation as it has been prescribed – and I call that 'the symbolic'. (Kristeva 1989a: 19)

The symbolic never conclusively succeeds in replacing and dominating the semiotic. Indeed, its supposedly rational criteria and rigorous syntactical rules can never have it all their own way insofar as the territory of reason is continually criss-crossed by corporeal and irrational impulses and desires.

'Discrete quantities of energy move through the body of the subject,' Kristeva writes in *Revolution*, 'who is not yet constituted as such and, in the course of his development, they are arranged according to the various constraints imposed on this body – always already in the semiotic process – by family and social structures' (Kristeva 1984: 25). However, such familial and societal constraints never manage to repress entirely the budding subject's pre-linguistic energies and traces thereof, accordingly, go on disrupting the mature adult's language. They manifest themselves through forms of discourse which subvert the rules of syntax, such as experimental writing, and through noises, intonations, gestures, rhythmic patterns, nonsense, wordplay and laughter that are reminiscent of the infant's first attempts at self-expression. The semiotic thus remains capable of disrupting the relatively crystallized categories of symbolic language by creating a playful, indeed carnivalesque, excess over precise meaning and by shunning the criteria of coherence and stability beloved of symbolic law. According to Carol Mastrangelo Bové, the resurgence of the semiotic in poetic discourse gives rise to a 'new language ... defined in opposition to traditional language where logically connected clauses and denotation are primary. Instinctual language highlights connotations and creates patterns that are more rhythmical than logical' (Mastrangelo Bové 1984: 219).

Laughter, in this context, represents a particularly intriguing phenomenon. As Martha J. Reineke observes:

> [it] demonstrates a linkage of expression between the body (out of which language wells, explodes, overflows and bursts forth), the subject, and 'a material outside'. What previous epistemologies have divided now are joined in a single economy. As such, laughter offers preliminary lessons in understanding the development of an economy of signification and emerging subjectivity. (Reineke 1997: 60)

Laughter is also a vital component of creative literature as the first symptom of a crisis in signification, of the rupture of the orderly structures and stable identities prescribed by the Symbolic. To substantiate this point, Kristeva cites Charles Baudelaire, who views laughter as belonging to the kind of artistic experience that conveys 'the power of being oneself and someone else at one and the same time' (Kristeva 1984: 223).

One of the most traumatic aspects of the subject's entry into language coincides with its separation from the maternal body. This is rendered inevitable by the fact that we need to perceive the world as distinct, as Other, in order to be able to relate to it and to other people, and that any relationship based on the denial of difference, indeed on *undifferentiation*, is bound to hinder our socialization and enculturement: 'Dependence on the mother is severed, and transformed into a symbolic relation to an other; the constitution of the Other is indispensable for communicating with an other' (p. 48). Furthermore, at a certain stage of its psychosexual evolution the subject might well feel trapped by the maternal body and perceive it not as protective but rather as oppressive and engulfing. In their extreme physical closeness, mother and child constitute a double body that obfuscates any clear distinction between one person and another, one category and another, and is therefore incompatible with the operations of adult language insofar as these pivot on principles of separation, classification and compartmentalization. Kristeva argues that there is a close analogy between the process through which the child separates itself from the mother and the process through which it acquires language. This is borne out by the incidence, in both experiences, of strategies of *incorporation* and collusion between *presence* and *absence*. The infant incorporates the maternal body, for example in the experience of being breast-fed, and, at a later stage, the child incorporates the signs of language which enable it to function in the adult world. At first, the infant relates to the maternal body as if it were a part of its own body that could never be taken away. Gradually, it realizes that, in fact, the mother may withdraw, go away, and that it must learn to cope with the possibility of her absence. The very structure of language is based on this early experience: in symbolic discourse, presence and absence are inseparable insofar as a sign which is present in an utterance is always traversed by absence, namely by the traces of other signs which could have been used instead and by the ghosts of signs which we consciously or unconsciously associate with it.

What makes the process of self-differentiation particularly painful is the fact that when the child first experiences the urge to distinguish itself from the other, it is not yet in possession of adult language and is incapable, therefore, of articulating that urge. As a result, the child expresses its efforts to create a boundary between itself and others *through the body*. These efforts often manifest themselves in violent ways, as frustration, fear, anger and, primarily, a visceral resentment against the physical *stuff* that threatens the body's self-containedness, such as milk, slime, blood, ooze and tears. The child's sense of disorientation is amplified by its fear that all attempts at separation may be vain and that it may become indistinguishable from the murky and polluting materials it longs to shed. What is hard to ignore, as this anguished psychodrama hurtles towards its denouement, is that identity is only ever achieved at great cost and that its attainment does not exempt us from an ongoing subjection to both external cultural forces, which aim at shaping us in particular ways, and no less oppressive internal forces, such as intense feelings of self-fragmentation, depression and horror. These affects can never be fully tamed because they are basic components of our being and it is precisely this realization, for Kristeva, that makes the speaking-subject a *wounded body*.

PATRIARCHAL PHILOSOPHY, FEMININE LANGUAGE: SYMBOLIC NORMS AND THEIR TRANSGRESSION

One of the most conspicuous facets of French feminist theory since the 1970s has consisted of sustained efforts to expose the pitfalls of patriarchal forms of expression and their deleterious impact on the subject's agency. This has entailed a questioning of the codes and conventions regulating what is considered an *acceptable* or *legitimate* form of language, as well as speculations about the plausibility of formulating *alternative* linguistic modalities. Antoinette Fouque subscribes to this critical project by emphasizing that a radical modification of ideas requires an equally drastic reconfiguration of the words employed to convey them and concludes that what is needed is no less than a 'revolution of the symbolic' (Fouque 1987: 54). C. G. Burke, likewise, argues that 'to find and use an appropriate female language ... a *prise de conscience* [capture of consciousness] must be followed by a *prise de la parole* [capture of speech]' (Burke 1978: 844). According to Annie Leclerc, the primary aim of such a *prise de la parole* ought to be 'to invent a language that is not oppressive, a language that does not leave speechless but that loosens the tongue' (Leclerc 1980: 179).

The quest for an emancipating idiom has been consistently pursued by Chantal Chawaf, who maintains that 'feminine language must ... work on life passionately, scientifically, poetically, politically' (Chawaf 1980: 177–8) and indeed endeavours to articulate this conviction through her own fictional writing. For some critics, Chawaf's 'dazzling combinations of words, images and metaphors forge new possibilities for conceptualizing the body, particularly the female body'. Others 'insist that traditional archetypes of woman and established literary convention contaminate her avant-garde practice' (Droppleman 1985). Thus, her originality notwithstanding, Chawaf has sometimes been said to perpetuate disabling images of the feminine as coterminous with inertia and passivity. However, as argued earlier in relation to Kristeva's approach to literary experimentation, innovation should not be measured exclusively with reference to content and it could be argued that Chawaf's work is most challenging and irreverent towards generic norms not when it explicitly departs from established procedures but when it displaces them through parodic manipulation and, specifically, an anti-mimetic, 'hyperbolic performance of gender and genre norms' (ibid.). A visual analogy of this strategy can be found in many of Cindy Sherman's photographs, where the artist appears to conform to familiar clichés in the representation of women but actually exaggerates them to the point that they require us to look at the image with a heightened sense of its artificiality and implicit subversion of conventions. The techniques utilized by both Chawaf and Sherman suggest that a work is more radically transgressive, at least potentially, when it relies on ironical distortions than when it claims to propose altogether novel themes and stylistic devices which, given sufficient usage, would themselves rapidly become conventions in any case.

Since the critics who have militated most eloquently in favour of a feminine language have, in various ways, tended to emphasize the latter's connection with the female body and female libido, the topics mentioned in the preceding paragraphs will be examined in more detail in *Chapter 5, Writing and the Body*. What the present discussion seeks to highlight is the broadly political significance of feminist interventions intent on problematizing the authority of patriarchally oriented speaking and writing practices. The concept of *écriture féminine* advocated by Cixous, in particular, can be described as having political cogency insofar as it is based on the assumption that there is an area of textual production that courses beneath the surface of masculine discourse and occasionally disrupts it, thereby challenging not only the subject positions imposed upon women by patriarchy but also, more broadly, patriarchal *institutions* committed to ideals of unity, rationalism and the strict regulation of the relationship between Self and Other. In this context:

> [The] political does not stem simply from the political scene, from the political events reported by the media; it begins obviously by the discourse of the speaking subject on him or herself, which is to say that all that makes the political scene – relations of power, of oppression, enslaving, exploitation – all of this begins with me: first of all in the family and in the interior of myself. Tyrants, despots, dictators, capitalism, all that forms the visible political space for us is only the visible and theatrical, photographable projection of the Self-with-against-the-other. I suggest we add the preposition 'withagainst' to the English language. The equivalent in French being '*contre*'. (O'Grady 1996)

The oppressive systems to which Cixous refers have traditionally relied on the support of disciplines deemed quintessentially masculine, and hence infallible by virtue of their intellectual and methodological precision. Therefore, an apposite target for feminist theorists committed to the interrogation of phallogocentrism is precisely the Temple of Western Philosophy with its Inner Sanctum of thoroughly *enlightened* male thinkers. Michèle Le Doeuff's writings, in particular, indicate that the construction of gendered subjectivity by language in patriarchal cultures has depended to a considerable extent on the distinction between a discourse supposedly based on reason and intellectual thoroughness, conventionally associated with philosophy and masculinity, and a discourse emanating from imagination and impressionism, habitually linked with fantasy literature and femininity. Cixous corroborates this proposition by stressing that, as a corollary, 'woman is always associated with passivity in philosophy' (Cixous and Clément 1987: 64). Le Doeuff questions the dichotomy described above by casting doubt on the very tendency to prioritize the masculine discourse of philosophy as somehow unerring. In *Hipparchia's Choice* (Le Doeuff 2000), in particular, she alerts us to the dangers inherent in the investment of the principle of 'rigour' with undisputable authority. Indeed this principle, in discouraging people 'from advancing something which has not yet been entirely thought through and well-founded', risks blocking the speculative thrust in the absence of which nothing truly novel may be contemplated. By contrast, 'impressionism' allows us to ideate new scenarios and possibilities, to voice 'little perceptions and intuitions, no matter how faltering' which might, by and by, generate fresh ways of seeing and understanding our worlds (p. 48).

The Philosophical Imaginary provides the theoretical premises for this position by arguing that no philosophical argument is ever wholly rational and consistent, due to the persistent intrusion in its folds of *imaginary* elements: 'Philosophical discourse is inscribed and declares its status as philosophy through a break with myth, fable, the poetic, the domain of the image' (Le Doeuff 1989: 1). Le Doeuff's approach consists of exposing 'strands of the imaginary operating in places where, in principle, they are supposed not to belong and yet where, without them, nothing would have been accomplished' (p. 2). A paradigmatic example is supplied by Galileo's revolutionary redefinition of time as a scientific discovery in which rational speculation colludes with traditional motifs derived from astrology and alchemy and cannot, therefore, 'be thought of in terms of a rigorously scientific break, an act by which the scientific detaches itself radically from the non-scientific, from reverie, the imaginary, the obscure and the confused' (p. 43). The methodology adopted by Le Doeuff is akin to Derridean deconstruction in the sense that it aims at showing how philosophical systems contradict their own basic premises by relying on textual elements, specifically images, that are presumed to be incompatible with their abstract parameters. Moreover, images do not serve merely ornamental purposes; nor do they work instrumentally to clarify complex ideas for the sake of their recipients. In fact, they sustain and further intellectual reflection in ways of which reason alone is incapable. The domain of consciousness is thus both punctured and enhanced by unconscious fantasies, barely formalized apprehensions and dreamlike visions and emblems.

Le Doeuff's principal objective, therefore, lies with foregrounding the existence of an ongoing tension between a philosophical system's intentions and its outcomes, between the materials it deliberately includes and those it is unable to exclude in spite of its strenuous efforts to this effect. As a result, we witness 'no closure of discourse, discourse only ever being a compromise – or bricolage – between what it is legitimate to say, what one would like to contend or argue, and what one is forced to recognize' (p. 19). This open-endedness also has the effect of suspending interpretation, of endlessly deferring the reader's progress towards the possession and ascertaining of sense. Indeed, texts which pre-empt the closure of discourse evince a 'polysemy', namely a state of affairs in which 'no *one* immediate meaning prevails', that ultimately renders them unsituatable as well: '*Atopos* means that which has no place, but also that which is bizarre, extravagant, strange. An atopia is a text which cannot immediately be given one single correct meaning by its reader' (p. 54).

Textual boundlessness is also a recurring theme in Sarah Kofman's work, lack of closure resulting from the fact that the subject's engagement with language is a never-ending process, a mobile exchange of signifiers divorced from any uncontestable signifieds. The moment we force the movement of meaning to stall, thought itself comes to an end and a stagnant ideology enthrones itself in its place. The ongoing deferral of sense is epitomized by intertextual operations whereby any ensemble of signs is ultimately liable to be appropriated and transformed by an indefinite series of *other* texts. Kofman illustrates this idea in her reading of E. T. A. Hoffmann's *Life and Opinions of Murr the Tomcat* (1999), where a feline autodidact pens his memoirs upon sheets he has torn out of his master's autobiography. In Kofman's analysis, Hoffmann's work problematizes the relationship between language and subjectivity by using a hybrid narrative and thereby producing a comparably composite, indeed schizophrenic subject: the story represents 'an unclassifiable, atopic book belonging to no determinable genre: a bastard text that mixes with the life of the cat pages that are quite foreign to it ... . A book that is about neither a man nor an animal, that, furthermore, breaks the order of the logos – a book with neither beginning nor end' (Kofman 1984: 72).

Furthermore, Kofman, like Le Doeuff, underscores philosophy's inability to extricate itself conclusively from the realm of fantasy. Her reading of Friedrich Nietzsche's critique of logic, for instance, intimates that philosophical abstractions frequently amount to a kind of consolatory therapy. In *Nietzsche et la scène philosophique*, specifically, she highlights the German philosopher's exposure of the Aristotelian principles of non-contradiction and identity as safety valves designed to allow humans to live in an illusion of unity and stability that effaces reality's ever-shifting character: logic is an 'anthropomorphic fiction' that falsifies the "real" to render it 'formulatable and foreseeable' (Kofman 1986a: 124). Both Le Doeuff and Kofman, therefore, draw attention to the plural nature of textuality and subjectivity alike in positing the Imaginary as the point of tension at which philosophy defines itself *against itself* through the implicit acknowledgement of its weaknesses, and through its dependence on elements of fiction, corporeality and narrativity, which it is held to resist: something that philosophy effaces and yet needs, the *alien stuff* it brings into its constructs in spite of itself. This view is further expounded by Le Doeuff in *Le sexe du savoir* (Le Doeuff 1998), where it is maintained that argumentative structures cannot abide by the tenets of rational coherence alone, for they inevitably require the incorporation of non-argumentative components in order to appear to function. These imaginary facets ultimately achieve what the argument is powerless to accomplish in and by itself.

Le Doeuff has also consistently argued that Western philosophy, as a male-dominated discourse, is proverbially wary of women arrogating the right to philosophize and hence sets itself up as a sealed system, deeply unsympathetic to the voices of *others*: not just women, of course, but also supposedly uncivilized beings such as non-Western subjects and children. The frailty of these presuppositions is easily exposed, however, by the realization that the male philosopher requires the existence of either a literally female or a figuratively feminized 'pupil', namely an inferior party upon whom knowledge may be imparted, in order 'to confirm his mastery'. It is only in the presence of a more or less ignorant subject that the putatively eminent thinker may shine forth as 'the depositary and proprietor of "great texts", the legate of "great authors"' (Le Doeuff 1989: 99). Cixous is likewise concerned with the issue of mastery and with revealing its intrinsic weakness. Both critics, in this regard, hark back to G. W. F. Hegel's theorization of the Master/Slave dialectic and its contention that the Master's power would be undemonstrable and hence void in the absence of the Slave. According to Cixous, we need to dispute mastery by rethinking the very concept of *strength* with which it is conventionally associated. This notion ought not to be unproblematically equated to principles of control, domination, possession and, above all, knowledge. In fact, being strong may well amount to a willingness to accept that one does *not* know: an admission of impotence, an act of self-dispossession. Moreover, strength is generally conducive to violence, both physical and psychological, when it is merely a performance, a fake, a show of force 'which is only fear's other face, and which, in order to reassure itself, produces only deeds of death and aggression' (Cixous and Clément 1987: 115–16), while indulging in 'an inflated narcissism' (p. 144).

What Cixous describes as 'true strength', conversely, 'has no need to protect itself, or to flaunt or prove itself, ... makes no use of tools or arms and ... is secure enough to be a source of peace' (pp. 115–16). Relatedly, Cixous is reluctant 'to use the term "mastery" as it is currently used because of the repression it implies. ... The one who is in the master's place, even if not the master of a knowledge, is in a position of power. ... The person who transmits has to be able to function on the level of knowledge without knowing.' 'I'm not at all referring to Socrates now,' Cixous hastens to add. 'Just that one should be in a state of weakness, as we all are, and that *it be evident*' (pp. 139–40). This unorthodox definition of strength as a faculty predicated on the acceptance and frank display of one's failings may only be achieved if we are prepared to embrace a view of ourselves, as subjects, and of the language that unremittingly articulates *us* as we articulate *it* – as palimpsests rather than monolithic entities.

Le Doeuff advocates a germane position in emphasizing that neither subjectivity nor language in any of their guises can ultimately be conceived of as discrete and insulated constructs. Accordingly, in exposing philosophy's circuitous trafficking in the domains of fantasy and myth, she is concurrently intent on demonstrating that it is spurious to assume that neat lines of demarcation can be drawn between disparate discourses: all thought is inter-disciplinary insofar as it proceeds from subjects that are themselves compo-site. Grappling with the cultural, psychological and broadly discursive attributes of identity presupposes a readiness to appreciate the subject's multiaccentuality against any temptation to yield to seductively reductive maps. Indeed, 'We need to push disorientation to its limits, to try to realize that the very categories in terms of which we ordinarily see politics must be transformed' (Le Doeuff 2000: 56). This radical programme requires us to quiz *all* forms of language: not just the registers favoured by mainstream male philosophers but also those adopted by female theorists whose perspec-tives risk perpetuating limiting definitions of femininity. Le Doeuff is parti-cularly unsympathetic to codifications of womanhood based on the assumption that a direct connection must exist between a female subject and a female language. The notion of *a* language for all women to appropriate, while seemingly undermining patriarchal hegemony, actually panders to its passion for unitary labels by negating the polyphony of the feminine. As Jennifer Hansen points out, the phenomenon of 'women's oppression' must be studied without recourse to foundationalist tenets if justice is to be done to the 'plurality of voices' hosted therein (Hansen 2000a: 37).

Luce Irigaray has undertaken a deconstructive project akin to Le Doeuff's in her own explorations of language and subjectivity. *The Forgetting of Air* (Irigaray 1999), specifically, proposes a drastic reinterpretation of Western metaphysics by interrogating the very ideal of discursive coherence as a dubious means of paralysing the flow of thought. It does so by foregrounding that what is most often forgotten in Western phallogocentric cultures is that aspect of Being which tenaciously eludes classification and framing, that which circulates endlessly without ever reaching, or indeed seeking to reach, any stable anchoring points. "Air", as both a physical element and a concept, encapsulates the principle of fluidity. Furthermore, it is associated by Irigaray with the feminine body and its rhythms as fundamentally *different* from the inflexible taxonomies resulting from masculine strategies of appro-priation of the elements and of their symbolic connotations. As Irigaray observes:

Metaphysics always supposes ... a solid crust from which to raise a construction. Thus, a physics that gives privilege to ... the solid plane. ... The metaphysical is written neither on/in water, nor on/in air, nor on/in fire. ... And its abysses ... doubtless find their explanation in the forgetting of those elements that do not have the same density [as solid earth]. (p. 2)

Air is the most intriguing of the neglected elements cited by Irigaray, because it invites us, by virtue of its apparent impalpability, to address the coexistence of 'presence and absence' (p. 9), as well as the ongoing interplay of visibility and invisibility.

Commenting on Martin Heidegger, whose theories of Being Irigaray is specifically concerned with in *The Forgetting of Air*, Terry Eagleton remarks:

> what we see when we contemplate something is merely a kind of snapshot or frozen moment of the temporal process which goes to make up its true nature. ... No object ever swims into view other than against the background of some 'world'. ... But this supportive context which makes possible the sighting of any particular thing is always itself elusive, fading into indeterminacy as the thing itself surges forward. (Eagleton 1990: 288)

Visibility is thus a function of the isolation of an individual element from its context, "context" signifying the space from which the individual element derives meaning, and which, however, it arrogantly strives to conceal. Hence, visibility may be something of a hoax: what is visible is only visible insofar as it is capable of lying, or is allowed to lie, about its fortuitous status, in an effort to hide any visible entity's inherent invisibility:

> we can see something because it is present to us; but what we cannot usually see is what enables this presentness in the first place. ... Finally, what we do not see in an object is that it might just as well never have been. How come that this uniquely particular thing has replaced the nothingness that would otherwise have been there, a nothingness which in certain moments of boredom or anxiety we imagine that we can still get a glimpse of? (p. 289)

The Forgetting of Air foregrounds the marginality of visibility and presence, and their derivative status as by-products of invisibility and absence, of an incalculable number of might-have-beens which empirical reality struggles to keep at bay but cannot ultimately account for. Irigaray draws attention to the radical contingency of all objects by supporting the idea that, in a sense, 'nothing actually needs to exist' (Eagleton 1990: 289) and that what does exist, therefore, is inevitably crossed by the nothingness which it may easily have been instead. The objects through which space is constructed are only visible as fragments against a context which is simultaneously necessary and elusive. We see what is present but cannot perceive the sources of this presence: while the present object may be visible, presence itself is obstinately invisible; presence is always shot through with an element of absence, for what *is* might as well *not have been*. Moreover, as Irigaray stresses, 'the constitution of intersubjectivity' depends on a willingness to concede, and eventually value, the fact that what any two subjects share is 'a nothingness – "an almost absolute silence"' (Irigaray 1999: 51–2). The "forgetting of air", in this respect, epitomizes the imposition upon Being of rigid metaphysical tenets and of related forms of language which aim at effacing the relative absence and invisibility of which all objects partake.

The *logos* only ever grasps and names the world reductively and despotically, according to what its champions are prepared to see as authentically existing and categorizable in their own terms. Air is disorienting because it is capable of 'thwarting all categories ... and transgressing the thinker's existing methods' (p. 11). However, while acknowledging that the guardians of Western logocentrism are generally male, it is also vital to realize that *man* himself is depleted by his culture's intransigent commitment to the logic of solidity, to what Irigaray describes as the 'peremptory and preemptive law' of 'one single language' (p. 39). On the one hand, man 'occupies his language more than he does his living body. He wants this language he uses to ensure him a solid foundation' (p. 38), and feels entitled to succeed due to his inveterate 'ascendancy' (p. 25). On the other, he does not enjoy incontrovertible control over his environment because he is unrelentingly, albeit liminally, haunted by 'something ever unpresentable, indemonstrable, and unpronounceable' hauling him 'along a path that leads ever farther into the depths, and binding with this attraction all of his words and monsters' (p. 119). No male subject can consider himself safe as long as he relies dogmatically on 'the set of grooves ... laid out so that his rays of light may appear there' (p. 133), for the traces of the primordial darkness from which everybody comes are indelible, and emergence into the realm of light inevitably coincides with the obligation to confront impenetrable mysteries. Any attempt to negotiate such imponderables will depend not upon enlightening tools but upon the ever-obfuscating media of speech and writing. Irigaray poignantly conveys this point in *Elemental Passions* by rhetorically asking her imaginary interlocutor: 'My child of night, you have known nothing but a cold, dark womb, how can I console you? Even your tears are black. ... They are drowned in ink' (Irigaray [1982] 1992: 23).

CHAPTER 4

Patriarchal Institutions

The notion of 'Woman' is imbricated in the materiality of existence: women are *enclosed* in the family circle and work *for free*. The patriarchal order is not only ideological, it is not in the simple domain of 'value'; it constitutes a specific, material oppression. To reveal its existence and lay bare its mechanisms, it is necessary to bring down the idea of 'woman', that is, to denounce the fact that the category of sex has invaded gigantic territories for oppressive ends. (Plaza 1978: 26)

The institutions with which French feminist theory is concerned do not merely include sociopolitical apparatuses such as the familial, educational, religious, medical, legal and commercial systems underpinning human cultures. In fact, they encompass two further fields of collective organization: namely, overarching power structures such as states and governments and attendant constructions of territorial and national identities; and apparently natural phenomena, such as sexuality, desire and reproduction, which are ultimately as culturally determined as any explicitly human-made system. It is vital to acknowledge the breadth of the interpretations to which the concept of *institution* lends itself in order to identify the diverse ways in which patriarchal ideologies infiltrate, more or less overtly, both microcosmic and macrocosmic cultural formations. The multiaccentuality of patriarchal institutions is borne out by the often very different approaches to their definition and interrogation exhibited by various strands of French feminism. Thus, Monique Wittig discusses marriage as a typical embodiment of the patriarchal institutionalization of asymmetrical power relations; Julia Kristeva frequently brackets the nuclear family, the state and the church together as related incarnations of the Symbolic order; Paola Tabet examines the politics of reproduction as illustrative of the patriarchal appropriation of supposedly natural processes. These different, albeit interconnected, projects warn us against the tendency to draw neat lines between the constructed and the natural by emphasizing the artificiality of *all* discourses centred on patriarchal definitions of power and on the assertion of sex-based and gender-based dichotomies separating normality from deviance.

The speciousness of the appeal to nature upon which patriarchy has insistently relied for the purposes of self-legitimation and self-perpetuation is attested to by the peculiar character of the discourse of *sexology*, the so-called science of sexuality that first emerged in the late nineteenth century. Sexology's theoretical maps and reports about the putatively scientific classification of both bodies and psyches are haunted by two incongruities. Firstly, there is a contradiction between sexology's emancipating and repressive potentialities. As Joseph Bristow observes, sexology 'has played a major role in enabling sex to be debated more widely and seriously at all levels of society'. 'On the other hand', he writes, 'sexology often remains worryingly insensitive to the historical contingency of the scientific methods it employs to estimate sexual adequacy or inadequacy.' Secondly, sexology's claims to accuracy are internally undermined by a commitment to the unearthing of 'some everlasting truth about the sexual capacity of human beings' (Bristow 1997: 15). No discipline ought to presume to be in a position to glean naturally ordained precepts from contingent cultural scenarios. Socialized expressions of sexual desire and behaviour, specifically, cannot be supposed to proceed unproblematically from primitive urges, and the institutions created to deal with the regulation of human desire and behaviour, sexual or otherwise, should likewise become objects of ongoing scrutiny.

THE HOME AND THE MARKET: DOMESTIC AND ECONOMIC APPROPRIATIONS OF FEMININITY

According to Wittig, the institution of marriage is the principal culprit in the enslavement and objectification of women in patriarchal societies: 'men appropriate for themselves the reproduction and production of women, and also their physical persons by means of a contract called the marriage contract', which 'assigns the woman certain obligations' (Wittig 1996: 27). As Doris Mitterbacher observes, Wittig's leading contention is that 'by the marriage contract they [women] have been given to a husband who has the right to demand unpaid work (housework, raising of children) and other obligations (cohabitation, forced coitus)' (Mitterbacher, 'Monique Wittig'). Christine Delphy and Diana Leonard are also concerned with the issue of domestic oppression and, drawing on a Marxist frame of reference, stress that women's unremunerated housework holds an economically unique status because it has no overt *exchange value* (Delphy and Leonard 1992). That is to say, it is not perceived as part of a broader network of production, circulation and consumption of commodities. In fact, as Doris Rita Alphonso observes, it is expected to supply 'services' that 'are highly personalized to the individual family members' needs', it lacks 'discrete boundaries', and it requires the female labourer to perform satisfactorily without her efforts being 'reflected in the resources that are available to her' (Alphonso 2000: 60). It is also noteworthy that in utilizing theoretical concepts introduced by Marx and in foregrounding important points of contact between feminism and Marxism, a number of materialist feminists are concurrently eager to show that the Communist Manifesto is far too vague about the role of women, children and family structures and that it potentially idealizes the bourgeois domestic model. Delphy, specifically, states: 'Marx denounces the official and unofficial prostitution characteristic of the bourgeois family, the fact that in the eyes of bourgeois men, women are only an instrument of production, but one does not know exactly of what production he is talking.' 'Furthermore', she adds, 'he seems to admire that bourgeois family' as an alternative to the scenario of pervasive 'self-interest' and 'brutal exploitation' ushered in by the erasure of feudal bonds and indeed tends 'to exalt the "free work" of women' in contrast with 'the alienated work of the worker'. Relatedly, 'women's right to financial autonomy, to financial independence, and thus to work, is absent from this analysis' (Delphy, 'Capitalist exploitation and patriarchal exploitation in the Communist Manifesto').

Outside the private institutions of marriage and the family, Wittig argues, women are no less persistently abused, for 'wherever they are, whatever they do (including working in the public sector), they are seen (and made) sexually available to men, and they, breasts, buttocks, costume, must be visible'. The institutionalized appropriation of the female body becomes a form of compulsory service comparable to 'the military one' (Wittig 1996: 28). Women, moreover, cannot expect to receive protection from quintessentially male institutions such as the army, or indeed the 'police', who are notorious for 'not intervening when a husband beats his wife. The police intervene with the specific charge of assault and battery when one citizen beats another citizen. But a woman who has signed a marriage contract has thereby ceased to be an ordinary citizen (protected by law)' (p. 27). As Mitterbacher comments, if women are not 'properly protected from domestic violence by the police', this is essentially 'because the authority of the husband has to a certain extent replaced the authority of the state' (Mitterbacher, 'Monique Wittig'). The asymmetry highlighted by Wittig is a direct corollary, according to Delphy, of the fundamentally hierarchical character of patriarchal institutions. The principle of hierarchy is indeed responsible for the iniquitous distribution of power at all levels of social existence, prior to both sex-based and gender-based distinctions. Whatever values may be associated with femininity and masculinity, in this context, are always tailored to fit the requirements of a particular society and, 'insofar as our society is hierarchical', its 'values are also hierarchically arranged' (Delphy 1996: 38). It is crucial, therefore, to appreciate that *'division* and *hierarchy'* (p. 30) are not interchangeable terms: the former merely points to traits that separate men and women with no obvious attempt to prioritize either party, whereas the latter refers to an institutionalized history that thrives on guaranteeing the 'domination' and 'exploitation' of one group by another (Delphy 1980: 87–8).

A somewhat debatable aspect of the social materialist critique of patriarchal institutions should be noted at this point: namely, its occasional tendency to deliver sweeping generalizations about the balance of power between the sexes. For example, Wittig, in stating that 'women do not know that they are totally dominated by men' and that 'men, on the other hand, know perfectly well that they are dominating women', appears to be subscribing to a conspiracy theory of society where *all* female subjects are unremittingly plotted against by *all* male subjects. There is a danger, here, of promulgating a monolithic view of ideology and a concomitant universalization of the categories of femininity and masculinity that are quite incongruous with Wittig's main objective: that is, the exposure of the culturally contingent character of sexual conflict and hence of its inscription in a 'material order' as the precondition of any possibility of struggle and change (Wittig 1996: 25). Surely, if Wittig's project were to be consistently pursued, it would rapidly become clear that neither men nor women are uniformly aware or ignorant of their conditions over time and that their cognitive standing, therefore, alters according to the material contexts to which they belong.

Analogously to the critics cited above, Colette Guillaumin argues that in all areas of social and embodied existence, from the family to the market, from the church to the law, the health service and the educational system, woman is an object of collective usage. By means of the marriage contract, she apparently ceases to function as common property and enters the sphere of private ownership. However, although marriage restricts the 'collective use' of female subjects in principle, there remains a sense in which women are presumed to belong not merely to men as individuals but also to broad categories of both literal and symbolic masculinity:

> in practice the *enjoyment* of the common right belongs either to God (nuns), to fathers (daughters, in which state one remains until one becomes a wife, according to the Civil Code), or to pimps (for women who are officially 'common property'). The contradiction at the centre of social appropriation itself operates between collective appropriation and private appropriation. (Guillaumin 1996: 82)

According to Guillaumin, the principal 'expressions' of this pervasive phenomenon consist of the confiscation of women's 'time', which 'is *explicitly* appropriated in the marriage "contract", insofar as there is no measurement of it and no limit placed on its use' (pp. 75–6); of 'products of the body' through modalities of reproduction which dictate that '*the number of children is not the subject of contract*: it is neither fixed nor subjected to the wife's approval' (p. 76); of 'sexual obligation' through both marriage and prostitution (p. 77); of the female body's value other than as a 'tool' (p. 78); and, finally, of 'individuality' itself (p. 79). The main 'means' adopted by patriarchy to ensure the successful outcome of these defrauding moves are the market, where women's inferior status is epitomized by their receipt of lower wages; the home, where 'spatial confinement' secures women's segregation from the public world and public action (p. 84); and 'violence', especially in the forms of 'rape, provocation, cruising, harassment' (p. 85). Guillaumin places special emphasis on the exclusion of women's labour power from payment and measurement: 'Unlike other dominated groups with labour power,' she writes, 'we women are, in the relations between the sexes, non-sellers of our labour power.' She then adduces the following reasons for this economic peculiarity:

> If it [women's labour] is non-paid, it is because it is not 'payable'. If it cannot be measured or converted into money ... this means that it is acquired in another way. And this other way implies that it is acquired in aggregate, once and for all, and that it no longer has to be evaluated in terms of money or timetables or by the job. (p. 80)

Nicole-Claude Mathieu is also concerned with the intersection of the sexual and economic realms and contends that the two cannot be treated separately. In her study of a wide variety of customs and laws underpinning marriage and other ritualized relations, discussed in some detail in *Chapter 2*, Mathieu consistently stresses the pivotal part played by the discourse of reproduction as an ensemble of beliefs and opinions pertaining not merely to the propagation of the species but also to the preservation and consolidation of the institutions through which power perpetuates itself by recourse to the 'concept of sex'. This designates concurrently 'the mental organization of ideas' and sets of 'practices', namely, '"thought" sex' and '"acted" sex' (Mathieu 1996: 42).

The institutionalization of reproduction is likewise central to Tabet's materialist critique of patriarchal institutions. Her argument proceeds from the basic premise that reproduction always takes place within specific structures of domination in the context of which the discipline of demography plays a vital part in differentiating between '*natural fertility*' and '*controlled fertility*'. The former is supposed to occur 'where no conscious effort is made to space births or to limit their number' whereas the latter pivots on 'interference on births'. Significantly, in demographic parlance, '"control" is generally only used in the sense of *limitation*' (Tabet 1996: 110), which suggests that if one acts upon a putatively natural phenomenon, it is only ever in order to subjugate or curb it, not to enhance human opportunities for the expression of pleasure and desire. In discussing various 'Interventions into the capacity to reproduce' (p. 113), Tabet differentiates between 'generalized interventions', such as coital training, the enforcement of conjugal duty, the maximization of chances of copulability and conception and the sustained surveillance of conception, pregnancy and childbirth, and 'specific interventions', such as the determination of fertile periods and the planned interruption of the sequence of reproduction (p. 123). The marriage contract is instrumental to the implementation of these strategies but would not be capable of guaranteeing their effectiveness were it not abetted by varyingly intense forms of institutionalized violence: 'if marriage represents the potentially optimal place for women's permanent exposure to impregnation, this can be effected only by a complex (and variable) apparatus of ideological pressures and physical and psychological coercion' (p. 116).

Above all, disparate societies rely on initiation rituals designed to ensure that 'women's sexual impulses are channelled, by socialization, towards one single type of sexuality, that of coitus' and women 'are coerced into it even when they feel no desire'. Tabet sees the 'training for the acceptance of conjugal sexual relations and reproduction', in many diverse cultures, as an 'institutional apprenticeship' often entailing the 'threat of violence and the use of force' (p. 117). She cites, as recurrent terrorizing tactics, 'widespread forms of rape' used as 'shock treatments' meant to 'break down [women's] resistance', to tame 'the recalcitrant spirit' and to punish any kind of 'insubordination'. Paradoxically, this strategy is said to be especially pervasive in Polynesian cultuses: namely, 'what are thought of as the paradise zones of sexuality'! Even societies that do not employ rape as an institutionalized aspect of coital apprenticeship repeatedly resort to 'the threat of rape' in order to 'forestall resistance'. This, Tabet argues, 'also applies to initiations based on sexual mutilation of girls, as with Australian rites where a girl is forcibly carried away by a group of men, deflowered with a stone knife, and then submitted to copulation by several men, in order to make her "quiet" once and for all' (p. 118). The 'domestication of women's sexuality' (p. 132), which is the ultimate aim of multifarious forms of coercion and repression, also hinges on the definition of 'categories of women' on the basis of reproductive and non-reproductive sexualities, and on the basis of familiar stereotypes such as the whore/madonna and courtesan/wife binary oppositions (pp. 134–5). At the same time, a neat distinction is drawn between supposedly incompatible 'life stages' separating juvenile sexuality from conjugal sexuality (p. 137).

Tabet is also concerned with the exploitation of reproduction in concurrently economic and psychological terms. Firstly, she posits the notion of 'reproduction as work' (p. 144) and, specifically, as a type of labour which, as in the classic Marxist definition of labour, involves an intimate relationship between the worker's body and her productive tasks. Secondly, Tabet further refines this position by describing 'reproduction as exploited work' (p. 147), the female body representing not an autonomous apparatus but a reified 'reproductive machine' whose products, from eggs to milk, can be treated as so much merchandise (p. 148). Thirdly, Tabet examines the recent 'transformation of relations of reproduction' brought about by the practice of 'womb-renting', whereby women agreeing to be artificially inseminated to produce children on behalf of others are ultimately involved in *'a sale, in which procreative power is exchanged in the same way as labour power'* (p. 153). This phenomenon could be regarded as emancipatory insofar as it disengages women's reproductive function from traditional 'marital ties' (p. 155) and indeed severs procreation from its conventional connection with the marriage contract and with relations based on 'private appropriation' (p. 154). However, it is also noteworthy that the 'weakening of the marital institution' tends, in many cases, to engender 'a deterioration in the situation of women', since one of its principal corollaries is the increasing number of 'women-headed single-parent families' made economically vulnerable by the fact that women are still discriminated against by the existing 'socio-economic relations of the sexes': the 'poverty risk rises steadily with the degree of "autonomy" of women' (p. 155).

It is arduous, in this scenario, to disentangle women's losses from their gains: although autonomy remains a primary objective, it is impossible to ignore that its achievement entails the assumption of additional responsibilities and burdens. Kristeva emphasizes this point in her assessment of the changing role of the couple as the traditional core institution of Western patriarchy: 'Since the couple, as a unity of production, is much less necessary now than it was in the past,' she writes, 'we have become increasingly aware of the psychic autonomy and divergent psychic interests of the two sexes' (Kristeva 1996b: 70). If these interests are to be fostered and protected, contemporary Western cultures must adequately recognize sexual difference and the *specificity* of both the economic and the affective needs of women and men *as* women, *as* men. Indeed, if old familial ties of a private kind undergo a process of transformation without any parallel change occurring in our collective, broadly cultural understanding of the relations of the sexes, no felicitous outcome can be anticipated.

Like both Tabet and Guillaumin, Luce Irigaray is concerned with the strategies of appropriation and manipulation of female bodies by patriarchal institutions that simultaneously impinge on women's individuality and intervene into natural processes and functions for regulatory purposes. In 'Women on the Market', in particular, she focuses on 'the appropriation of nature by man; the transformation of nature according to "human" criteria, defined by men alone; the submission of nature to labour and technology' (Irigaray 2000c: 221), and argues that in order to disassociate themselves from the overtly corporeal aspects of nature, of which woman acts as a constant reminder, men have endeavoured to translate femininity into symbolic roles whereby woman's 'natural body disappears into its representative function'. The 'mother', the 'virgin' and the 'prostitute' are the principal roles discussed by Irigaray as signifiers, respectively, of woman as private property, woman as a desirable acquisition, and woman as the epitome of forbidden fantasies (p. 222).

Drawing on the anthropological model elaborated by Claude Lévi-Strauss in *The Elementary Structures of Kinship* (1969), Irigaray observes that the inscription of the female body and of female labour in patriarchal formations hinges on 'the exchange of women' and that the Symbolic order itself 'is assured by the fact that men, or groups of men, circulate women among themselves, according to a rule known as the incest taboo' (Irigaray 2000c: 211). In this scenario, argues Irigaray, women simply constitute 'objects of transaction' to be passed from one man to another, while 'productive work' is emplaced exclusively as 'men's business' (p. 212). In economic terms, therefore, *'woman has value on the market by virtue of one single quality: that of being a product of man's "labour"'*. Thus, female subjects as emblematized by patriarchy are fundamentally *products* of a concurrently financial and psychological economy that accords significance not to their material bodies as such but to the abstract connotations of those bodies as commodities. Their worth, accordingly, does not depend on their 'intrinsic, immanent value' but on 'their current price in gold, or phalluses' (p. 214).

DECODING THE CODES: LAWS, RITUALS, CUSTOMS

Of all institutional ensembles, the legal system is arguably the one that feminist theorists of diverse orientations have often found most wanting in its lack of recognition of the gender-inflected character of specific offences. The issue of rape has been especially controversial in this respect, as demonstrated, for instance, by Monique Plaza's 'Our Costs and Their Benefits' ([1978] 1996). Plaza is specifically concerned with highlighting the shortcomings of the approach to rape promulgated by Michel Foucault. In seeking to separate violence from sexuality, Foucault argues that while violence in rape is unacceptable, sexuality itself must never be condemned. In a volume published in 1977 by the 'Change Collective' entitled *La folie encerclée* (*Encircling Madness*), Foucault states that 'sexuality cannot, under any circumstances, be subject to punishment'. If rape is conceived of as a sexual act and punished as such, it is sexuality itself that comes under attack and this serves to perpetuate the disciplinary strategies that repress human beings, as shown in *Chapter 1*, by curbing precisely their sexual drives. Hence, Foucault contends, 'when rape is punished, it should be exclusively the physical violence that is penalized' (Change Collective 1977: 99). In commenting on Foucault's position, Plaza observes that 'it is an issue of finding a way for "sexuality" to escape the criminal law, by not forbidding sexuality but only "violence"' (Plaza 1996: 180) and then proceeds to pose a harrowing question: 'Rape should not be punished as sexuality. So as what should it be punished, since it seems uniquely sexual?' (p. 181).

For Plaza, rape, as '*an oppressive act by a (social) man against a (social) woman*' (p. 182), is ineluctably sexual even when it does not involve genital penetration because it always pivots on men's brutal appropriation of female bodies. This appropriation, moreover, is somehow justified by the notion that 'women as a class belong to men as a class': what the rapist violates is not merely an individual of the female gender but a whole category of being which men 'have learned to consider is their property' (p. 182). Relatedly, 'to make rape a "simple" matter of civil responsibility would be quite simply to *permit rape*' (p. 183). Biddy Martin corroborates Plaza's point by arguing that Foucault's attempt to remove sexuality from control by the legal system 'evidences a denial of the power differences that characterize relations between the sexes in society' (Martin 1988: 17). It is also noteworthy, as Winifred Woodhull suggests, that several feminist critics have pursued a line of argument akin to Foucault's in endeavouring to redefine rape as a crime of power rather than a sexual crime. As a corollary, they have often subscribed to a spurious separation of sex and power, which suggests that sexual relations exist in a nebulous area beyond dominant relations of power, and that they strike their roots in some pre-social realm rather than in contingent discursive formations. This approach

rests on a notion of power divorced from sex, as if sex preexisted the social, from which power is said to derive. In so doing, it falls prey to the ruse of power cited by Foucault, namely, the designation of 'sex' as a biological and ontological given whose function is to guarantee that sexuality appears to have its origin outside of and prior to power. (Woodhull 1988: 170)

Irigaray agrees with Plaza in drawing attention to the vagueness of dominant definitions of rape which, in merely labelling it a *crime*, serve to efface its sexual specificity: 'rape was categorized as a crime, is still termed a crime, which effectively eliminates the problem of respect for the female body as such and in no way alerts the potential rapist to the felony that his action represents' (Irigaray 2000a: 31–2). Thus, although the sexual offences to which female subjects are exposed stem precisely from their sex, 'women are not protected by the law as women' (p. 181). This argument is put forward in the context of a much broader discussion of the relationship between the law and sexual difference undertaken in *Democracy Begins Between Two*. As we saw in *Chapter 2* and *Chapter 3*, Irigaray regards the recognition and cultivation of sexual difference as instrumental to the achievement of genuine intersubjectivity. In *Democracy*, she extends this view from private to civil relations and maintains that it is vital for the putatively democratic bases of Western culture to acknowledge the needs of both men and women in their distinctiveness and specificity. Women, in particular, must be granted civil rights that correspond to their separate civil identity and that are equivalent, rather than equal, to those accorded to men. The ideal of equality is inadequate since, while claiming that men and women can be subjected to the same laws, it almost invariably benefits patriarchal priorities and neglects gender-specific requirements and aspirations. As Jennifer Hansen observes, Irigaray works on the assumption that 'the legal code operates with the masculine sex as its norm, insidiously protecting male bodies and desires while ignoring the needs and contributions of the other sex'. At the same time, in endeavouring to make sure that masculine rights are advocated and conquered without their beneficiaries being interfered with by wider political apparatuses such as the state, it functions according to an ethos of negativity: namely, through exclusions and limitations. According to Irigaray, conversely, 'laws should function as positive rights, empowering men and women to achieve to their fullest capacities' (Hansen 2000b: 204).

Erasing the reality of difference ultimately amounts to a colonial project of appropriation and commodification, whereas 'renouncing the desire to possess the other, in order to recognize him as other, is perhaps the most useful and the most beautiful of the tasks which fall to us' (Irigaray 2000a: 7). To this effect, Irigaray maintains, a 'sexually-marked civil code is the minimal guarantee needed to protect the singularity of man, that of woman, and the relation between them' (p. 9). In order to produce a code that recognizes and respects the specificity of each sex, 'we have to define objective methods of guaranteeing rights and duties for different subjectivities' (p. 10). A revised code of the kind proposed by Irigaray would not only 'protect the identity of women' but also 'offer a means of defining a level of equality between women without diminishing their diversity' (p. 11). At the same time, although femininity and masculinity are the principal categories whose distinctive requirements must be acknowledged in the endorsement of a more equitable distribution of power, a code centred on the recognition of sexual difference would also be conducive to the recognition of 'other forms of diversity' (p. 12) by fully taking into account 'the cohabitation of traditions and cultures' (p. 68). This is particularly important in the context of a prismatic social ensemble such as contemporary Europe: 'Constructing a European citizenship requires assuring the passage from natural to civil identity which presupposes taking certain differences into account in the construction of civil identity' (p. 66). For Irigaray, these differences pertain not only to 'the sexes' but also to 'the generations' and to the 'cultural families' based on 'race' and 'religion' that constitute an ethnic grouping as 'multinational, multicultural and multiracial' as 'the European Union' (p. 67). Kristeva corroborates this idea by maintaining that Europe cannot be conceived of as a monolithic entity because its nations' shared baggage of 'art, philosophy, and religion', while operating as a connective tissue, cannot 'aspire to universality' as it is constantly infiltrated, challenged and reshaped by 'other sociocultural memories' (Kristeva 2000a: 182). Hence, any definition of a European '*identity*' will inevitably entail a confrontation of the possibility of the '*loss of identity*' (p. 183).

Dominant structures of power consolidate themselves not only through institutions designed to enforce and symbolize *order* but also through the *institutionalization* of signifiers of *dis*order. Catherine Clément documents this phenomenon by focusing on two parallel moments in a long history of institutionalization of supposedly deviant female figures, with specific reference to the figures of the sorceress and the hysteric. Both are said to live simultaneously in the past and in the present: the 'sorceress ... incarnates the reinscription of the traces of paganism that triumphant Christianity repressed. The hysteric, whose body is transformed into a theatre for forgotten scenes, relives the past, bearing witness to a lost childhood that survives in suffering.' Both, moreover, play concurrently reactionary and transgressive functions by being enlisted to the preservation of cultural stability even as they threaten it through their disruptive behaviour:

the role of sorceress, of hysteric, is ambiguous, antiestablishment, and conservative at the same time. Antiestablishment because the symptoms ...

revolt and shake up the public. The sorceress heals, against the Church's canon; she performs abortions, favours nonconjugal love .... The hysteric unties familiar bonds, introduces disorder into the well-regulated unfolding of everyday life. ... These roles are *conservative* because every sorceress ends up being destroyed .... Every hysteric ends up inuring others to her symptoms, and the family closes around her again. (Cixous and Clément 1987: 5)

Thus, although these figures are 'dangerous', they are concurrently 'productive' for the 'social order' since they emblematize syntheses and compromises which could never be realized in their absence (p. 7). They are, moreover, quasi-magical creatures of inversion that make 'it possible to see what cannot be represented'; yet, the imaginary realm they evoke is also a paradoxical manifestation of 'orderly displacements of the proportions of the real world' which, like carnivals, may harness disorder to the preservation of order (p. 23). Ultimately, what virtually any culture needs is some opportunity for the institutional demonization of certain categories of people as a means of giving form to otherwise amorphous threats and inchoate fears coursing through its fabric. The sorceress and the hysteric, specifically, come to incarnate the ubiquitous sense of 'guilt' of whole societies stifled by their own social, moral and religious constraints (p. 52).

Echoing Plaza and Irigaray, Kristeva, too, has consistently examined Western culture's institutional approaches to acts of violence perpetrated upon women and pondered the sexual specificity of such offences. At the same time, analogously to Clément, she has drawn attention to the part played by designated scapegoats in the institutionalization of social notions of order and transgression. As Martha J. Reineke observes, central to Kristeva's analysis of violence is the idea that this pervasive phenomenon 'does not always present itself in terms of physical assault' but 'transpires also as paralysis', as a freezing of being 'which immobilizes women in cultural bonds not of their own making' (Reineke 1997: 2). Concomitantly, Kristeva emphasizes that violence does not unproblematically constitute a subversion of law and order, since countless rituals intended to secure social cohesiveness and stability rely precisely on symbolic acts of violence. This is typified by a ubiquitous 'sacrificial economy' whereby people protect themselves against threats of chaos and pain by invoking 'the most ancient of gestures: they cut, kill, and eat bodies to create community' (p. 11). Thus, legion ceremonies, taboos and prohibitions associated with disparate religions serve to institutionalize violence by translating it from the most unpalatable reminder of human vulnerability into a symbol of ritualistic and ritualized *control*.

In highlighting the pervasiveness of sacrificial violence, Kristeva is also eager to show that it is woman who has most regularly featured as its victim or scapegoat. According to Reineke, the two categories of femininity that have persistently and eloquently operated as ideal sacrificial bodies are witches and starving women, their symbolic usefulness deriving largely from their uncomfortably paradoxical admixture of an apparently unlimited urge for freedom and a no less extreme proclivity for self-destruction. The witch is an ambiguous and controversial cultural scapegoat, embodying the repressed drives of entire cultures. Throughout history, she has been made to coincide with the prototypically aberrant female and her persecution, accordingly, has been justified as a holy crusade against all forms of depravity and degeneration. It is no coincidence, in this regard, that the women singled out as Satan's associates were *unconventional* types in breach of patriarchal norms. While women in general could be deemed 'prone to the devil's seduction' on the basis of an inveterate belief in their being 'both more lustful and weaker than men' (p. 132), one should not underestimate the fact that 'widows and spinsters number high among the initial victims of witchcraft charges' because 'unmarried women were outside the key institution – the family – that would offer them protection' (p. 133).

The witch's symbolic precursors, according to Reineke, are the medieval mystics: 'women who, in saintly asceticism, deliberately abstained from all food but God's food: the Eucharist' (p. 111). What makes these women comparable to the victims of ruthless witch hunts is the fact that they, too, embody the anxieties and crises of the wider social body. The cultures by which they were produced were torn between the longing to transcend the flesh and an equally ardent desire to intensify corporeal experience. The female mystics' own conduct encapsulates this contradiction: in seeking to shed the mortal coil, their self-sacrificial devotion belies a yearning for physical *jouissance*, lack of basic nourishment often leading to ecstatic rapture of a quasi-erotic kind and of indubitably hallucinogenic proportions. The modern replica of the starving mystic is the anorectic subject as a woman (primarily if not exclusively) who, in pursuing freedom through self-imposed starvation and often finding pain or even death instead, epitomizes the contradictory logic of capitalism. Indeed, as Bryan Turner points out, the anorectic's entrapment in a world wherein desire and reason, the body and the intellect, appear irreconcilable echoes the unresolved conflicts that pervade modern Western culture in its entirety (Turner 1984: 201). Moreover, insofar as she simultaneously opposes and complies with the myth of the body perfect, the starving female stands out as an institutionalized icon of discordant patriarchal expectations.

UNEQUIPPED TO THINK, BORN TO SWOT: WOMEN, PHILOSOPHY AND EDUCATION

Over the centuries, educational systems have insistently ranked among the patriarchal institutions least favourable to female emancipation. Women's access to education has indubitably widened, in the West at least, in recent decades, yet the current situation does not warrant undiluted enthusiasm. Indeed, women still constitute a minority in the upper echelons of academia, where the most prestigious titles and most desirable earnings are to be found. Moreover, the claim that today female pupils and students at virtually all levels of their educational programmes tend to outshine, or *outperform*, their male colleagues cannot be seen as an incontrovertible victory for women. It could, in fact, be argued that women excel more often than men in educational terms because they have been more thoroughly programmed by patriarchal hegemony to be hard-working and industrious and, ultimately, to pursue diligence rather than brilliance. In other words, women have been persistently trained, through both overt and subliminal tactics, to make themselves marketable. Therefore, although it would be preposterous not to recognize the obvious advantages of improved educational opportunities for both young and mature females, it should also be noted that in endeavouring to maximize their marketability, women risk perpetuating the patriarchal ruse of power that has traditionally induced them to quantify their self-worth in terms of their value as commodities.

According to Irigaray, reforms in the domain of education are the precondition of the establishment of a genuinely democratic basis for contemporary Western cultures. Furthermore, any effective reform will have to take adequately into account the irreducible reality of sexual difference. As Irigaray writes in *Democracy Begins Between Two*:

> training in citizenship involves changes in, or at least additions to, educational programmes. It has to be borne in mind that the subject is two, not one, and that it is a question of educating two subjects, without forgetting to develop coexistence, dialogue, and even love between them, since this is the task that falls to each citizen, male and female. (Irigaray 2000a: 16)

However appealing, the liberal project promoted by Irigaray will hardly be feasible as long as women are discriminated against through the deployment of both explicitly and implicitly marginalizing strategies. Hélène Cixous persuasively conveys this message in 'Castration or Decapitation?' (Cixous [1981] 2000c), where it is argued that the castration anxiety posited by Freudian psychoanalysis as a key aspect of the emergence of masculinity results in a backlash against women, which manifests itself in the form of a symbolic decapitation: namely, the routine exclusion of women from the masculine realms of history and philosophy. Whereas men are in a position to sublimate their fear of mutilation, women live constantly on the brink of loss, are often consigned to silence and inertia, and are either deemed incapable of using thought and language satisfactorily or only deemed capable of hysterical outbursts. The punishment to which the female subject is unrelentingly subjected, then, is a form of decapitation precisely to the extent that what she is deprived of is her very 'head': namely, the right to exercise her reasoning and creative faculties. Her predicament is typified by the figure of 'Sleeping Beauty. Woman, if you look for her, has a strong chance of always being found in one position: in bed. In bed and asleep' (p. 277). In relegating femininity to an institutionalized state of passivity, patriarchy denies women's signifying powers:

> It is said, in philosophical texts, that women's weapon is the word, because they talk, talk endlessly, chatter, overflow with sound, mouthsound: but they don't actually *speak*, they have nothing to say. They always inhabit the place of silence, or at most make it echo with their singing. And neither is to their benefit, for they remain outside knowledge. (pp. 283–4)

Thus, female subjects have repeatedly been fashioned according to the premise that they do not possess adequate linguistic tools, that this lack renders them unable to contribute to philosophical speculation or indeed to historical developments of any kind, and that education is hardly likely to compensate for this abysmal gap in their being.

Both Sarah Kofman and Michèle Le Doeuff are also concerned with patriarchy's tenacious banishment of women from the realm of philosophy both as a discipline and as an institution. Kofman's critique of patriarchy cannot be described as overtly "feminist" insofar as she does not engage directly with women writers and is not explicitly involved with the women's movement. Nevertheless, Kofman *does* conceive of her writings on the positioning of female subjects by and in the discipline of philosophy as implicated with feminism. In an interview conducted by Evelyne Ender, she states: 'My position as a woman philosopher marks itself in this manner, and my feminist position can be found in these kinds of readings' (Kofman 1993: 14). That is to say, Kofman's exposure of the iniquities of patriarchy and of its speculative and academic foundations is, ultimately, feminist in the sense that it exhaustively documents, by recourse to close deconstructive examinations of mainstream male thinkers, both their demonization and/or exclusion of the feminine and their gender-based prejudices. As Penelope

Deutscher and Kelly Oliver observe, Kofman's 'methodological approach' involves, among other things, 'analyzing a philosopher's sexual economy', whereby she seeks 'to destabilize separations between rational philosophy and the author's life, blood, drives, and desires', namely, the 'murky domains' that 'the life of the mind' can never conclusively transcend (Deutscher and Oliver 1999: 4–5). Accordingly, Kofman refuses to 'take her philosophers at face value' and insists instead on highlighting 'the pathology of their systems' (p. 16).

A recurrent aspect of this pathology is the tendency to neglect the question of sexual difference and hence to relegate femininity to the ghostly regions of the unspeaking and the unspeakable. Indeed, institutionalized philosophy stubbornly dismisses the feminine as a valid object of study and wipes out the possibility of women themselves formulating innovative philosophical models. According to Françoise Duroux, Kofman challenges this tradition by foregrounding the basic weaknesses of the institutions on which it rests: flaws that can be led back to the subtextual anxieties of the major representatives of those institutions. Thus, at the same time as she declines to worship 'the rules of the "professors", those who make the history of philosophy in the form of courses' (Duroux 1999: 135), Kofman also delves into the writings of *Great Masters* such as Descartes, Leibniz, Kant and Rousseau to demonstrate that their systems are neither 'uniform' nor 'pure' (p. 136). This is borne out by their almost superstitious aversion to 'mention', let alone treat seriously, the subject of 'women'. As creatures tainted by their association with the diverse, the earthly and the impure, females are simply deemed incongruous with intellectual programmes devoted to the rational and the transcendent: 'as a matter of principle sexual difference does not constitute a theoretical object because it would risk jamming the direct line of communication with Being, the Pope, and the Others' (p. 137). Yet, Kofman contends, the issues of femininity and sexual difference inexorably insert themselves into the interstices of philosophy by virtue of their very absence. Exclusionary policies, ultimately, only serve to make us wonder why and how something or somebody has been ostracized in the first place.

Not only has the discipline of philosophy traditionally marginalized women through the institution of eminently sexist academies and enclaves: it also relies on a veritably patrilineal system of both acknowledged and subterranean influences and borrowings, which has inevitably assisted the endurance of male solidarity to the detriment of female thinkers. Kofman elaborates this idea by tracing powerful connecting threads linking Western male philosophers across the centuries. In 'Mirror and Oneiric Images: Plato, Precursor of Freud' (Kofman 1999a), for instance, she highlights Freud's connection with Plato to show how, ironically, the man reputed to have *discovered* the unconscious, thereby calling the authority of vigilant reason radically into question, is closely linked to the very forefather of idealistic rationalism. Plato undoubtedly foreshadows Freud in asserting that:

> in this state (the state of sleep), the soul dares all, as if it were detached and disencumbered from all shame and reason . . .; it does not hesitate to attempt in thought to rape its mother, or any other . . .; there is neither a murder it shies away from, nor a food it abstains from; in short, it does not restrain itself from any madness or immodesty. (p. 5)

According to Kofman, if Freud chose to 'turn his eyes from Plato to Sophocles', it could be precisely because 'the former anticipated too clearly Freud's own discoveries, depriving him of his priority, of which he was so jealous' (ibid.). Ultimately, Platonism and Freudianism, for all their differences, come to constitute a two-headed and intrinsically patriarchal *institution* committed to the identification and normalization of lawful, as opposed to illicit, fantasies and desires. In viewing dreams as coded fulfilments of repressed wishes that could not be allowed free rein in conscious life, Freud echoes Plato. Plato is far stricter than Freud in commending the need to keep our wildest urges at bay, and indeed maintains that 'it is possible to control oneiric delirium, to escape the illusion and the brutish visions, so long as one knows how to master his desires during waking life' (p. 8). Yet, Freud's own emphasis on the inevitability of repression – which dreams themselves bear witness to in the operations of secondary revision whereby the dream's latent meanings are *edited* and made more palatable – definitely harks back to the Greek philosopher.

The controlling agency of numerous institutions is, by and large, difficult to detect and defuse because it does not depend so much on overtly brutal strategies of coercion as on surreptitious forms of ideological mystification. Ideologies, in turn, are hard to unmask because they thrive less by explicitly enforcing their values than they do by dressing up cultural fabrications as natural *facts*. Kofman's exploration of ideology underscores this phenomenon by foregrounding its implication with the discourse of spectrality, most notably in *Camera Obscura* (1973). As Pierre Lamarche observes, central to Kofman's critique of ideology is its ambiguous etymology and implicit association with unrepresentable, spectral entities: 'The *eidos* is the form, figure, shape, or that which is seen, and it figures the *eidolon*, which is the phantasmal, ghostly, unsubstantial spectre of the seeable.' The *eidolon*, therefore, 'is the ghost of the *eidos*' (Lamarche 1999: 125). In its connection with the *eidolon* as a near-hallucinatory simulacrum and, by extension, with '*eidolatria* – idolatry, the idolization/idealization inherent in the fetish' (p. 123), ideology reveals its own illusory status: the apparitional and hence deceptive character of what it aims at passing off as reality. This line of argumentation bears affinities to the writings of Roland Barthes, particularly *Mythologies*, where considerable emphasis is placed on the mystifying power of ideology as the mechanism whereby 'petit-bourgeois culture' is transformed 'into a universal nature' (Barthes [1957] 2000a: 9), and *Camera Lucida* ([1981] 2000b), where attention is drawn to the collusion of the real and the simulated. Indeed for Barthes, the 'referent' of a representation is comparable to 'a kind of little simulacrum', or '*eidolon*', which he likes to term '*Spectrum*' insofar as 'this word retains, through its root, a relation to "spectacle"' while also hinting at the disturbing notion of 'the return of the dead' (Barthes 2000b: 9).

Finally, Kofman is committed to the exploration of the tactics deployed by patriarchal institutions in order to compartmentalize and ultimately repress human beings' imaginative faculties and, specifically, the more subversive facets thereof. In her reading of Oscar Wilde's *The Picture of Dorian Gray*, for example, she concentrates on the systematic repression of the Dionysian principle, namely the pole of experience associated by Friedrich Nietzsche with the irrational and with psychological abandonment in contrast with the Apollonian, that is to say, a mentality committed to order and control. The picture mercilessly recording Dorian's deterioration while his own body remains miraculously unscathed by his depravity is an '"Apollonian" impostor' (Kofman 1999b: 48): an artefact which, despite its horror, retains the controlling power of art and thus serves to contain the true horror of Dionysian excess. According to Kofman, this Apollonian mask represents an institutionalization of the Dionysian through art that reflects the 'mutilating puritanism' (p. 47) imposed by society on all passions and desires which refuse to be accommodated within comfortable, albeit specious, categories of 'beauty and serenity' (p. 41). Kofman also shows that the taming, or masking, of the Dionysian carries sexist connotations. Indeed, Dorian is not merely eager to retain *his own* beauty but also 'to keep intact in himself his mother's beauty': the attractive aura of a woman despised, banned, 'marked with a scarlet letter' (p. 47) precisely because of her passionate nature. Dorian's most treasured image of his mother displays her, importantly, in the guise of a bacchante, a follower of the god Dionysus. Therefore, the repression of the Dionysian could be said to be intimately connected with the repression of the feminine at its most tantalizing.

Le Doeuff, too, examines the relationship between definitions of femininity and patriarchal institutions with an emphasis on the discriminatory strategies insistently utilized by Western philosophy as a discipline and as a discourse underpinning traditional academic structures. As we saw in *Chapter 3* in the context of a discussion of philosophy's ambivalent relation to the cultural imaginary, Le Doeuff maintains that 'the discourse which we call "philosophical" produces itself through the fact that it represses, excludes and dissolves, or claims to dissolve, another discourse, other forms of knowledge' (Le Doeuff 1989: 114). These forms of knowledge are associated with the hazy areas of fantasy, myth and narrative and are considered incompatible with philosophy's pretensions to the conquest of truth via wholly rational procedures. However, philosophy can be shown to rely, circuitously, on these secreted discourses in order to illustrate and substantiate its findings. Indeed, it has no choice but to resort to the imaginary because its arguments cannot be pursued by reason alone. Philosophy's own objectives are riddled with enigmas and imponderables akin to the ones explored by fiction and legend, and a collusion between the two discourses is therefore inevitable. Nonetheless, Western philosophers have been, by and large, quite reluctant to acknowledge the ineluctability of such an interplay and, instead of admitting to the elements of uncertainty haunting the very core of their enterprises, have endeavoured to keep 'the indefinite at bay'. Furthermore, unable to give 'this nameless, undefined object, this indeterminable otherness' a transparent name, they have chosen to describe it 'metaphorically': that is, to posit it as 'the hostile principle'. Femininity, in particular, has time and again been constructed as the quintessentially adversarial pole, the 'inner enemy' (p. 115).

This world-view has been sustained by academic institutions based on rigid hierarchies wherein patriarchal masculinity is invariably on the side of mastery. However, Le Doeuff is unsympathetic to feminist approaches that amount to 'a mere lament' about women being 'forbidden all access to philosophy' (p. 100), and encourages her readers to consider not simply how or why women have been alienated and disenfranchised by patriarchal institutions but also the measures to be taken to guarantee female participation in all sorts of male-dominated apparatuses. In her contribution to the Conference on 'Knowledge and Learning for a Sustainable Society' held in Göteborg, Sweden, in 2001, for instance, Le Doeuff argues that while women's engagement in the study of science and in scientific research should be promoted, it is first of all crucial to identify 'the social mechanism which discourages or even blocks individual vocations' (Le Doeuff 2001).

Moreover, Le Doeuff invites women to engage in group-based philosophical and broadly educational activities that would challenge the individualistic bias of patriarchal thought. It could be argued that, by implication, the shift from the individual to the group will discourage women themselves from adhering to a cult of the Self and of self-aggrandizement, which ultimately just mimics the patriarchal model and its ungenerous proclivities:

if the subject of the enterprise is no longer a person – or, better still, if each person involved in the enterprise is no longer in the position of being the subject of the enterprise but in that of being a worker, engaged in and committed to an enterprise which is seen from the outset as collective – it seems to me that the relationship to knowledge – and to gaps in knowledge – can be transformed. (Le Doeuff 1989: 127)

The major advantage of such a project would, ideally, be an acceptance of, and enthusiastic willingness to work with, a 'penumbra of knowledge', a form of speculation and analysis 'which does not claim to reconstruct and explain everything, which slides along the verge of the unthought' (ibid.).

CHAPTER 5

Writing and the Body

The advantage of life (or a story) in the shape of a star – in which things may move without necessarily intersecting and advance without necessarily meeting, and where every day (or chapter) is a different world pretending to forget the one before – is that it corresponds to what seems to be an essential tendency in the world itself: its tendency to expand, to dilate. The big bang, which has made us what we are and will destroy us in order to write a new chapter, remembering very little of our own, is never seen more closely than in the countless rays spreading outward in a biography full of new departures. The same movement is reflected in a story that keeps making new starts, leaving the reader half disappointed, half eager: he may never find what he's looking for ... (Kristeva 1992: 214–15)

It would be years before I learned that females possessed the only organ in the human body with no function other than to feel pleasure. (If such an organ were unique to the male body, can you imagine how much we would hear about it – and what it would be used to justify?) Thus, whether I was learning to talk, to spell, or to take care of my own body, I was told the name of each of its amazing parts – except in one unmentionable area. (Steinem 2001: xi)

Issues surrounding the relationship between language and the body were touched upon in *Chapter 3*. However, the earlier chapter was primarily concerned with examining the status of language as the backbone of the Symbolic order, namely, the ensemble of cultural codes and conventions that assign particular subject positions to the members of a society or community. Concurrently, *Chapter 3* highlighted the encoding of sexist world-views in semantic habits and linguistic stereotypes; the part played by language in the constitution of a socialized subject; and the political significance of feminist interrogations of patriarchal configurations of meaning. The present chapter, by contrast, focuses on the relationship between language and the *material* dimensions of the subject's existence. Subjectivity, it is here argued, is inconceivable independently of the symbolic systems in which it emerges: that is, cultural values and institutions that invest people with identities by placing them into shared structures. Nevertheless, several French feminist theorists are also concerned with exploring the extent to which the specifically corporeal aspects of a person's being may be expressed in language. Given that we never exist solely as pure consciousnesses or symbolic entities, insofar as we are embroiled at all times in a membrane of flesh and blood, it is plausible to assume that our physical existence may affect the ways in which we express ourselves and attempt to communicate with others.

REINVENTING LANGUAGE?

Feminist theory has repeatedly speculated about the relationship between textuality and corporeality, frequently suggesting that texts and bodies are analogous. As Julia Kristeva suggests in the above quotation from her novel *The Samurai*, affinities can be found between the ever-changing body of the cosmos and the body of an open text. Moreover, bodies can be *read* insofar as our experiences are invariably written on the body. Concurrently, eminently physical and erotic drives come into play in both the reading and the writing of texts. It is also vital to acknowledge, as Gloria Steinem indicates, that the body is not simply a text but also, more specifically, a *gendered* text, elements of which may be obscured or repressed by various forms of cultural censorship. A number of French authors have elaborated these ideas by arguing that the redefinition of conventional understandings of gender and sexuality requires a radical reassessment of language itself.

Monique Wittig, for example, maintains that we should endeavour to create language anew and her fictional output encapsulates her own attempt to do so. In her first novel, *L'Opoponax* (1964), in particular, she articulates her experience of emotional attachment to another girl at the age of twelve by deploying a highly experimental form that foregrounds the narrative's own status as a body. The complexity and multifacetedness of the experience itself is conveyed through a discontinuous textual form that rejects linearity, plays with cinematic techniques, and uses a self-reflexive style intended to mock the conventions of traditional autobiography. According to Cheryl Johnston, it is in *The Lesbian Body* (1973) that Wittig demonstrates most vividly her commitment to the reinvention of language: 'she describes in painful, clinical detail the bonding of two women lovers – their very viscera entwining and disentangling as the relationship ebbs and flows' (Johnston, 'Wittig: *The Lesbian Body*'). Images such as the following are quite characteristic of Wittig's style: 'I see your bones covered with flesh the iliacs the kneecaps the shoulders. I remove the muscles ... I take each one between my fingers the long muscles the round muscles the short muscles' (Wittig 1973: 31). *The Lesbian Body* builds on the project undertaken in *L'Opoponax* both by highlighting the physical properties of language and by intimating that the disruption of Symbolic discourse can lead to an invigorating explosion of the Western myth of unitary identity. As Felice Aull observes, *The Lesbian Body* is

> a sensual, image-rich picture of one (or, perhaps, many) lesbian affairs. The images are rich in anatomical detail, even employing medical language to describe the lover's body. Wittig re-imagines the act of love, the boundaries of the body, and masculine language. The lovers literally take apart each other's bodies as an act of love. ... Every personal pronoun in the book is 'split'. In French, for example, *je* became *j/e* and *tu*, *t/u*. ... Wittig's point is that no person is a coherent, self-sustaining element. We are all internally divided and made up of many dissimilar characteristics. (Aull, 'The Lesbian Body').

Marguerite Duras is also eager to expose the illusory status of all supposedly coherent identities and does so by recourse to techniques of defamiliarization and destabilization of conventional gender roles. In *The Lover* (Duras, 1997), specifically, she utilizes the unnamed protagonists as a means of transgressing legion cultural, sexual and racial boundaries and of interrogating the very categories from which such boundaries ensue. The novel does not merely reverse conventional subject positions but also conveys a sense of apocalyptic dissolution of standard roles and patterns of conduct, whereby Duras's characters and readers alike are left with 'all contraries confounded' (p. 8). Most importantly, as Rich Campbell points out, 'The young girl and her lover each have their gender identity deliberately blurred and entangled. They are not, however, created as mere reversals of their respective genders (and thus as accomplices to the binary), but rather as "others"' who, in 'denying classification as male or female', ultimately 'destroy the category itself' (Campbell 1999). In this respect, Duras's main characters embody the notion of *transvestism* as theorized by Marjorie Garber: namely, a drastic redefinition of the gender and sexual distinctions erected by binary thought, which does not only make 'such distinctions reversible' but also, more significantly, 'denaturalizes, destabilizes, and defamiliarizes sex and gender signs' (Garber 1997: 147).

Vestimentary codes are used throughout the novel to evoke graphically a potent sense of gender ambiguity. As Campbell notices, the girl's hat 'itself is a gender crisis in that it is a man's "fedora", while sporting the traditionally "feminine" shade of pink'. Thus, Duras 'does not dress the young girl as a man or as a woman, but as a combination, an ambiguity' (Campbell 1999). As for the lover, he is often defined by reference to physical attributes that would conventionally be thought of as feminine: his 'skin is sumptuously soft. The body is thin, lacking in strength, in muscle, he may have been ill, may be convalescent, he's hairless, nothing masculine about him but his sex' (Duras 1997: 38). Clothes and accessories contribute to the character's relative demasculinization: he is described as 'elegant' and as emanating the fragrance of 'expensive perfume, honey, ... the scent of silk' (p. 42). Thus, Duras could be said to have created a textual form in which writing and the body are inseparable to the extent that narrative and descriptive techniques designed to convey a pervasive sense of uncertainty, nebulousness and even undifferentiation consistently translate into ambiguous and fundamentally undecipherable bodies.

Annie Leclerc proposes a further approach to the collusion of textuality and corporeality based on the celebration of difference in both female language and the female body. Leclerc seeks to revalue the physical dimension of the feminine not simply by *writing about it* through a focus on psycho-physiological experiences specific to women but also by *writing it*: that is to say, inscribing femininity in the very texture of written discourse. Thus, she advocates the right to release the 'vigorous voices' radiating from a 'woman's belly' (Leclerc 1987: 59) as a vital means of rectifying the disabling effects of a long history of sexual imperialism fostered by a 'deafening tumult of important voices; and not one a woman's voice' (p. 58). Leclerc concurrently wishes to bring out in writing the 'adventure' entailed by 'the cyclical changes' undergone by the female body (p. 61) and to challenge those women who themselves cultivate crippling stereotypes of femininity: the 'dis-incarnated women, de-sexualized women, disinfected, dis-affected, glossy magazine women, puppet women, ... women the dragon of the family', who are inevitably 'in complicity with man's oppressions', by underscoring the irreducibility of sexual difference and its eminently bodily manifestations (p. 63).

This model has been fiercely criticized by Christine Delphy, who accuses Leclerc of abstracting the body from social and political reality:

When trying to 'revalue' our bodies, [Leclerc] uses only words which denote very physical things and acts: vaginas, childbirth, menstruation, etc. However, while there is a certain physical, non-social element in our bodies and actions, there is also a social component. It is essential to recognize that the meaning of periods, for instance, is not *given* with and by the flow of blood, but, like *all* meaning, by consciousness and thus by society. (Delphy 1984: 195).

If Delphy is fundamentally dissatisfied with the depoliticization of corporeality implicitly fostered by the proponents of a distinctively feminine discourse, another materialist critic, Colette Guillaumin, opposes the principle of *difference* itself as the basis upon which alternative modes of expression may be developed: difference does not give women a new language and tools for writing but merely perpetuates familiar patterns of oppression and exploitation. Guillaumin does, however, maintain that an intimate connection exists between writing and corporeality and that patriarchal language is visibly inscribed on women's bodies. This inscription is most blatantly evidenced by sartorial codes. In 'The Question of Difference', Guillaumin draws attention to the female body's entrapment by '*skirts*, destined to keep women in a state of permanent sexual accessibility'; '*high-heeled shoes*' assuring the 'limitation of bodily independence'; and '*diverse prostheses of the lace-up family*' (Guillaumin 2000a: 101) which, in 'hindering or reducing normal breathing' and in making 'stretching difficult and distressing', never 'let a woman forget her body'. The body which we are not allowed to *forget* is not the diffuse, flowing and multiple body idealized by the likes of Leclerc but a bound and bounded site of discomfort and pain. For Guillaumin, these vestimentary shackles sustain a discourse of sexual difference that does not allow women to voice and write out their uniqueness and specificity but actually 'wear down any tendencies a woman might have to think herself free' (p. 102).

Michèle Le Doeuff has also drawn attention to the shortcomings of certain approaches to the female body and its relation to language. Le Doeuff has highlighted the body's significance as an ensemble of narrative elements that constitutes an important part of the *philosophical imaginary* insistently suppressed by Western thought, and hence as instrumental to the puncturing of rationalist pretences. However, she is also wary of all projects intent on idealizing a female language supposedly issuing from the female body. Her critique is levelled primarily at the notion that we should endeavour to rediscover a submerged female discourse censored by patriarchy: in seeking to identify *a* language for women, we merely risk perpetuating a hegemonic situation wherein the multiplicity and diversity of female voices is effaced. Concurrently, Le Doeuff questions the proposition that women can articulate their essential femininity through a totally novel discourse, by pointing out that this 'supposes that one can purely and simply repudiate an old system of signs ... and invent a new language which, far from being conventional, would be invented by nature and secreted by "womanhood"' (Le Doeuff 2000: 53). According to Le Doeuff, a critical evaluation of the relationship between writing and the body can only adequately proceed from the awareness that if 'sexual difference has always been largely a business of signs', the signs themselves 'are truly difficult to revoke' and it is both spurious and dangerous to assume that 'one can be an absolutely free spirit, soaring high above convention and paying no attention to the "rest of humanity"' (p. 52).

ÉCRITURE FÉMININE: IRIGARAY'S AND CIXOUS'S PSYCHOLINGUISTIC PERSPECTIVES

An important theoretical formulation in French feminist thought is *écriture féminine* or "feminine writing". This concept involves the inscription of the female body and female sexuality in textuality and discourse. A concurrently utopian and experimental practice, *écriture féminine* seeks to write that for which no language yet exists – namely, the silenced, the marginalized and the repressed – while rejecting the principles of rationality and logic fostered by the masculine Symbolic order, traditional concepts of progression and linearity and the conventional subordination of the body to the mind. This segment offers a range of descriptions of *écriture féminine* that varyingly validate or question its existence.

Luce Irigaray contends that feminine language is tied up with the female body and with female libido as a non-phallic, plural and heterogeneous economy. Male sexuality has been constructed as a form of control based on the symbol of the phallus, whereby the '"differentiation" into two sexes derives from the *a priori* assumption that the little girl is, must become a man minus certain attributes whose paradigm is morphological – attributes capable of determining, of assuring, the reproduction-specularization of the same' (Irigaray 1985: 27). Female sexuality, in fact, is plural, for women's sexual organs are multiple and just about *everywhere*. Patriarchy and Freudianism, in establishing male sexuality as the norm, have caused women to lose touch with their bodies. Asserting a female identity, therefore, means regaining contact with our physical selves: that is to say, allowing our bodies to express themselves through a feminine writing that defies the standards of coherence and common sense treasured by patriarchal language, and is determined to 'reject all closure' and 'any constitution of *archē* or of *tēlos*' (Irigaray 2000d: 210).

According to some critics, there is a danger, in emphasizing the relationship between writing and the body, of *essentializing* woman: of reducing femininity once again to a biological and anatomical *substance* and thus implicitly reinforcing phallocentrism. This is not necessarily the case, however, since the "body" of which philosophers such as Irigaray speak is not so much a flesh-and-blood organism as a *text*: that is, both the fictional version of femininity constructed by patriarchy in order to legitimize its oppressive practices and the alternative construct ushered in by the practice of *écriture féminine*. Moreover, Diana Fuss argues, it is possible to see Irigaray's position as 'a politically strategic gesture of displacement' intended to expose how, throughout the history of Western thought, 'woman' has been persistently posited as a 'site of contradiction' (Fuss 1989: 72), endowed with essential characteristics, on the one hand, and reduced to the essence-lacking status of brute matter, on the other. Thus, far from essentializing woman, the notion of *écriture féminine* could be said to explode the myth of essence by arguing that all identities are textual and that, like all texts, they are inevitably riddled by internal tensions and paradoxes. An enthusiastic supporter of the liberating potentialities of feminine writing, Lynda Nead maintains that in Irigaray's prose, as indeed in Hélène Cixous's, 'the feminine text has an exhilarating and unbounded energy that shatters masculine institutions and values' (Nead 1992: 30). Moreover, due to its penchant for disrupting both formal and conceptual boundaries, this type of textuality bears affinities to the aesthetic notion of the *sublime*: that is, the undefinable and unrepresentable qualities of certain aspects of both nature and art, which elude classification and rational explanation and may only be apprehended, paradoxically, as long as we are able to grasp their incomprehensibility. This happens most characteristically when reason fleetingly gives way to the imagination and so-called certainties concede ground to tentative hypotheses. As a result, Jean-François Lyotard observes, 'the sublime sentiment' is 'a strong and equivocal emotion: it carries with it both pleasure and pain. Better still, in it pleasure derives from pain' (Lyotard 1984: 77).

It is also noteworthy that Irigaray resists the essentializing fallacy by refusing to posit a unitary, sealed or universal model of femininity and by underscoring instead women's boundlessness, polyphony and diversity:

> Because we are always open, the horizon will never be circumscribed. Stretching out, never ceasing to unfold ourselves, we must invent so many different voices to speak all of 'us', including our cracks and faults, that forever won't be enough time. We will never travel all the way round our periphery: we have so many dimensions. (Irigaray 1980: 75)

What is therefore central to Irigaray's project is the exploration of 'the multiplicity of new positions opened up by the realization of feminine power' (Nead 1992: 30).

In promoting feminine writing, Irigaray encourages the emergence of an innovative textual body that is capable not only of disrupting the conventions of classic realism on the formal plane but also of rescuing women from a cultural history of systematic marginalization in thematic terms. Indeed, refuting Sigmund Freud's contention that 'the murder of the father' represents 'the founding act for the primal horde', Irigaray argues that the Western imaginary, specifically in the guise of myths and legends, has repeatedly enacted and justified 'an even more ancient murder, that of the woman-mother'. An illuminating analysis of Aeschylus's *Oresteia* exemplifies this position. In this dramatic trilogy, Clytemnestra is killed by her son Orestes because she 'does not conform to that image of the virgin-mother which has been promoted as our ideal for centuries', is passionate, dares take up a lover, and indeed kills the husband who has been willing to sacrifice her daughter, has deserted her for several years and eventually returned home with a mistress. While both Orestes and his sister Electra are driven mad in retaliation for the son's nefarious act, Electra remains insane, whereas Orestes 'must be saved from madness so that he can found the patriarchal order' (Irigaray 2000e: 243). Apollo and Athena, the deities most overtly associated with reason and order, aid Orestes's escape from his guilt-induced lunacy and persecution by the 'horde of angry women, the Erinyes' who 'howl for revenge' at his heels. The moral Irigaray draws from this torrid saga is that 'the murder of the mother is rewarded by letting the son go scot free, by burying the madness of women – and burying women in madness – and by introducing the image of the virgin goddess, born of the Father [Athena], obedient to his laws at the expense of the mother' (p. 244). Western writing is replete with instances of brutal suppression of the female body which evince a phobic dread of 'retreating into the original matrix' (p. 246). (*Matrix*, incidentally, means "womb" in Latin.) Thus, the tendency exhibited by patriarchal texts to terrorize feminine corporeality goes hand in hand with an anxious yearning to demonize the primary locus of procreation itself. Relatedly, Irigaray observes, the 'womb is never thought of as the primal place in which we become body. Therefore for many men it is variously phantasized as a devouring mouth, as a sewer, ... as a threat to the phallus' (p. 247).

Cixous echoes Irigaray in maintaining that whereas 'masculine sexuality gravitates around the penis, engendering that centralized body (in political anatomy) under the dictatorship of its parts, woman does not bring about the same regionalization' (Cixous 2000a: 270). Eminently non-phallic and non-penetrative, woman's 'light', accordingly, 'doesn't come from above, doesn't fall, doesn't strike, doesn't go through. It radiates' (Cixous and Clément 1987: 88). Moreover, a parallel can be traced between female sexuality and female textuality: just as woman's 'libido is cosmic', so 'her writing can only keep going, without ever inscribing or discerning contours' and indeed releasing 'the language of 1,000 tongues which knows neither closure nor death' (Cixous 2000a: 270). However, Cixous does not incontrovertibly associate feminine and masculine forms of language with the human anatomy because she views both masculinity and femininity as linguistic fabrications:

> Great care must be taken in working on feminine writing not to get trapped by names: to be signed with a woman's name doesn't necessarily make a piece of writing feminine. It could quite well be masculine writing, and, conversely, the fact that a piece of writing is signed with a man's name does not in itself exclude femininity. It's rare but you can sometimes find femininity in writings signed by men: it does happen. (Cixous 2000c: 286)

Furthermore, as Mary Klages emphasizes, it is important to recognize that when Cixous claims that 'women are less fixed in the Symbolic than men' and that 'women – and their language – are more fluid, more flowing, more unstable than men', the term *woman* 'means both the literal woman, the person, and the signifier "woman"' (Klages 1998).

In celebrating the emancipatory value of a feminine language, Cixous's work often evinces a confidently hortative tone: 'Write your self. Your body must be heard. Only then will the immense resources of the unconscious spring forth. Our naphtha will spread, throughout the world, without dollars – black or gold – nonassessed values that will change the rules of the old game' (Cixous 2000a: 262). Cixous's enthusiastic encouragement to embrace *écriture féminine* posits this practice as capable of challenging the boundaries of the Symbolic by releasing feminine *jouissance*: 'a phenomenon that confounds, defies and exceeds the phallic order' (Bristow 1997: 96). What is here at stake is nothing less than woman's liberation from a prolonged history of both physical and psychological enslavement:

> It is in writing, from woman and toward woman, and in accepting the challenge of the discourse controlled by the phallus, that woman will affirm woman somewhere other than in silence, the place reserved for her in and through the Symbolic. May she get out of booby-trapped silence! And not have the margin or the harem foisted on her as her domain! (Cixous and Clément 1987: 93)

One of Cixous's main objectives is the dissociation of the 'history of writing' from the 'history of reason' insofar as the philosophical perspective that conventionally presents these two histories as inseparable and somehow interchangeable only serves to promote a 'self-congratulatory phallocentrism' (Cixous 2000a: 261). As writing is rescued from the imperialism of reason, its connection with corporeality is correspondingly strengthened. Concomi-

tantly, since women are supposed to be more closely connected than men
with the physical realm, they are potentially capable of a greater and deeper
involvement in body-oriented textual activities: 'More so than men who are
coaxed toward social success, toward sublimation, women are body. More
body, hence more writing' (p. 268). At the same time, following the deconstructive approach, Cixous steers clear of dogmatic categorizations by
arguing that no form of writing can be neatly labelled:

> it is impossible to define a feminine practice of writing, and this is an
> impossibility that will remain, for this practice can never be theorized,
> enclosed, coded – which doesn't mean that it doesn't exist. But it will
> always surpass the discourse that regulates the phallocentric system; it
> does and will take place in areas other than those subordinated to philoso-
> phico-theoretical domination. It will be conceived of only by subjects who
> are breakers of automatism, by peripheral figures that no authority can
> ever subjugate. (pp. 264–5)

Writing, therefore, is a practice with immense potential for feminist
politics, but we must be aware that at the same time as it flows from the
body, writing is also culturally and ideologically determined. Toril Moi
argues that Cixous's recognition of the political implications of *écriture
féminine* is inadequate insofar as her work does not offer 'any specific analysis
of the material factors preventing women from writing' and 'can say nothing
of the actual inequities, deprivations and violations that women, as social
beings rather than as mythological archetypes, must constantly suffer' (Moi
1985: 123). While Moi's criticism is indubitably cogent and an issue for
serious consideration, it is still feasible, as Klages states, that 'feminine
writing will serve as a rupture, or a site of transformation and change',
rupture signifying, 'in the Derridean sense, a place where the totality of the
system breaks down and one can see a system as a system or structure, rather
than simply as "the truth"'. 'Feminine writing', she suggests, will show the
structure of the Symbolic as a structure, not as an inevitable order' (Klages
1998).

It must also be noted that Cixous addresses the politics of textuality in
setting the emancipatory thrust of *écriture féminine* against the background of
an imposing corpus of narratives that have aimed at domesticating woman's
sexuality and, by extension, her very ability to *act* in the social sphere.
Female characters ostensibly endowed with strength and self-determination
are invariably destroyed, since such faculties contravene the patriarchal codification of the feminine. Citing the legends surrounding Penthesilea and
Clorinda as illustrative cases, Cixous states: 'a woman warrior is not a

woman; it is a woman who has killed the woman in her. Only through death does she return to femininity' (Cixous and Clément 1987: 118). A 'woman who is neither doll nor corpse nor dumb nor weak. But beautiful, lofty, powerful, brilliant' (p. 122) is only lovable once she has been annihilated and her perceived unfemininity has thus been vanquished. A further strategy frequently employed to contain the menace embodied by assertive females consists of translating them into exotic objects of both desire and dread. Their power may then be explained away as an aberration, coterminous with the outlandish nature of their cultures, and merely tolerated as long as it does not interfere with the laws of the *civilized* world. The story of Cleopatra exemplifies this point:

> She had to be from the Orient to be so lofty, so much the mistress of herself and *recognized* as such by her contemporaries. She had to be foreign. The 'great women' who pass through history or the historical imagination of the western side of the world come, can come only from an elsewhere one expects always to be holding a surprise – good or bad. Queen, entirely radiant, woman, on the condition that she rule from the other side of the world. (p. 125)

What is most problematic, in any assessment of *écriture féminine*, is simply establishing what this *is* beyond the level of abstract definitions. This difficulty ensues largely from the fact that the writings of Cixous and Irigaray provide descriptions of feminine writing more than they cite examples of this practice. This occasionally conveys a sense of vagueness and even tentativeness. In 'The Laugh of the Medusa', for instance, Cixous only addresses the question of illustrative cases in a footnote: 'Which works, then, might be called feminine? I'll just point out some examples. ... In France ... the only inscriptions of femininity that I have seen were by Colette, Marguerite Duras, ... and Jean Genet' (Cixous 2000a: 275). Arguably, it is in the style used by Cixous herself, with its propensity for breaking the conventions of the theoretical essay, that one finds one of the most vivid illustrations of *écriture féminine* at work. This is borne out by the following passage depicting the repression of female creativity:

> I, too, overflow; my desires have invented new desires, my body knows unheard-of songs. Time and again I, too, have felt so full of luminous torrents that I could burst – burst with forms much more beautiful than those which are put up in frames and sold for a stinking fortune. And I, too, said nothing, showed nothing. I didn't open my mouth, I didn't repaint my half of the world. ... I said to myself: You are mad! Where's

the meaning of these waves, these floods, these outbursts? Where is the ebullient, infinite woman . . .? (p. 258)

A further example of *écriture féminine*, according to Timothy H. Scherman, is supplied by Toni Morrison's *Beloved* (1997). It is hardly deniable that formal fluidity plays a prominent role in this text, as indeed in the majority of Morrison's works. At the same time, it is noteworthy that *Beloved* consistently weaves a dense web of poetic images that frequently foreground intensely physical sensations and bodily experiences. A fairly typical illustration of Morrison's style can be found in the closing section of *Beloved*:

There is a loneliness that can be rocked. Arms crossed, knees drawn up; holding, holding on, this motion, unlike a ship's, smooths and contains the rocker. It's an inside kind – wrapped tight like skin. Then there is a loneliness that roams. No rocking can hold it down. It is alive, on its own. A dry and spreading thing that makes the sound of one's feet going seem to come from a far-off place. (p. 274)

It should be noted, however, that not all critics would automatically agree with the definition of the type of writing theorized by Cixous as "feminine". Indeed, texts employing the very same linguistic strategies which Cixous regards as distinctive of *écriture féminine* have, in different contexts, been designated as experimental, poetic, modernist or postmodernist (and this list is by no means exhaustive). It is therefore necessary, in light of these potential criticisms, to emphasize that the term "feminine" is used by Cixous to designate not a textual modality incontrovertibly associated with women but rather a form that is metaphorically feminine insofar as it opposes patriarchal notions of order and logic. This form is supposed to mirror symbolically the physiological rhythms of the female body and female libido, and to foster a language that is neither linear nor goal-oriented but insistently conveys the fluid interweaving of thought, memory and voice.

INSCRIPTIONS OF THE BODY

This final segment examines two further levels at which writing and the body intersect, with specific reference to the theories of Julia Kristeva and Sarah Kofman. On the one hand, it focuses on some of the ways in which corporeality is textually articulated in writing: particularly, in religious, mythological and anthropological discourses devoted to the production of certain models of masculinity, femininity and gender relations. On the other hand, it indicates that while adult language cuts us off from the eminently physical experiences of the pre-adult realm, writing and related creative activities can help us re-experience and resurrect what we have lost in symbolic form. Thus, the body is culturally inscribed on two counts: firstly, because particular body images are brought into existence by writing; and secondly, because writing supplies a means of revisiting a submerged world in which the physical dimension once prevailed.

According to Kristeva, there is no full sense of the body as such before cultural inscription, for humans only endeavour to establish their corporeal boundaries at the point when they begin to develop a sense of themselves as subjects of the Symbolic. However, the body cannot be described merely as a product of culture. Indeed, Kristeva talks of *another body*, which is actually ungraspable by society and its discourses, and incompatible with rigid linguistic categories. As language endeavours, and by and large fails, to achieve stable and plenary meanings, some elusive traces always slip through its flimsy nets. This *remnant*, according to Kristeva, 'is experienced as the body' (Kristeva 1988: 215). The body, then, is not simply the concept we create when we enter culture and language: it is also an *excess* which signs cannot capture.

The most confusing corporeal configuration is, arguably, the maternal body. According to Kristeva, this has been warded off by many cultures as a symbol of boundary-confusion because, as Kelly Oliver observes, it functions as 'the very embodiment of alterity-within. It cannot be neatly divided into subject and object. ... The other cannot be separated from the self' (Oliver 1993: 4). Furthermore, the maternal subject refers to 'an identity that splits, turns in on itself and changes without becoming other' (Kristeva 1986a: 297). Attempts to contain this puzzling entity abound throughout history. Paganism is full of complex rituals meant to separate the pure from the impure, the latter being frequently associated with the female body, female blood, and even food touched by a woman's hands. In this context, 'religious rites' consist fundamentally of 'purification rites whose function is to separate this or that social, sexual, or age group from another one, by means of prohibiting a filthy, defiling element' (Kristeva 2000b: 168). Judaism, in turn, expresses its distaste of the maternal body by sanctioning circumcision, a ritual re-enactment of the cutting of the umbilical cord, as a means of protecting the male body from pollution, and preaches codes of purity meant to exclude everything that threatens to breach the body's boundaries: tabooed foodstuff, the corpse, sickness, the nourishing mother. Significantly, the objects which are considered most overtly and perniciously defiling are 'excremental and menstrual': namely, corporeal products associated with 'the *maternal* and/or the feminine'. Indeed, 'neither tears nor sperm, ... although they belong to the borders of the body, have any polluting value'. The connection between menstrual blood and femininity is quite obvious. The one between excremental waste and the mother is explained by Kristeva by recourse to the notion that 'maternal authority is experienced first and above all, after the first essentially oral frustrations, as sphincteral training' (p. 173).

Christianity does not exclude the mother but transforms her through purging into a paradoxical creature capable of giving birth without the *taint* of sexual intercourse. Insofar as Mary conceives immaculately, her body is cleansed of the carnal attributes of femininity which Western culture has repeatedly found so menacing. In a sense, the Christian mother could be said to lack a real body. Nothing is mentioned in the Scripture about the pain Mary must have experienced in the hours leading to the birth of Christ, and one may feasibly feel more aggrieved about Joseph, knocking on unwelcoming door after unwelcoming door, and for the donkey bearing the couple/triad, than for the heavily pregnant woman. Canonical versions of the Virgin Birth thus suggest that one of the most intractable aspects of human experience lies with the unresolved tension between the mortal body and the immortal one. While the former is unquestionably a potential site of pleasure, it also connotes decay and vulnerability, while the latter, though supposedly perfect and eternal, is also remote, beyond our grasp. Hence, religions have resorted to numerous hybrids intended to bridge the gap between the two bodies: incarnate deities, part-beings that combine human and non-human elements and, of course, virgin mothers.

Kristeva examines the cult of the Virgin Mary in the essay 'Stabat Mater', where it is argued that 'we live in a civilization in which the *consecrated* (religious or secular) representation of femininity is subsumed under maternity. ... this maternity turns out to be an adult (male and female) fantasy of a lost continent: ... not so much an idealized primitive mother as an idealization of the – unlocalizable – *relationship* between her and us' (Kristeva [1977] 1986b: 99). Since the Middle Ages, the Western idealization of the relationship between the Christian subject and the Virgin as the archetypal mother has 'served', as Allison Weir points out, 'to absorb the economy of the maternal ... into the social order, under the Law of the Father' and 'to absorb the pagan belief in the Mother Goddess ... into Catholicism' (Weir 1993: 82). Furthermore, this idealizing strategy pivots on the simultaneous elevation and brutalization of the feminine. Mary is celebrated as 'Queen of Heaven' (Kristeva 1986b: 114) and as 'unique among women, unique among mothers, and, since she is without sin, unique also among humans of both sexes'. However, Kristeva stresses that this 'uniqueness is achieved only by way of exacerbated masochism: an actual woman worthy of the feminine ideal embodied in inaccessible perfection by the Virgin could not be anything other than a nun or a martyr' (p. 115). Thus, the Marian myth bears witness to the Symbolic's ability to appropriate the affective qualities of the maternal body by enlisting them to the preservation of an order that categorically excludes the possibility of feminine excellence except as a prodigious deviation from the phallic norm. The prospect of a woman being genuinely *creative*, moreover, is denied out of a 'fear of the archaic mother' that ultimately 'turns out to be essentially fear of her generative power' (Kristeva 2000b: 174).

Kristeva contrasts this inflexible idealization of Mary with representations which free motherhood from cultural and religious dogma and experiment instead with *form*. She is particularly interested in images which do not frame the mother figure as a fixed cultural icon but actually show her as fluid and vibrant. In the essay 'Motherhood According to Giovanni Bellini', taken from *Desire in Language: A Semiotic Approach to Literature and Art* (Kristeva 1980), Kristeva commends the fifteenth-century Venetian painter's interpretations of the Madonna-and-Child theme, because they refuse to be constrained by their subject matter and choose instead to foreground resplendent colour, light, air and rhythm. Bellini's paintings exhibit rich chromatic harmonies and a uniquely radiant atmosphere, which together convey a heightened sense of tenderness and warmth. Kristeva celebrates their depiction of motherhood as 'a luminous spatialization, the ultimate language of a *jouissance* at the limits of repression, whence bodies, identities, and signs are begotten' (p. 269). The writing of the maternal body may only transcend the authority of the Symbolic by allowing the repressed energies of the Semiotic to surface, albeit temporarily. This occurs in Bellini's representations of the Madonna and Child to the extent that dominant cultural meanings conventionally ascribed to the Virgin and to the baby Jesus are subordinated to the imaginative *play* of non-verbal signs.

As shown in *Chapter 3*, Kristeva argues that in order to access the Symbolic and a sense of individuality, the budding subject must *act upon* its own body and, primarily, define its corporeal boundaries by shedding the borderline materials that threaten its self-containedness: that is, everything that flows, oozes, spills out – the *abject*. Insofar as the child is required to extricate itself from all external objects and people that threaten to engulf its subjectivity by tearing itself away from them, it could be argued that we become adult subjects through the experience of *violence*. Kristeva uses the idea of *horror* to describe the ways in which we revolt violently against aspects of our being which society deems unacceptable:

Abjection is something that disgusts you, for example, you see something rotting and you want to vomit – it is an extremely strong feeling that is at once somatic and symbolic, which is above all a revolt against an external menace from which one wants to distance oneself, but of which one has the impression that it may menace us from the inside. (Kristeva 1996e: 118)

Kofman explicitly relates the experience of abjection to the consumption of food and to the cultural imperatives and taboos associated with the latter in her autobiographical writings. While the freedom to eat items 'decreed impure' by religious and paternal authority, specifically in the context of Judaism, may prove 'delicious' (Kofman 1986b: 8), forced ingestion of food-stuff deemed good for one's 'health' can induce intense feelings of repugnance. When 'the food of [her] childhood' is 'decreed bad' and she is put 'on a totally different diet' by her substitute mother, she painfully finds that she can 'no longer swallow anything' and is compelled to vomit 'after each meal' (p. 9). As Tina Chanter points out, this manifestation of abjection is not merely a response to contingent forms of nourishment but also, more impor-tantly, a turbulent expression of Kofman's concurrent inability and unwill-ingness to 'stomach anything, ... to introject permanently ... or to successfully sublate her father's death, a death that is abandoned by a nation-state that saw his/her religion, his/her race, his/her Jewish identity as unpala-table. Kofman vomits. What has been buried inside her mind cannot be sustained by her body' (Chanter 1999: 201).

Kristeva argues that there is a danger of violence becoming the governing principle of our entire lives. Having become subjects by means of acts of violence perpetrated on our own bodies, we may find ourselves in a position where we are only capable of retaining our subjectivity by doing violence to others. Kristeva's views on this subject exhibit several points of contact with those of René Girard, as theorized in his book *Violence and the Sacred* (1977). Girard maintains that the primary reason for which human beings desire is that they acutely perceive a sense of lack but do not know what it is that they lack. As a result, they turn to others in the hope of identifying the object of their consuming, yet directionless, longing. In this process, they set out by trusting and respecting others as sources of authority and of knowl-edge, yet eventually end up envying, resenting and rejecting them precisely because they fear their putatively superior wisdom. This rejection is often vehement and brutal.

Kristeva's views on violence are also related to the theories put forward by Freud in *Totem and Taboo* (Freud 1913). Freud links the roots of violence to a mythical familial conflict. The young males of the primitive tribe team together to destroy an authoritarian father-chief – who has absolute power over all the women of the community – because they want the women for themselves. However, once the father has been eliminated, another threat arises: now all the young males are potentially one another's rivals in the struggle to possess the women. Clearly, if these hypothetical men were to devote their whole lives to the dicta of assassination and retaliation, no form of human society would be possible. Freud sees a way of bypassing this obstacle in the *incest taboo*: men will not fight unrelentingly over *all* the women available in a group as long as they are taught that certain women, namely those closest to them in the kinship structure, are not culturally available and may not be carnally possessed. Thus, in Freud's version of the origins of the law:

> the archaic father and master of the primeval horde is killed by the conspiring sons who, later seized with a sense of guilt for an act that was upon the whole inspired by ambivalent feelings, end up restoring paternal authority, no longer as an arbitrary power but as a right; thus renouncing the possession of all women in their turn, they establish at one stroke the sacred, exogamy, and society. (Kristeva 2000b: 166)

In examining Freud's claim that human morality strikes its roots in the taboos of murder and incest, Kristeva endeavours to establish a viable link between the two, and observes that while murder becomes taboo, quite unproblematically, through the experience of remorse, the desire to atone and the erection of laws able to accommodate and quantify these feelings, incest is a more elusive phenomenon. Although it can, and indeed is, prohibited by specific laws, it remains, like the abject, an active source of both fascination and revulsion due to its proclivity to challenge culturally constructed compartments and lines of demarcation, and hence the Symbolic itself. Kristeva also problematizes the Freudian perspective by arguing that murder is not merely a mythical point which precedes the law and the Symbolic order but a real and physical phenomenon: the *suppression of bodily drives*. As we have seen, the first experience of violence is written on the body by the vicissitudes that inevitably accompany the process of abjection. This initial, metaphorical *murder* is repeated whenever the subject's identity is threatened and its boundaries must be reinforced. Indeed, our mastery of the abject is always incomplete: the unsavoury aspects of ourselves, which we strive to shed as emerging individuals, unremittingly go on affecting our lives, and violence, therefore, has to be enacted again and again throughout adult existence to reaffirm the precarious edifice of subjectivity. A black hole on the edge of being into which the subject may implode any second, the abject's ghostly threat ceaselessly returns, to challenge the self-containedness of our psyches and bodies. 'Abjection' writes Kristeva, is 'the journey to the end of the night' (p. 168): a journey as never-ending as the night itself.

In combining intense physicality and the qualities of a figurative murder meant to assure our coming into being as subjects of the Symbolic, Kristeva's concept of abjection is reminiscent of Georges Bataille's notion of eroticism as a phenomenon in which the continuation of life is paradoxically guaranteed by a symbolic death, and in which sensuous experience is dominated, as in abjection, by 'violence', 'excess' and 'disorder' (Bataille 1962: 170). However, whereas abjection is supposed to secure the emergence of discrete subjectivities, the erotic as theorized by Bataille would ideally achieve the exact opposite by removing the divides between individual subjects and allowing Self and Other to merge in mutual suffusion. This ideal is directly inspired by Bataille's belief that humans are '*discontinuous* beings' (p. 12), separated by impervious barriers that preclude authentic intersubjectivity to develop. Although Kristeva does not celebrate the condition of discontinuity diagnosed in Bataille's *Eroticism*, she argues for its inevitability and emphasizes, moreover, that in order to accomplish satisfactorily the task of self-separation, upon which the attainment of an individual subjectivity depends, we must be able to come to terms with *loss*. This ability, in turn, requires us to learn how to *mourn* what we have lost: that is to say, the state of plenitude and undifferentiation that characterizes the pre-Symbolic realm, epitomized by the fusion of subject and object, Self and Other, child and mother. If we are incapable of mourning, we are doomed to the depressive/psychotic condition of *melancholia*. Let us consider the implications of this proposition in some detail.

In *Mourning and Melancholia* (Freud 1917), Freud linked melancholia to a sense of loss that is never properly worked through insofar as the pleasure principle is overwhelmed by *death-drives*. This leads to the disintegration of all positive human relationships. The melancholic subject refuses to separate itself from the lost object of desire and strives to incorporate this object into itself. This move is simultaneously cannibalistic and self-destructive for, in incorporating the other, the subject also creates conflicts and divisions within its own ego: it becomes alienated from itself. Kristeva, for her part, views melancholia as a consequence of the subject's inability to sever itself from the pre-Symbolic domain, and attendant failure to relate to others. Indeed, we can only interact with others if we are aware of our separateness from them. In melancholia, relatedly, we are unable to mourn: we pine over a lack that cannot be symbolized, cannot be given a name. Therefore, this condition involves a total devaluation of social bonds and of language, whereby *everything becomes meaningless*.

In 'The Imposture of Beauty' (Kofman 1999b), Kofman examines the predicament experienced by the protagonist of Oscar Wilde's *The Picture of Dorian Gray* as precisely a case of melancholia precipitated by the inability to mourn. What Dorian Gray 'fails to mourn', in particular, is 'beauty. *His* beauty, to be sure, but behind his own, what he does not manage to tolerate … is the loss of his mother's beauty, with which he identified.' Kofman corroborates this hypothesis in the following observation:

> the room in which Dorian banished his picture … is … the room in which he spent the majority of his boyhood and adolescence. Here it is that he 'exhibits' (without exhibiting) his picture, the progressive blemishing of his soul, deliberately, monstrously scorning and mocking the stainless 'rose-white' purity of this boyhood and the man who strove to preserve it for him by his stern prohibitions: his grandfather, the representative of the Law. (p. 43)

An unusually beautiful and unconventional woman prepared to risk everything for a delirious passion, Dorian's mother typifies the threat of voracious and unbridled femininity so intensely abhorred by the phallocentric order upheld by Dorian's grandfather. Implicitly echoing Kristeva, Kofman thus links the melancholic subject's narcissistic and self-debilitating clinging to the pre-Symbolic domain to the mother figure, as the epitome of a baffling corporeality that stubbornly eludes containment by the patriarchal law.

One of Kristeva's main concerns lies with how, given that the melancholic person rejects language and retreats into a silent crypt of pain, one may help her or him *express* this pain. A way of accessing the mind of the melancholic is to move beyond conventional language and focus instead on non-linguistic forms of expression: for example, semiotic and corporeal signs of the kind discussed in *Chapter 3*. Kristeva also believes that chemicals can be helpful. It remains to be proved whether a *depression gene* is transmitted by the X-chromosome (the female one), as some argue, and whether this gene may be scientifically altered. However, Kristeva contends that psychiatric drugs may enable the patient to articulate her/his predicament by lifting certain inhibitions. For example, some patients only think they have dreams when they are under the influence of chemicals. Since oneiric images can be regarded as a kind of writing issuing from the body's darkest recesses, forms of therapy that aim at unburdening the physical being may also create scope for textual productivity.

It could also be argued that in rejecting dominant forms of language, melancholia challenges the Symbolic order by drawing attention to the incidence of feelings, fantasies and emotions which the latter is simply incapable of encoding. These, in fact, may only be expressed through material, bodily and semiotic qualities of language that irreverently criss-cross, pluralize and pulverize phallocentric discourse, and thus reveal its exposure to blank spots of non-meaning. What should be emphasized, however, is that the mourning subject agrees to name its desires by using the words which the Symbolic imposes upon it in what Ewa Ziarek terms 'an economy of losses and compensations' (Ziarek 1993: 72), whereas the melancholic refuses 'to accept any compensation for that loss [the loss of wholeness], especially in terms of symbolic mastery' (p. 73), and shuns the tyranny of words which s/he finds arbitrary, conventional, and totally indifferent to individual desires.

In *Black Sun* (Kristeva [1987] 1989b), Kristeva argues that a powerful means of giving the experience of loss a form is art. Art cannot *represent* the drama of melancholia because, as we have seen, this condition resists conventional language and its signs. Yet, at times, it becomes so minimalistic that it at least approximates melancholia by refusing to idealize the body, passions, feelings and aesthetic notions such as beauty. Kristeva discusses Holbein's painting *The Corpse of Christ in the Tomb* (1521) as an example of this type of art, and emphasizes its ability to put the viewer in touch with pure, undiluted sorrow. As John Lechte observes, Holbein's painting

> takes us very close to a presentation of signs completely bereft of drive affect typical of melancholia. ... This effect is achieved in the painting in question through a 'minimalism' which, firstly, isolates the figure of Christ through depicting the body entirely alone in its crypt; and, secondly, gives no hint at an idealization of the body, no sign of transcendence, or of passion (semiotic features). ... it is not a sign of grief, it *is* grief. (Lechte 1990: 188)

A literary example of this minimalism can be found in the writings of Duras, where psychological disturbance is repeatedly addressed coldly, unsentimentally and without any trace of sentimentalistic idealism. Duras, Lechte contends, conveys the 'erasure of all signs of transcendence' (p. 193).

> [Her] writing, as Kristeva presents it, contains no ideal, no music ... only a cold, logical, totally lucid self .... Such writing is symptomatic of a world where people have gone mad quite rationally, in full command of their faculties. Indeed, we are witness to a growing worthlessness of meaning and sentiment accompanied by complete lucidity. (p. 194)

It is also noteworthy that Kristeva links creativity with depression and melancholia on a further level, too. In creating artworks, she argues, we are productive but we simultaneously deplete ourselves, drain our bodies and minds of vital energies. Artistic creation is thus a way of reiterating the initial experience of loss from which all subjectivity stems. This re-evocation of the primal psychodrama is not without advantages, however. It is by deploying our creativity that we may devise a means of counteracting the disabling effects of socialization and enculturement. The entry into the Symbolic is painful because it subjects us to the despotic authority of disembodied signs, yet also the precondition of our ability to function as adult subjects and, relatedly, to interact with other beings. We have no choice, ultimately, but to accept the Symbolic and the figurative death it brings: namely, the repression of bodily drives. Nonetheless, we remain in possession of an inalienable right to resort to art and writing as ways of metaphorically reliving and negotiating the ancestral state of lost plenitude *through signs*. These will inevitably lack the actual body's sensuous immediacy but, in that body's irretrievable absence, will at least enable us to relate to it via a symbolic substitute.

CHAPTER 6

Power, Race and the Stranger

I consider women's literature as a specific category, not because of biology, but because it is, in a sense, the literature of the colonized. (Rochefort in Showalter 1988: 344)

critical inquiries into sexuality must be sensitive to the non-uniformity between miscellaneous types of privilege and deprivation. Class, genera-tion, race, and sex – just to give some of the main categories for mapping understandings of sexuality – are factors that can complicate our knowl-edge of how power is distributed in the West. Therefore it becomes possible to grasp exceptionally complex reconfigurations of dominance and subordination when we explore the interfaces between these multiple coor-dinates of power. (Bristow 1997: 172–3)

SEXISM AND RACISM

A pressing concern for French feminist theorists, particularly in the social/materialist camp, lies with the endeavour to establish whether sexual oppres-sion and racial oppression are analogous or comparable and, if so, what the cultural and economic repercussions of this collusion might be. According to Monique Wittig, sexism and racism are inextricably intertwined insofar as they deploy closely related forms of objectification and exploitation of both the physical and intellectual resources of the enslaved race or gender:

The category of sex is a totalitarian one. ... it shapes the mind as well as the body since it controls all mental production. ... [It] is the category that ordains slavery for women, and it works specifically, as it did for black slaves, through an operation of reduction, by taking the part for the whole, a part (colour, sex) through which the whole human group has to pass as through a screen. (Wittig 1996: 28)

One of the most comprehensive discussions of race from a radical feminist viewpoint can be found in Colette Guillaumin's 'Race and Nature: The

System of Marks' ([1982] 2000b), where it is argued that the concept of race in the modern sense of the term did not exist prior to the social and economic reality of black slavery. Indeed, up to that point, it generally referred to family lineage. The invention of the current notion in conjunction with the phenomenon of slavery was further supported by the social taxonomies created in the late eighteenth century to classify humans into groups. What is crucially significant, according to Guillaumin, is that 'race' as an indicator of 'a social group' has been insistently distorted insofar as this group has come to be *perceived as natural* (p. 82). Race is thus regarded as a *given* inherent in the natural order of things. As a result, we are encouraged to take as an essential truth something which is, in fact, a mythological/ideological fabrication. Moreover, Guillaumin stresses, if blackness is apprehended in specifically racist ways, this has less to do with what blackness *is* than with what it is *construed* as being.

As Wittig points out in her commentary of Guillaumin's work on this subject, black people 'are seen as *black*, therefore they *are* black' but 'before being *seen* that way, they first had to be *made* that way'. An analogous process of distortion animates sexist agendas: female subjects 'are seen as *women*, therefore, they *are* women' (Wittig 2000b: 130). The patriarchal construction of femininity is thus effaced and "woman" presented as a natural substance rather than the cultural category it actually is. The burden of Guillaumin's theories on the relationship between race and sex, then, is that just as the idea of a *natural race* does not precede racism but is, in fact, the *product* of racist ideologies, so the idea of a *natural sexuality* is the *result*, not the *origin*, of sexism. In both cases, the 'invention of the idea of nature cannot be separated from domination and the appropriation of human beings' (Guillaumin 2000b: 97). It is because blacks and women are kept in a subordinate position that they can be arbitrarily attributed a certain nature: this represents a radical inversion of the commonsense assumption that it is because those groups are endowed with a certain nature in the first place that they can, indeed must, be subordinated.

Guillaumin also emphasizes that although racist belief systems consist fundamentally of imaginary formulations, they acquire reality and authority by virtue of their institutionalization as laws: 'the law is the expression of the ideology ... of the system of *domination*' (p. 96). Some of the most notorious instances of the institutional naturalization of the idea of race by legal systems are the laws produced 'at the end of the nineteenth century in the United States (the Jim Crow law), in 1935 in Nazi Germany (the Nuremberg laws), and in 1948 in South Africa (the apartheid laws)'. All these 'discriminatory, interdictory, segregating laws which touch practically all areas of life (marriage, work, domicile, moving about, education, etc.)' stem from the institutionalization of race '*as a category of nature*' (p. 94).

Racial and sexual issues can also be shown to coalesce in the context of materialist feminist research in the fields of anthropology and ethnography: particularly, *vis-à-vis* the study of the cultural construction of gendered and sexual identities, of reproduction and of laws, customs and rituals designed to regulate and monitor these complex phenomena. Nicole-Claude Mathieu indicates that the systematic gathering and processing of an ample body of documents and data is instrumental to the achievement of an adequate understanding of the cultural, ethnic and racial distinctiveness of the contexts within which gender and sex interact with and complicate each other (Mathieu 1996). In the absence of such documentation, anthropological and ethnographic enquiry risks deteriorating into the production of sweeping generalizations and reductively opinionated statements which pay scanty attention to racial specificities. In her assessment of the cultural and ideological dimensions of the procreative process, Paola Tabet likewise points out that the history of reproduction is patchily recorded due to limited anthropological perspectives marred by racism. In order to supply an accurate analysis of 'the control of the reproductive body', and of 'the agents intervening at different stages in the *sequence or process of reproduction*', one would need 'systematic and detailed documentation' of these factors across 'many societies'. Yet, 'the available qualitative and quantitative information on reproduction is far from satisfactory' (Tabet 1996: 110). Tabet suggests that this scarcity of data is a direct corollary of 'ordinary sexism, redoubled by racism, with authors reproducing stereotypes, such as that women in "primitive societies" do not experience pain during labour because they are more "natural"' (p. 156).

THE STRANGER WITHIN

Why is it that we find some people *foreign*, and what makes them so threatening? Why does difference beget fear and violence, and can we ever move to an ethics of respect for those different from us? (McAfee 1993: 116)

According to Julia Kristeva, we are only capable of living with others to the extent that we are capable of seeing *ourselves* as Other. Political movements based on a group identity, be this linked to gender, race or class, have done much to fight discrimination and oppression. Yet, they must be careful not to practise politics of exclusion, promote that group identity and brand those who do not partake of it as *alien*. Kristeva's commitment to the investigation of these issues spans the early 1970s to the present. In recent years, her writing on foreignness has developed in the context of various redefinitions of the concept of national identity brought about, for example, by massive waves of immigration; problems concerning the European federation; the disintegration of Eastern Europe into conflicting communities. Speculating specifically on contemporary French culture, Kristeva asks:

> where does one start to open up this very phobic notion of national identity, to permit the mixture of races and to welcome others, in order to proceed to what I call 'puzzle' states, that is, states that are constituted from several types of citizens – immigrants, people who are part of the European community, people who come from Africa and Asia in addition to those in France – and then perhaps one day to proceed toward the disappearance of the notion of the foreigner?' (Kristeva 1996d: 40)

In attempting to address this challenging question, Kristeva contends that 'we cannot look for the answer in religion' (ibid.). This is because religious movements only accept the Other if its alterity can be either legitimated or erased, either turned into some kind of cultural norm or totally repressed through conversion. Thus, they 'are discourses that welcome the other only on condition of delegitimating or annulling him. "You are accepted if you accept our moral code as Christian or Jew. The moment you do this, there is no problem. You are like us. We accept you".' Concurrently, Kristeva maintains, 'the great monotheistic religions like Islam are extremely reactionary and persecutory – look at the Rushdie affair' (pp. 40–1). In *Thinking the Difference* (Irigaray [1989] 1994), Luce Irigaray embraces an analogous perspective and seeks to show that racial discrimination frequently stems from dogmatic religious systems that afford no scope for difference, whether ethnic or sexual. This is evinced by the fact that 'established religions' rely on fundamentally 'patriarchal churches' (p. 10) that have ruthlessly 'deprived women of their own gods or divinity(ies)' (p. 11) and promulgated an androcentric world-view which invariably celebrates a masculine deity and masculine privilege: 'respect for the father and for God the Father' (p. 33), in this regard, is the cardinal obligation.

Although the ideas outlined above could be said to make Kristeva's writings overtly political, critics are by no means in agreement over the exact ideological significance of the theories proposed therein. Indeed, some have argued that even though Kristeva's approach to the notion of the foreigner is helpful in questioning racial stereotypes, it does not actually offer any practical political solutions. Others have gone even further, by arguing that in valorizing the Other, Kristeva falls into the trap of idealizing it in a purely utopian fashion. A text often cited by these critics as evidence for the danger of idealization in Kristeva's work is *About Chinese Women* (Kristeva 1977). The book was shaped by cultural debates of the early 1970s initiated by the feminist movement, psychoanalysis, Marxism and structuralism, as well as by many intellectuals' disillusionment in the wake of *les événements* of 1968. China was often seen as a model world where radical politics yielded practical results, in contrast with the thwarted revolutionary aspirations of Europe, and particularly France. As Lisa Lowe observes, 'the French construction of China in the 1970s was central to a counterideological politics; China was constituted as an object of desire' (Lowe 1993: 150). China was thus romanticized and rather uncritically construed 'as a utopian site of revolution outside Europe'. Kristeva's book commends the Chinese political system by concentrating specifically on the role played by women in Chinese history and society, and describes the origins of Chinese culture in relation to commanding female personages symbolically capable of challenging and subverting the patriarchal foundations of Western culture, as well as Judaism and Christianity: '*Des Chinoises* [*About Chinese Women*] invokes the powerful figure of an ancient Chinese matriarch as the disrupting exception to Western patriarchy and psychoanalysis, and the People's Republic of China is praised as a political antithesis to contemporary France.' This reading, some commentators have argued, is problematic. It breaks with a long tradition of imperialist thought which could only think of the oriental Other as a colonized space. Yet, it still treats it as *Other*: 'the examples of China and Chinese women are cited only in terms of Western debates, are invented as solutions to Western political and theoretical problems' (Lowe 1993: 151).

However, Kristeva is aware that when we encounter other cultures, we can never leave our own culture totally behind and that there is therefore always a risk of reading the Other through Western eyes, from the perspective of an orientalist gaze. Kristeva knows that she herself is not immune from this danger and articulates this position in her later writings on the subject of otherness, where a rather more complex argument than the one pursued in *About Chinese Women* comes to the fore. These texts do not focus on one ideal or idealized site of revolutionary politics but rather address the psychological roots of our attitudes to alterity. Difference, it is argued, is not the gap between the identity of an individual or a group and what is foreign to it. In fact, difference is an internal condition: *the stranger is in us*. As we have seen, Kristeva maintains that the Self is neither stable nor unified, for conflicting forces are unrelentingly at work in our minds and bodies. This condition makes us feel vulnerable and uncertain and in order to fend off this sense of insecurity, we create distinctions between those parts of ourselves which we cherish and wish to retain as ours, and those which we loathe and wish to expel. The excluded parts become the *Other*.

When a society, community or nation ostracizes certain people, what it is attempting to exclude is actually a part of its own identity. That is to say, its own inherent otherness is projected onto the people whom it discriminates against, and the Other is thereby transformed into an *external* dimension of being. Kristeva emphasizes that we should always bear in mind that when we abuse other people, we are really abusing parts of ourselves which we have cast off in the search for wholeness and safety. We regard some people as *foreign*, find them menacing and react to them violently because we have problems with the *foreigner within us*. This alien domain is the unconscious itself, as the region of psychic life which we most stubbornly fail to acknowledge:

> 'Hell,' said Sartre, 'is other people.' Perhaps, but because hell is my unconscious and I do not recognize it. Therefore, recognizing what is not doing well in myself – my death drives, my eroticism, my bizarreness, my particularity, my femininity, all these uncoded marginalities that are not recognized by consensus – I would tend less to constitute enemies from those phenomena, which I now project to the exterior, making scapegoats of others. (Kristeva 1996d: 41)

Thus, we treat strangers in pretty much the same way in which we treat our unconscious desires: in both cases, we repress what we cannot come to terms with. Kristeva also stresses that it should never be a matter of trying to *make sense* of otherness. What we must learn, in fact, is how to value what we cannot know or understand. Insofar as the manner in which we treat foreigners is intimately connected with the manner in which we approach our own unconscious, 'it is only by coming to terms with the stranger within that we can come to terms with those in our midst'. Relatedly, coming to terms with our unconscious, and hence the Other outside the Self, does not mean 'eradicating difference and alterity' but rather 'developing an ethics of respect for what cannot be known' (McAfee 1993: 116). Kelly Oliver concurs: 'Psychoanalysis accepts, even invites, difference, nonmeaning, otherness. It can provide a new way of identifying the other, the stranger, not in order to reify or exclude it, but in order to welcome it' (Oliver 1993: 8).

Like the *abject*, as discussed in *Chapter 3* and *Chapter 5*, the stranger elicits anxiety because we cannot place it in any definite compartment. We find it disturbing not simply because of specific features of its being, such as the way it looks, speaks and behaves, but primarily because of its *indeterminate-*

ness. We are unable to assign it to a category with which we are familiar and therefore become anxious. The anxiety escalates, sometimes to the point of paranoia, as the stranger comes to remind us of our own strangeness to ourselves and of our incompleteness. In *Strangers to Ourselves*, Kristeva states: 'Confronting the foreigner whom I reject and with whom at the same time I identify, I lose my boundaries, I no longer have a container ... I lose my composure. I feel "lost", "indistinct", "hazy"' (Kristeva 1991a: 187). Politically, anxiety about the stranger can easily degenerate into blind hatred, as borne out by various forms of fascism, racism, genocide, and fetishistic attachment to national identities, languages and territories. A way of preventing these extreme dangers is to become reconciled with the Other: to see it as an integral component of our culture rather than a threat to it. However, Kristeva indicates that even this move is not without perils, since reconciliation may amount to the *absorption* of the Other into the so-called norms of our culture, and hence to integration, colonization and a denial of the right to be different. Kristeva believes that it is far healthier to accept the Other's difference and come to think imaginatively about cultures that are always and inevitably polyphonic and hybrid.

Kristeva explicitly argues in favour of multiracial societies in her *Lettre ouvert à Harlem Désir* (1991b), an open letter to the Head of the French human rights organization *S.O.S. Racisme*, which she wrote in 1990 as a contribution to debates unleashed by *l'affair du foulard* (the headscarf affair). This came about when, in the course of 1989, a group of young Arab women wearing headscarves (the *hijab*) were denied entry to their school. For Kristeva, this incident speaks volumes about Europe's repressive attitude to cultural and religious otherness, and specifically about France's anxieties about the infiltration of its national identity by Islamic immigrants from North Africa. In her letter, Kristeva argues for the *necessary* heterogeneity of national and political communities. The idea of a unitary nation or culture, like that of the unitary subject, is only ever an oppressive myth, fuelled by dogmatism and short-sightedness.

Kristeva's views on power, race and the stranger have been criticized by commentators who find her political stance vague and not sufficiently committed to the issue of local specificity. Clair Wills, for example, argues that in the context of Kristeva's work, racial and ethnic conflicts evaporate in a transhistorical grand narrative. This is supposedly corroborated by Kristeva's analysis of Meursault, the protagonist of Albert Camus's *L'Étranger*, undertaken in the first chapter of *Strangers to Ourselves*. Wills is particularly concerned with Kristeva's evaluation of the story's climax, the point at which Meursault, a French colonial settler in Algeria, shoots an Arab, and is alarmed by Kristeva's 'astonishing claim that it is not a matter of importance whether he kills a Frenchman or a Maghrebian' (Wills 1992: 289). From this claim, Wills extrapolates Kristeva's tendency to 'dissolve all differences of class, gender and ethnicity within an essential difference' (p. 290): namely, the fact that all people are intrinsically alienated from themselves. In other words, Kristeva's belief that 'since we are all foreigners, none are any more foreign than others' (p. 289) risks obfuscating the distinctive predicaments of specific groups within the social and cultural practices of colonialism and imperialism, in the service of a universal notion of endemic foreignness.

Norma Claire Moruzzi also criticizes Kristeva for endorsing a universalistic agenda, which she attributes primarily to the fact that her 'emphasis on the psychoanalytic elides the political' (Moruzzi 1993: 138). Like Wills, Moruzzi offers Kristeva's analysis of Meursault as evidence for this regrettable inclination to prioritize the inner, individual dimension over the social and collective one. Hence, Kristeva is accused of not paying any attention to the specific differences that obtain in particular societies, to the specific forms which racism tends to take in such societies, and, relatedly, to the practices that construct strangers as context-bound beings rather than abstract, universal entities. Kristeva, Moruzzi argues, ignores the fact that 'Meursault is a *pied noir* in Algeria' (p. 137), namely a colonial settler rather than a mere visitor, that his status is fundamentally that of 'an interloper among more clearly defined national identities', and that his own identity 'has been fractured and misplaced, not only through the personal details of his life, but also by the vague political and social facts among which he, despite himself, has made his life'. In neglecting Meursault's 'political and social circumstances' by focusing exclusively on his 'psychoanalytic alienation' (p. 138), Kristeva exhibits a tendency to gloss over the historical specificities of 'social heterogeneity' (p. 141).

Martha J. Reineke offers a counter-reading of these issues which stems from the conviction that both 'Wills and Moruzzi misread Kristeva' (Reineke 1997: 191). For Reineke, Kristeva is actually 'attuned ... to signifying practices that produce and support specific political, religious, and familial structures' and, relatedly, eager to pose 'a thoroughgoing challenge to identity politics out of which are constructed exclusionary practices, such as racism, sexism, and colonialism' (p. 192). What Kristeva prioritizes, therefore, is the need to understand and confront these practices as an ensemble capable of producing cumulative effects, not as discrete discourses. That is to say, the various practices cited by Reineke must be grasped as interrelated components of a complex network, rather than as monadic entities, if we are to comprehend the far-reaching repercussions of discrimination and oppression at all levels of both personal and social existence. Furthermore, Reineke is keen to emphasize the following point:

Whereas Wills and Moruzzi claim that the ethnic identity of the person Meursault murders makes no difference *to Kristeva*, Kristeva actually says that it makes no difference *to Meursault* whom he kills ... . Kristeva most definitely is not indifferent toward Meursault's indifference. She wants to know what has produced indifference in Meursault. (p. 193)

Indeed, in remarking on the character's 'anesthetized indifference' (Kristeva 1991a: 26), his cold and unemotional language and his spiritual hollowness, Kristeva wants to know what has *made* him into what he is by the signifying practices – social, cultural, racial and sexual – that interweave in all areas of our lives.

It could be argued, moreover, that Kristeva does not propose universality, as opposed to specificity, since she rejects the classic foundation of all Western universal rubrics: namely, 'the autonomous subject of humanism in which an other and its social world is always embraced as an afterthought or an addendum in the subject's life'. In fact, as we have seen, Kristeva's subject is always already inhabited by an irreducible alterity and somehow dependent on the latter's existence for its own survival. Indeed, the stranger within constitutes an ineradicable part of ourselves: fantasies, desires and anxieties, often unconscious, which may terrify us but which, at the same time, need to be articulated if we are to retain a modicum of sanity. A total repression of the unconscious, of the otherness which we host and which we are, assuming this were at all possible, would transform us into either ghosts or automatons. It would make us victims of totalitarian acts analogous to those routinely perpetrated by colonial and imperial rule. In this respect, it is also vital to develop an ability to recognize the imaginative and creative opportunities afforded by strangers, both *without* and *within*. Indeed, as McAfee emphasizes, 'the foreigner presents an opportunity and not an abyss'. That is to say, in confronting what is strange, alien and, very possibly, disorienting, we are reminded that the subject is never permanent or whole. Identity is endlessly transformable and its transformability increases in proportion to its openness to the Other: 'Without completion, possibility thrives' (McAfee 1993: 132). The acceptance of our own self-division and incompleteness is what makes us go on *trying*, and hence the guarantee of creativity and change.

It is also noteworthy, in this context, that although Kristeva's discourse of the Other is not based specifically on a critique of sexual politics but rather on the broad body of fantasies and myths surrounding the stranger, she does state that woman has traditionally been construed as something of a prototypical other. Grounding this affirmation in the terrain of legend from which conventional wisdom characteristically stems, Kristeva cites the myth of the *sacred cow* as a case in point:

the first foreigners about which occidental history speaks were foreign *women* ... the Danaïdes ... who descend from the sacred cow, Io. What did she do this sacred cow? She was a person who fell in love with Zeus, and who thus committed an illegitimate act because she seduced the husband of Hera. ... And Hera, obviously, is furious. She sends a sort of insect, a horsefly, which crazes Io, who is turned into a cow and chased from her native land. So she becomes foreign from that moment on; there are no more lands that can become her own because she is condemned to wander in the world. (Kristeva 1996d: 47)

When Zeus eventually calms her and she gives birth to the fifty Danaïdes, the daughters repeat their mother's story of feminine recklessness: 'forced to marry their fifty cousins', they prove 'resistant to marriage, and in certain variants of the myth, on the day of the marriage ceremony, they kill the cousins' (ibid). We are thus presented with a signifying chain in which foreignness almost automatically translates into femininity and the latter, in turn, into the epitome of an unruly sexuality unproblematically liable to harsh divine punishment in the familiar guise of madness. At the same time, we are warned about the likely perpetuation of this nefarious cycle by the bestial woman's proclivity to produce yet more foreign and intemperate women.

In examining Kristeva's positions on the foreigner, it is arguably important to bear her own background in mind. Born in Bulgaria, she moved to Paris at the age of twenty-four as a result of what could be termed a form of cultural and educational colonialism. In the mid-1960s, Charles de Gaulle's government was keen on the idea of an integrated Europe and, as a means of achieving this objective, on awarding scholarships to Eastern European students to study in Western Europe. Having received one such grant, Kristeva began working in Paris. Since then, she has done all her theoretical work in French. Kristeva had already been exposed to the French language from an early age as a result of having been enrolled in a French kindergarten. Working in a foreign language is an important part of Kristeva's critical career and personality because it has encouraged her to reflect on the idea of foreignness and on the various ways in which this manifests itself in culture and art. Kristeva believes that foreigners and immigrants always carry in themselves the spectre of another place. This sometimes creates a sense of confusion in the foreigner's mind but also constitutes an exciting challenge, an invitation to understand the element of otherness which dwells in all of us, regardless of whether or not we live in a culture other than our native one. Kristeva also stresses that we all carry memories of childhood connected with places, their colours, smells and sounds, and that the reason for which these recollections are often hazy is that we find it difficult to express them in words: as adults, we have lost touch with the language of childhood. A foreign language can help us translate those early impressions of the world into words because it is more distanced from them than our mother tongue is. It is for this reason that Kristeva found her analysis, which was conducted in French, helpful in transposing her images of childhood onto her new culture.

As in Kristeva's case, possibly even more so, personal experience plays an important part in Hélène Cixous's views on race, power and foreignness. Born in Oran from a physician of Sephardic origins and a midwife of Austro-Czechoslovakian and German descent, and brought up bilingual in French and German while also being exposed to Arabic and Spanish, Cixous was never quite at home in the colonial environment in which she grew up. This is attested to, as Verena Andermatt Conley points out, by the fact that

> subsequently, Cixous never lost her desire to fight the encroachment of power in all its forms upon the human body and the human mind. She felt the need to break out of the world in which she was born and look for other worlds or realities less marked by the horrors of the political events of her childhood. She found these worlds in fiction. ... The causes she espouses vary. From a need for personal liberation through a reading of psychoanalysis, she moves on to more collective struggles, the woman's cause, an interest in the Third World, ... the German and Russian death camps. (Conley, 'Hélène Cixous')

Cixous comments eloquently on both the political reality and the symbolic connotations of racial identity in 'Sorties', a section within *The Newly Born Woman* (Cixous and Clément 1987), where she states that 'the paradox of otherness is that, of course, at no moment in History is it tolerated or possible as such. The other is there only to be reappropriated, recaptured and destroyed as other.' Commenting on the specific context of colonial France, she then adds: 'Even the exclusion [of otherness] is not an exclusion. Algeria was not France, but it was "French".' Cixous comments thus on her own sense of cultural polyvalence and displacement:

> The routine 'our ancestors, the Gauls' was pulled on me. But I was born in Algeria, and my ancestors lived in Spain, Morocco, Austria, Hungary, Czechoslovakia, Germany; my brothers by birth are Arab. So where are we in history? I side with those who are injured, trespassed upon, colonized. I am (not) Arab. Who am I? I am 'doing' French history. I am a Jewish woman. ... Who is this 'I'? Where is my place? ... Which language is mine? ... Who spoke for me throughout the generations?' (p. 71)

It is futile to strive to answer any of these questions more than tentatively, provisionally, experimentally. Infinitely more important than our possible answers are our unlimited attempts to understand the questions themselves, their implications for people's lived and embodied experience and their openness to constant renegotiation.

There is only one 'place', according to Cixous, that allows for such an 'exploration' without being 'indebted to all the vileness and compromise' of official history and its recursive appropriation of the Other: 'This is writing.' Writing is 'a somewhere else that can escape the infernal repetition' of the same, namely the colonial master's continuous reassertion of his supremacy, and hence 'invents new worlds'. Cixous is eager to emphasize the significance of writing as a political weapon not only capable of producing knowledge of one's conditions and an informed understanding of their ethical and ideological significance but also of fostering a sense of solidarity among variously oppressed people. She vividly conveys this idea by recalling her own experience of reading as a young girl beset by uncertainty and anger about her ambiguous cultural standing:

> I take books; I leave the real, colonial space; I go away. Often I go read in a tree. Far from the ground and the shit. I don't go and read just to read, to forget – No! Not to shut myself up in some imaginary paradise. I am searching: somewhere there must be people who are like me in their rebellion and in their hope. Because I don't despair ... if I can't be alive without being angry, there must be others like me. I don't know who, but when I am big, I'll find them and I'll join them, I don't yet know where. (p. 72)

These hypothetical others, whose existence the young Cixous is only too right to infer, ultimately constitute a multifaceted, polyphonic and hybrid *race*: what Kristeva would possibly tag a *puzzle* race. The predecessors and allies about whom Cixous speculates epitomize the non-French Other in the form of all people condemned to iniquitous domination, deprivation and rape:

> While waiting, I want to have only my true ancestors for company (and even at that I forgive the Gauls a great deal, thanks to their defeat; they, too, were alienated, deceived, enslaved, it's true) – my true allies, my true 'race'. Not this comical, repulsive species that exercises power in the place where I was born. (ibid.)

Echoing Kristeva's suggestion that the stranger and the unconscious mirror each other, Sarah Kofman addresses the issue of foreignness as intimately connected with the psychological mechanisms of repression and censorship. In so doing, she supplies an innovative interpretation of the Freudian concept of negativity, to show that the assertion of self and national identity hinges on a twofold process of negation. As Penelope Deutscher and Kelly Oliver observe, negation works 'by expelling or denying elements that threaten the stability of identity', on the one hand, and by transforming 'the self-preserving instinct into an instinct for mastery that turns against the subject', on the other (Deutscher and Oliver 1999: 21). As Diane Morgan points out in her analysis of Kofman's response to Freud, the subject's 'primitive' attitude to the outside amounts to a rather crude 'What is good is what I want to incorporate into me; what is bad, what threatens me, is what I want to expel from me.' She then observes that such an 'unsophisticated and impulsive method of deciding has many inconveniences. It prematurely disallows the encounter with new material, the foreign, the unknown. The external is prejudged' (Morgan 1999: 221). This method must be transcended, according to Sigmund Freud, because the psyche's main aim should be precisely the conquest of increasing portions of the external world. Indeed, Freud's work is driven by a 'colonizing spirit': namely, 'winning territory from the id and turning it into productive, progressive consciousness' (p. 223).

Freud alludes to the colonial connotations of his project by asserting that 'the repressed is foreign territory to the ego – internal foreign territory – just as reality (if you will forgive the unusual expression) is external foreign territory' (Freud 1975: 88). Commenting on Freud's statement, Thomas Mann observes: 'As for the ego itself, its situation is pathetic, well-nigh alarming. It is an alert, prominent, and enlightened little part of the id – much as Europe is a small and lively province of the greater Asia' (Mann 1947: 417). Morgan vividly highlights the racial implications of the Freudian enterprise:

> The conscious vigilance of 'Europe' is constructed out of terrain won from the expanse of 'Asia', which stands in geographically for 'external foreign territory' and psychically for 'internal foreign territory'. ... The ego, or 'Europe', is besieged on both sides ... . It is precariously and artificially carved out of the very forces to which it belongs and that threaten to undermine its constitution. (Morgan 1999: 222)

However, the murky id can never be conclusively conquered and controlled, which is why self-assertion is virtually inseparable from self-depletion. Indeed, Kofman argues that while endeavouring to protect ourselves and hence affirm our impregnability, we concurrently risk making ourselves more vulnerable. This is because the instinct for mastery cannot ultimately guarantee our safety: we may feel in control of others but we can never achieve total control over our own psyches and bodies. Indeed, we need to recognize that the most intractable menace that we struggle to keep at bay is not external to the Self but actually emanates from within, from the dark, repressed and silenced recesses of our minds that insistently threaten to fragment and divide us. The trials of a split psyche are exemplified by Kofman's own life and its tragic landmarks: the experience of the German occupation, the death in a concentration camp of the father whose pen is the only extant vestige, and her concealment to avoid capture. These and many other painful and intricate experiences are documented in the autobiographical work *Rue Ordener, Rue Labat* (Kofman 1996), where Kofman's inner division is epitomized by her relationships with two mothers: the natural Jewish mother whom the young Sarah is increasingly inclined to negate as the representative of a stifling law and as inseparable from the danger of Nazi persecution and the pain of war; and the adoptive Christian *Mémé*, who is, by contrast, increasingly perceived as the provider of pleasure, freedom and safety.

FEMINISM AND ALGERIA

... wrap the nubile girl in veils. Make her invisible. Make her more unseeing than the sightless, destroy in her every memory of the world without. And what if she has learned to write? The jailer who guards a body that has no words – and written words can travel – may sleep in peace: it will suffice to brick up the windows, padlock the sole entrance door, and erect a blank wall rising up to heaven. And what if the maiden does write? Her voice, albeit silenced, will circulate. A scrap of paper. A crumpled cloth. ... The jailer must keep watch day and night. The written word will take flight from the patio, will be tossed from a terrace. The blue of heaven is suddenly limitless. The precautions have all been in vain. (Djebar 1993: 3)

In examining the interrelations of issues of power, race and foreignness, consideration must be given not only to theorists working in the context of metropolitan France but also to the feminist voices that have emerged in postcolonial societies, and specifically Algeria, as well as to the distinctiveness of their concerns. Attempting to deal exhaustively with the historical, cultural and political status of Algerian feminism in the present context would be quite preposterous. Indeed, entire volumes could be devoted to a topic of such complexity, and to cognate issues such as the impact of decolonization on the conditions of Maghrebian women and the relationship between feminism and Islam. What this segment aims at, therefore, is the provision of a selective survey, intended to highlight some of the principal preoccupations voiced by a representative cross-section of Algerian women writers.

The question of feminism's relation to Islam has been the highly controversial focus of many heated debates. Even a cursory examination of feminism in Algeria demonstrates that there is no consensus about the aims of feminism *vis-à-vis* the Islamic world-view. Such debates have, in turn, raised challenging questions about the meaning of women's self-determination and the definition of a female subject's duties and rights. In order to understand how the rise of Islam as a means of asserting various, and frequently conflicting, national and cultural identities has impacted on feminist debates, certain historical circumstances and developments should be noted. As Marian Aguiar states:

[the] feminist movement in Islamic Africa draws on a rich tradition of women's political participation. ... The contribution of these women to nationalist struggles brought dangers unique to their sex: in Algeria, fighters such as Djamila Boupasha, raped by French military police while in custody, suffered sexual brutality during the quest for an independent nation. (Aguiar 1999)

It should also be emphasized that women's activism has often resulted in the perpetuation of rather conservative attitudes towards woman's role in domestic life and her familial responsibilities, which may suggest that female involvement in political causes has not led to momentous transformations of the social fabric. However, as the historian Mervat Hatem points out in relation to Algerian women's role in the struggle for independence, even contributions based on traditionally feminine activities such as nursing and cooking could be seen as an extension and repositioning of conventional duties (Hatem 1995).

After the achievement of independence, the emancipation of women by means of programmes providing elementary education, training in domestic management and contraception was in the first place connected with postcolonial governments. Subsequently, at least since the 1970s, further initiatives have been sponsored by international organizations such as the United Nations. Most importantly, 'in the last forty years, women throughout much of Islamic Africa have gained the right to work and to vote. In Algeria, women have been elected to the National Assembly' (Aguiar 1999). An indicator of how rapidly the campaign for women's emancipation has developed despite harsh opposition may be obtained by considering a few key moments in recent history. The first meeting of Algeria's new feminist movement was held on 30 November 1989; the following year, on International Women's Day, 10,000 women marched in protest against discriminating laws and terrorism; by 8 March 1994, the number of protesters had risen to 50,000, and on 8 March 1995, a women-led people's tribunal passed a symbolic sentence against Islamic leaders and their allies for crimes against humanity. It is crucial to recognize, however, that legal reforms and enhanced educational opportunities have not uniformly benefited *all* Algerian women, due to the persistence of cultural and class-based inequalities.

One of the most problematic issues, in assessing feminism's chances in the Islamic world, lies with the difficulty of quantifying and qualifying the specific forms of oppression imposed on its female population. An especially contentious point for feminism, in this regard, is the question of whether Islamic law and theology are intrinsically sexist and hence disadvantageous to women, or whether oppression stems from the ways in which the Koran has traditionally and rather uncritically been interpreted by patriarchal institutions. Such institutions, it must be emphasized, only acknowledge patrilineal succession and accord men unilaterally the privileges of divorce and polygamy. The critic Samia Kouidier is overtly sympathetic to Islamic codes and eager to valorize their positive effects for women:

> Islam is no more misogynous that other religions. Quite the contrary in fact: the position on sexuality, the body, male/female relationships as established by the Koran are much more human and natural than in other religions. This is because the space devoted to men and women is based on the practices of the prophet, on those of a man, therefore, and not a god, whose primary needs such as sexuality are taken into due consideration. (Quoted in Galesne and D'Asaro 1995)

Djezia Ben, quoted in the same volume, sounds rather more cautious: 'Everything is open to interpretation. When various societies have a blinkered and exclusive vision of their religion, women always suffer the effects of such a simplification. On the other hand, there is an open, illuminated interpretation of Islam', which may help women 'find a compromise between Islam and the modern world.' As Aguiar notes, analogous positions have developed in other parts of North Africa:

> feminist activists such as Malak Hifni Nassif and Huda Shaarawi in Egypt, and Bechira Mrad in Tunisia call for a 'synthesis' in contemporary Islamic society. They propose a model that would maintain the structure of traditional family life while affirming the value of women's education and employment outside the home. (Aguiar 1999)

Another pressing concern has to do with the rise of fundamentalism since the late 1980s. The impact of this phenomenon on female emancipation is patently borne out by the deterioration in the condition of Algerian women. While in 1984, feminists rightly felt entitled to fight against the newly established Family Code, 'which counteracted feminist gains concerning such issues as equal inheritance and equal divorce rights', less than two decades later 'women who stray outside the conservative norms dictating female dress and behaviour risk anything from public censure to state persecution to vigilante violence' (ibid.). Khalida Messaoudi is one of the most militant and ebulliently committed Algerian feminists. Her work as an activist started in 1981 with her resolute indictment of the aforementioned Family Code. When the latter was legalized, in 1984, Messaoudi became President of the Association for the Equality of Men and Women Before the Law, and in 1990, she founded the Independent Association for the Triumph of Women's Rights. Strongly opposed to the establishment of an Islamic state, Messaoudi spent the terror years between 1993 and 1996 touring Europe to raise consciousness about fundamentalist positions, and fighting, when in her homeland, merely 'to stay alive' by being 'constantly on the move, with no fixed points' (Swift 1995). In 1997, Messaoudi was elected to Parliament and in 2000 became President Abdelaziz Bouteflika's adviser.

Above all, Messaoudi is an unflinching critic of the fundamentalist Front for Islamic Salvation, whose members she describes as 'fascists who claim that Allah is on their side and that they are marching under the banner of righteousness'. As a result, they 'cannot allow difference. That is why they insist on veils to cover the difference' (ibid.). Colette Guillaumin corroborates this point in arguing that the veil is an 'extreme case' of the use of sartorial conventions and restrictions 'whose common function is to remind women that they are not men, that they must not confuse the two, and above all that they must never, *for a moment*, forget it' (Guillaumin 2000a: 102). According to Aguiar, attitudes to the veil are by no means uniform:

> many Islamic women see the veil as a symbol of the oppression of women's bodies and sexuality. In Algeria, women who refuse to wear the veil have been subject to discrimination and, sometimes, to violence. But others, including some feminists, value the veil as a form of cultural expression that also allows women to escape unwanted sexual attention. (Aguiar 1999)

What remains unexplained, however, is why women should be expected to hide behind a mask in order to 'escape unwanted sexual attention'; why they should not be granted the freedom to show themselves without this act automatically amounting to their putting themselves at risk; why they should submit to uncomfortable vestimentary codes as a means, paradoxically, of feeling more comfortable with themselves. In other words, who is asking these women to suffer in order, supposedly, to avoid worse suffering? Attempts to justify the appropriateness of oppressive garments is harrowingly redolent of attempts to justify the appropriateness of the practice, still common in many Muslim communities, of what is euphemistically termed female circumcision but is actually a barbarous form of mutilation. Arguably, if femininity had not been constructed in the first place as dangerous, unholy and unpresentable, there would be no need to enforce the concealment or removal of its visible signifiers. The only eye invested with authority by Islamic law is that of the patriarchal gaze at its most despotic and intolerant. Being seen is a crime for women, while seeing, as and when he chooses, is man's supreme, divinely ordained right.

Fundamentalists, according to Messaoudi, legitimize all their actions and discourses with reference to Islam and the Koran. However, this position is highly questionable for no religious text, in her view, carries within it explicit interpretive instructions. In an interview for the Italian publishers Mondadori, from which the extracts below are taken, she states that a text 'becomes what men make of it according to their political and social ambitions and to their psychological structures. A passage in the Koran, however, reminds the believers that all manner of readings are possible, none infallible' (Messaoudi, 'Una donna in piedi'; my translation). Behind fundamentalism's dogmatic stance, Messaoudi maintains, lies an obsession with sexuality. Echoing Michel Foucault, she argues that

> fundamentalism, like all totalitarian movements, aims at absolute possession of the social and has understood that this rests in the first place on the control of female sexuality. ... Moreover, like all extremists, fundamentalists hate and persecute diversity, the principal concomitant of democracy. And women represent time and again desire, seduction, mystery, trouble and diversity. ... This is why they are so eager to hide women, veil them, engineer the disappearance of biological difference in its external manifestations.

Concurrently, fundamentalists are most likely to gain ground in a culture when its members feel emotionally and sexually frustrated.

> In our societies, sexuality is taboo. ... Traditional structures of organization were destroyed by colonization and families, thereafter, by urbanization and industrialization. The clan was annihilated. The sense of balance women and men managed to find in marriage within the clan has disap-

peared. ... Since rules dictating sexual segregation regulate personal life
... today, many Algerians live without any knowledge of the other sex.

This is the state of affairs, for Messaoudi, that the Front for Islamic Salvation has striven to exploit to its own advantage. She also emphasizes that in a
repressive society such as Algeria, 'men are no freer than women to be themselves. ... Even the most progressive men evince a painful inability to talk
about affection and love. Mothers play a fundamental role in this respect by
imposing upon their sons the view that they will have of themselves.' Indeed,
from the age of five or six, when circumcision is normally performed in
Algeria, males are subjected to initiation rites designed to buttress their
virility. From that point onwards, 'the threat hanging on boys who do not
behave "like men" is that they might be compared to women'. Furthermore,
both men and women are victimized by intransigent laws ultimately conducive to sexual violence and thus continually exposed to the threat of rape.
Not surprisingly, perhaps, only a minority of victims dare to publicize the
abuse to which they have been subjected.

A rare example of a context allowing for freedom of expression is the
hammam (Turkish bath). Here, Messaoudi argues, 'a marvellous complicity
reigns: women tell one another everything' and 'no-one fears the possibility
of indiscretions'. The *hammam* is a temporary shelter for females condemned
by patriarchal law to a cloistered existence: a nurturing space enabling
mutually supporting relationships among women, which are in sharp contrast
with the reality of the home, where intimidation, surveillance and often even
violence are dominant. It is hardly surprising that the most militantly intolerant fundamentalist groups should have forbidden women's use of the
hammam. Nevertheless, despite this interdiction, women still frequent this
unique site of freedom, thus manifesting what Messaoudi describes as 'a
glorious form of resistance'.

Not unlike metropolitan French feminism, Algerian feminism has made
important cultural interventions through creative writing, as well as through
participation in overtly political debates. This is most strikingly exemplified
by the work of the novelist, playwright and film director Assia Djebar, whose
main objective since the 1960s has been an imaginative rereading of colonial
constructions of history through her distinctive brand of *écriture féminine*.
(This concept is discussed in detail in *Chapter 3, Language and the Subject*
with reference to feminist critiques of patriarchal forms of language and in
Chapter 5, Writing and the Body with a focus on experimental inscriptions of
femininity.) Djebar seeks to highlight women's active involvement in
Algerian political and cultural life in the face of history's persistent attempts
to obliterate their very presence. She does so by examining the fabric of

repression from the perspective of a postcolonial woman and by interweaving her own voice with the neglected testimonies of heroic Algerian women, stifled and silenced by the double tyranny of colonization and patriarchy. This is achieved by means of a provocatively experimental narrative form. Commenting on Djebar's *L'Amour, la fantasia* ([1985] 1993; translated as *Fantasia, an Algerian Cavalcade*), Jennifer Bernhardt observes: 'Djebar revises traditional history in the novel using several techniques which successfully decentre the colonizer's version of history and make space for the participation of women in the struggle for national independence' (Bernhardt 1996). *Fantasia* is an essentially polyphonic text vividly reminiscent of the *Arabian Nights*. Significantly, the legendary figure of Sheherazade becomes explicitly central in Djebar's next novel, *Ombre sultane*, translated into English with the title *Sister to Sheherazade* (Djebar 1987).

Fantasia combines personal and collective memory by interweaving autobiographical fragments, letters, diaries, published accounts of the conquest by French officials and soldiers and oral records of the revolution. The last often consist of transcriptions of words uttered by female revolutionaries, which Djebar herself has translated from Arabic into French. This has two important repercussions. Firstly, the author herself feels torn between different languages, traditions and modes of expression. Indeed, she draws a parallel between the guerrilla tactics of Algerian fighters and the struggle between the French tongue and her native language within the territory of her very body:

> The French tongue, with its body and voice, has established a proud presidio within me, while the mother-tongue, all oral tradition, all rags and tatters, resists and attacks between two breathing spaces. ... I am both besieged foreigner and the native swaggering off to die, in the illusory effervescence of the spoken and written word. (Djebar 1993: 215)

Moreover, Djebar is acutely aware of the ethical implications of writing in French – the colonizer's language that she has mastered through a Westernized education and which, simultaneously, exiles her or, at least, sets her apart from the world of traditional Algerian women. She describes French as the language 'formerly used to entomb [her] people' and comments thus on her own use of this potentially nefarious weapon: 'when I write it today I feel like the messenger of old, who bore a sealed missive which might sentence him to death or to the dungeon' (p. 215). Secondly, her text draws attention to

> [the] limitations of traditional history and the richness of her culture's oral tradition. Considering the French invasion of 1830 and the twentieth-

century War of Algerian Independence, as well as adding pieces of her own autobiography, Djebar complicates the notion of linear history, presenting an alternative view of the interdependence of the personal and the national, the past, the present and the future. (Bernhardt 1996)

Djebar endeavours to revive and bring to the foreground not only the voices but also the bodies of forgotten and marginalized women revolutionaries: namely, to convey a strong sense of the material implications of their struggle and not merely their abstract political agendas. As Bernhardt stresses, 'Speaking the self is linked in important ways to speaking the experience of female embodiment' (ibid.). Indeed, as Sidonie Smith argues in her study of autobiography, this form encourages an interplay of body and subjectivity:

When a specific woman approaches the scene of writing and the autobiographical 'I', she not only engages the discourses of subjectivity through which the universal human subject has been culturally secured; she also engages the complexities of her cultural assignment to an absorbing embodiment. And so the autobiographical subject carries a history of the body with her as she negotiates the autobiographical 'I', for autobiographical practice is one of those cultural occasions when the history of the body intersects the deployment of subjectivity. (Smith and Watson 1996: 22–3)

As indicated above, the very linguistic tension experienced by Djebar's narrator as a split cultural subject is inscribed on her body and turbulently manifests itself via this same body. At the same time, it is vital to acknowledge the *specific* difficulties and dilemmas faced by a woman embarking upon an autobiographical project in the context of a culture that condemns the expression of female subjectivity. As Mildred Mortimer observes:

Islamic culture is bound to the *non-dire*, or unspoken, in other words, to silence; it prohibits personal disclosure. If a Muslim woman is to be neither seen nor heard in public and divulges private matters, revealing in public the secret world neither men nor women should ever reveal, she is, in effect, involved in a double transgression. If the female writer dares to preserve for posterity the very secrets not to be revealed in public, is she not committing a triple transgression? (Mortimer 1996)

Relatedly, it could be argued that central to Djebar's enterprise is the determination not only to divulge occluded female voices and subjectivities but also to underscore the corporeal dimension of women's roles in Algerian history. Algeria itself is metaphorically conceived of as a body: a dismembered, abused and fundamentally *female* body. As Danielle Marx-Scouras observes, the image of the severed hand in the closing section of *Fantasia*, 'symbolizes Algeria, mutilated by a history written by the hands of others (French historians, writers, artists) but, perhaps more importantly for Djebar, it also represents Algerian women amputated in their desire to write or express themselves. The dominant images of the novel – abduction and rape – sexualize the representation of Algeria' (quoted in Bernhardt 1996). Moreover, Djebar's handling of themes directly related to her personal experience, such as her attitude to the veil, her escape from enclosure, her involvement in academic life and writing, vividly demonstrates that the female body is a site of contestation, rebellion, and cultural metamorphosis: that is to say, the site of a struggle for both power and knowledge.

> The fourth language, for all females, young or old, cloistered or half-emancipated, remains that of the body: the body which male neighbours' and cousins' eyes require to be deaf and blind, since they cannot completely incarcerate it, the body which, in trances, dances, or vociferations, in fits of hope and despair, rebels, and unable to read or write, seeks some unknown shore as destination for its message of love. (Djebar 1993: 180)

Conclusion

The survey of representative authors and texts in the field of French feminist thought conducted in this book has emphasized that the field does not constitute a uniform body of theories but is characterized, in fact, by both conceptual and methodological diversity. This is a factor that ought to be taken into consideration by anyone intending to undertake further research in the domain of French feminism and to explore possible connections between French and Anglo-American contexts. No less vital is a recognition of the ongoing interplay of theory and practice within feminist politics in France. This collusion entails an understanding of the political dimension of feminism not only in terms of militant activism but also in terms of philosophical positions and choices.

At the level of lived and historically recorded experience, the development of French feminism has been affected by ambivalent cultural attitudes to women's social, economic and legal status. As argued in this book, French history features many powerful female figures. Nonetheless, these personages tend to come across as exceptional cases against the background of a general propensity to marginalize women and to exclude them, specifically, from the public sphere and from numerous opportunities for educational and professional enhancement. France's Catholic legacy is largely responsible for perpetuating the connection between femininity and maternal/familial duties and responsibilities. Moreover, male politicians of a conservative orientation were eager, throughout the fight for the vote, to emphasize women's "natural" association with the private sphere and to advance this notion as the primary justification for their disenfranchisement. However, several female promoters of emancipation have also, at various points in history, celebrated the domestic dimension of women's existence as inextricable from their distinctive *nature*. Concurrently, even putatively progressive political movements and governments led by men tended to resist the cause of female emancipation despite their professed commitment to democratic and indeed, at times, socialist values. When women eventually won the vote, in 1944, the threat of marginalization was by no means conclusively averted. In the years that followed, only few parliamentary seats were held by female members. Furthermore, power relations between men and women belonging to left-wing organizations have often been marred by the enduring hold of male dominance. This is not to say that French women have made no political or economic gains, or that the theorists discussed in this book are merely isolated phenomena soon to be confined to the footnotes of history. In fact, these women have both initiated and pursued debates that have attained considerable prominence in contemporary philosophy. Several of them have also made important contributions to the cause for the amelioration of educational opportunities and the reformation of civil codes. However, it would be absurd to claim that French feminism has achieved *all* of its goals. The very plurality of objectives pursued by different critics allied to divergent political agendas renders any such claim utterly untenable.

It should also be noted that if women's conditions as theorized by French feminist thought are not uniform, neither are the philosophical perspectives on which the theorizations draw. Students and researchers in the area, therefore, ought to take into account the influence on, and appropriation by, French feminist theory of a wide variety of positions and movements. As indicated, Existentialism has played an important role by positing that human beings only come into existence through decisions and actions, the outcomes of which are inevitably provisional. The principal corollary to this proposition is that we are committed to the imperative to define ourselves incessantly, in the understanding that our identities may never be conclusively established. In terms of political action, Existentialism extends the notion of individual commitment to the collective domain by advocating the necessity of *engagement*, or involvement in revolutionary activities. Where feminist politics are specifically concerned, Existentialism fosters a constructivist approach to gender and sexuality whereby men and women do not constitute either metaphysical or biological essences. In fact, masculine and feminine subjects only *become* so as a result of societal pressures and expectations. Moreover, the principle of *engagement* provides a link between the theoretical promotion of feminist ideals and the translation of theory into practical political interventions.

Although Existentialism questions radically the humanist conception of the Self as stable and autonomous, it retains a humanist component in valorizing the individual's decisional powers and standing as a free actor in history. Several theoretical perspectives formulated thereafter undermine this residual endorsement of humanism by laying unprecedented emphasis on the culturally constructed status of all subject roles and positions. A range of theories clustered around the labels of structuralism, poststructuralism and psychoanalysis have played an especially significant part, in this respect, and

French feminist thought has acknowledged their influence on several planes. For example, the notion that subjectivity is a product of language – ushered in by structuralist linguistics and elaborated by deconstructive criticism and post-Freudian psychoanalysis – has supplied some French feminists with tools for examining the ways in which masculine and feminine subjects are socially fashioned and encultured by recourse to syntactical and semantic conventions. Concomitantly, the denaturalization of concepts of gender, sexuality and desire has fuelled feminist interrogations of the symbolic meanings that are often uncritically attached to masculinity and femininity. Particularly influential have been the ideas that putatively natural categories are actually imbricated at all times in structures of power and knowledge, and that a subject's self-perception is inexorably distorted by elements of misrecognition encouraged by a culture's ideology. In broad terms, structuralism, poststructuralism and psychoanalysis have attracted the interest of several French feminist theorists to the extent that they have provided perspectives from which feminist objectives may be complicated and enhanced. More specifically, they have emphasized the need to scrutinize patriarchal formations not only by recourse to a theory capable of describing particular types of sociopolitical organization but also in light of theories capable of relating a society's structures to the operations of language and ideology at both the personal and the communal levels.

In examining a variety of French feminist positions that have developed in conjunction with the theories outlined above, it is vital to recognize that multiple divergences exist within French feminism. Three issues are here worth pointing out as major sites of dissension. Firstly, French feminists are divided in their attitudes to the political left: while some view the latter's progressive agendas as supposedly beneficial to the advancement of women's causes, others are suspicious of its latent patriarchal leanings and predilection for rigidly hierarchical organizations. Secondly, not all female theorists favour the use of the term "feminism" to describe their propositions and activities insofar as they associate the employment of labels with ghettoizing proclivities inextricable from patriarchal and bourgeois values. Thirdly, some theorists advocate the principle of equality as a means of securing women's participation in dominant structures and relations of power through the acquisition of the same civil rights and cultural credentials accorded to men. Others, conversely, promote the ideal of difference insofar as they view the pursuit of equality as a normalizing strategy that reduces feminism to the advocacy of women's acceptance into patriarchal systems and thereby leaves the latter effectively unaltered.

The divisions just described pervade the two main trends into which French feminist theory branches: namely, social/materialist feminism, the strand that concentrates on the construction of concepts of gender, sexuality and desire by patriarchal social institutions; and psychoanalytic/linguistic feminism, the strand that focuses on the impact of symbolic representations of gender, sexuality and desire on the emergence of subjectivity and on the individual's psychosexual development. This bifurcation of interests has entailed diverse attempts to chart the processes through which sexual and gendered identities are produced and to highlight, in particular, the need to distinguish between the supposedly biological determinants of a person's sexuality and the cultural dimension of gender roles and relations. The materialist and psychoanalytic strands of French feminist theory repeatedly collude, in spite of several divergences, in their respective emphases on the culturally constructed status of both sex and gender. Materialist feminism focuses on the need to examine gender categories as ideological fabrications that cannot be unproblematically anchored to a person's biological sex. Psychoanalytic feminism, while also subscribing to the constructivist perspective, draws attention to the mobility of the categories within which gendered beings may fall by positing the notion of subjectivity as an open process. Most critics discussed in this book, moreover, acknowledge the pivotal role played by language in the construction of subjectivity. This recognition paves the way for two interrelated projects: a critique of the codes and conventions that sustain patriarchal language, on the one hand; and an exploration of the possibility of devising alternative forms of expression, on the other. In both cases, it is vital to remember that the practices through which dominant forms of subjectivity are fashioned and challenged always unfold in the context of both private and public institutions. These underpin the constitution and functioning of personal relationships at the microlevel of societal organization, and of collective structures of power at the macrolevel.

Finally, it is noteworthy that the diversity of French feminist theory is mirrored by the variety of responses which it has elicited in Anglo-American circles. Indeed, its reception outside France has been far from uniform. The issues and figures explored in this book have exerted an influence, though not always directly or explicitly, on feminist theory in the anglophone world. Both the social/materialist and the psychoanalytic/linguistic trends could be said to be in dialogue, in different fashions, with Anglo-American perspectives on sex, gender, language and subjectivity. The psychoanalytic strand has arguably attracted the attention of English-speaking theorists more pervasively than its social counterpart. This could be attributed to its greater openness to interpretation, encouraged by stylistic features no less than by content, and its concomitantly greater adaptability to both textual and contextual application. In any case, involvement with French feminist theory in anglophone contexts has been, by and large, patchy. As Nancy Fraser and

Sandra Bartky stress, the 'reception of "French feminism" has been partial and selective. It has focused almost exclusively on one or two strands ... of a much larger, more variegated field. The result is a curious synecdochic reduction' (Fraser and Bartky 1992: 1).

Some critics have been relatively ignored, perhaps due to the lack of translations or to the assumption that their positions were exclusively relevant to French society. Others, most notably within the linguistic camp, have been misunderstood as standing for French feminism in its entirety and hence misappropriated, particularly in academic enclaves. Indeed, there has been a widespread tendency to focus on 'psychoanalytic and deconstructive literary analyses, especially those by the French writers Luce Irigaray, Julia Kristeva and Hélène Cixous' (Adkins and Leonard 1996: 3), at the expense of 'French radical materialist feminism' (p. 2). This imbalance has sometimes resulted in the emplacement of so-called 'French feminism' as 'the body of anglophone commentary' (p. 3) on that privileged Trinity rather than an ensemble of diverse positions in its own right. Christine Delphy, for example, argues that the notion of French feminism has been invented in order to attribute to an outlandish Other the responsibility for creating ideas that the Anglo-American world finds alluring but dangerous (Delphy 1995: 194). A further problem affecting the reception of French feminism in English-speaking contexts stems from the scholarly credentials of the theorists involved. As Toril Moi observes, 'Steeped as they are in European philosophy ... French feminist theorists apparently take for granted an audience as Parisian as they are. Though rarely wilfully obscure, the fact that few pedagogical concessions are made to the reader without the "correct" intellectual co-ordinates smacks of elitism to the outsider' (Moi 1985: 96). Claire Duchen pursues a related argument in maintaining that

> feminist texts that are produced in France tend to find their way into English-speaking circles through French departments ... which are frequently literary, linguistic or philosophical in their focus. Both the texts that are likely to interest academic women and the kind of use made of them will exaggerate the tendency that we have to think of French feminism as highly theoretical and as having little in common with Anglo-Saxon feminism. (Duchen 1987: 11)

Nevertheless, French feminist theory in virtually all its manifestations *is* relevant to issues being tackled in the English-speaking world, and although it would be preposterous to attempt an indepth comparative analysis of French and Anglo-American feminisms in the present context, the *Appendix* is devoted precisely to the corroboration of this notion.

The selection of debates discussed in this book in order to illustrate the most salient features of various *feminisms* draws attention to the multiplicity and diversity of perspectives that have developed and go on developing within feminist thought. They concurrently indicate the continuing importance of engaging in and fostering the exploration of gender and sexuality in their multifold psychological, bodily, economic, political and linguistic manifestations. Indeed, following Mary Klages's (1999) proposition that 'thinking about gender happens in cultures where gender configurations – the social meaning systems that encode sexual difference – undergo changes or shifts', and her related contention that 'gender roles seem to shift in just about every time period, in relation to all kinds of factors', it can be argued that it is incumbent upon *all* societies at *all* times to address gender-related issues through whatever media may be available to them.

The ubiquity of gender as an object of study has been significantly encouraged, since at least the 1970s, by various tendencies to defamiliarize and deconstruct apparently stable gender categories. The debates outlined in this book hopefully demonstrate what can be achieved by interrogating ideas which have become so ingrained in a culture's collective imaginary as to have reached a point of stagnation, as well as ideas which risk becoming so. They also suggest that practice and theory, militant activism and intellectual study can be equally instrumental to the critical process. So-called abstract thought cannot be reduced to a scholarly pursuit, at best irrelevant and at worst inimical to action. As Klages observes, 'philosophical systems are worth thinking about ... not for some intrinsic "academic" value' but because they 'determine the conditions, the terms and premises and concepts, on which our daily lives as individuals, and our social institutions, are based' (ibid.).

Appendix: Anglo-American Connections

Adopting a thematic approach, this *Appendix* supplies a schematic description of theoretical positions, put forward by Anglo-American feminist critics, that are varyingly relevant to the main concerns of French feminist thought. Relatedly, it seeks to elucidate areas of confluence and cross-fertilization by focusing on a selection of illustrative authors and texts that have addressed questions analogous to the ones investigated in the main body of this volume. The *Appendix* does not intend, let alone claim, to provide an exhaustive survey of Anglo-American feminist theory, which would be quite incongruous with the scope and aims of the present study. It does, however, offer pointers for further study and research.

THEMES FOR DISCUSSION

1 Subjectivity and politics
2 Against universalization
3 Feminism and alterity
4 Feminism and psychoanalysis
5 Femininity and the body
6 Gender and performativity
7 Technology and reproduction

(Note: Where key theorists and/or concepts discussed in the main body of the book are mentioned, their names are highlighted in **bold**. Cross-references to earlier chapters are indicated in brackets.)

1. SUBJECTIVITY AND POLITICS

Drucilla Cornell
Chantal Mouffe

Nancy Fraser
Nancy Hartsock

In *The Imaginary Domain: Abortion, Pornography and Sexual Harassment* (Cornell 1995), *Drucilla Cornell* seeks to move beyond the adversarial relationship between equality feminism and difference feminism in the belief that both, if embraced dogmatically, risk 'reinforcing and reifying culturally constructed gender binaries' (Murphy 1998). Her main strategy consists of destabilizing identity by questioning the anchored subject of liberal humanism and by positing the 'person' as 'a possibility, an aspiration which ... can never be fulfilled once and for all' (Cornell 1995: 5). (This position is redolent of **Existentialist philosophy** as discussed in *Chapter 1*.) The notion of personhood as an ideal towards which people continually strive has important repercussions for the field of political philosophy: especially, as Sara Murphy observes, in relation to 'the concept of rights' and to 'the distinction between public and private' (Murphy 1998). Aspiring to become a person does not automatically mean that one is free to choose 'who one seeks to become' (Cornell 1995: 6). Indeed, the would-be person is politically situated at all times and its aspirations are not, by and large, fostered by either the state or the law: the 'state cannot give us the freedom to transform ourselves' and the 'law cannot guarantee us the success of our struggle' (Murphy 1998).

Cornell advocates an ethos of *equivalence*, rather than equality, and promotes the reformation of civil codes as the precondition of social and cultural change (see **Luce Irigaray**, *Chapter 4*). As Joseph Bristow points out, her project is based on the conviction that 'all human subjects should have the right to an "imaginary domain" in which they can operate on a day-to-day basis without being systematically oppressed because of their class, race, gender or any other perceived mark of difference'. Drawing on **Lacanian theory** (see *Chapter 1*), moreover, Cornell draws attention to the ongoing nature of 'the struggles each and every one of us endures in our search for a coherent and sustaining self-image' (Bristow 1997: 160). The legal system's principal responsibility, in this context, lies with securing that 'everyone has an equivalent chance at that struggle to transform her or himself into a person' (Murphy 1998). To this effect, three 'minimum conditions of individuation' (Cornell 1995: 7) must obtain. Firstly, the imaginary domain, namely the realm wherein subjects seek to achieve their personhood, must safeguard the bodily integrity and value the specific material conditions of each and every subject. Secondly, all subjects must be granted access to the symbolic structures through which their experiences are culturally shaped and classified. Thirdly, the sheer existence of the imaginary domain must be protected as an ideal in which the relationship between the private and the public spheres is never definitively established and is therefore always open to transformation. A human being's struggle for personhood happens in the public realm and it is this realm's responsibility to assure equivalent chances for all. Nevertheless, how each subject negotiates its situation, particularly when beset by doubts, insecurity or pain, is an eminently private process, the outcome of which no public structure may predict. Above all, Cornell argues for the expansion of the areas in which individuals may express themselves and maximize their potential without violating the domains of others. This somewhat utopian vision, redolent of certain aspects of **Christine Delphy**'s writings (see *Chapter 2*), is central to the argument pursued in *The Philosophy of the Limit* (Cornell 1992), the phrase coined by Cornell to designate **Derridean deconstruction** (see *Chapter 1*). In the text, the deconstructive project is evaluated in relation to juridical approaches to ethics and commended on the basis of its commitment to ethical principles that bypass or exceed legal codifications of putatively *normal* conduct. At the same time, in deconstructing traditional binaries such as the private-versus-public opposition, Cornell proposes a notion of *relative universalism* akin to the one advocated by **Michèle Le Doeuff**. Just as the latter rejects Existentialist and naturalist definitions of woman, yet endorses the overarching significance of feminist causes, so Cornell argues that we must recognize important differences in women's conditions while simultaneously retaining the conviction that women strive to oppose a common obstacle: oppressive patriarchal institutions. Developing this position, *At the Heart of Freedom* (Cornell 1998) maintains that the freedom to expand one's imaginary domain is ultimately more worthwhile an achievement than equality. Freedom is the precondition of women's ability to create more meaningful lives for themselves in the political, legal and broadly cultural spheres.

The emergence of disparate subject positions in the context of contemporary political formations is one of *Chantal Mouffe*'s principal concerns. Mouffe concentrates specifically on the changing character of social and cultural organizations and on their impact on current understandings of political identity. She draws on the theses proposed by deconstruction and pragmatism, as well as on the writings of Ludwig Wittgenstein and Carl Schmitt, in order to highlight the limitations of liberalism and democracy and to expose their internal contradictions. *The Return of the Political* (Mouffe 1993), in particular, argues that liberal democracy has a tendency to misunderstand the specific significance of diverse ethnic, nationalist and religious controversies and that a more comprehensive notion of democracy is accordingly necessary. Pluralism, however, cannot be expected to ensue merely from the politics of a *third way* negotiating between the Left and the Right.

The Challenge of Carl Schmitt (Mouffe 1999) indeed contends that if liberalism is constantly in danger of responding complacently and patronizingly to the demand for a plurality of viewpoints, the third-way approach suffers from a proclivity to neglect the intrinsically conflictual character of democratic formations. According to Mouffe, what is needed is an understanding of democracy that recognizes and takes on board the inevitability of adversarial and antagonistic forces within its cultural and political machinery.

Nancy Fraser focuses on the connection between various expressions of gender-based domination and subordination, on the one hand, and industrial and post-industrial economic and cultural formations, on the other. On this basis, she seeks to define a socialist-feminist model committed to the *politics of need interpretation* (Fraser 1990). This objective is elaborated further in *Justice Interruptus* (Fraser 1996), where a key role is assigned to the establishment of a cultural programme of *recognition* and a social programme of *redistribution* – of needs, means and welfare opportunities – in the light of growing multiculturalism.

The importance of identifying the specific needs of women *vis-à-vis* capitalist modes of production and consumption is emphatically stressed by *Nancy Hartsock*. Echoing **Monique Wittig** and **Christine Delphy** (see *Chapter 4*), Hartsock contends that those needs will not be adequately met as long as women, oppressed by the alliance of capitalism and patriarchy, remain the victims of 'exploitation both as unpaid reproducers of the labour force and as a sex-segregated labour force available for low wages' (Hartsock 1997: 159). Like **Paola Tabet** (see *Chapter 4*), moreover, Hartsock urges a recognition of 'motherhood as an institution' (p. 156).

2. AGAINST UNIVERSALIZATION

Elspeth Probyn
Michèle Barrett
Patricia Waugh

Elspeth Probyn argues that a genuinely feminist ethics must oppose the tendency to obfuscate the specificity of women's predicaments in the service of a universalistic conception of femininity. This spurious universalism causes 'women's stories of their lives' to be 'cancelled out by the larger narrative of gender' that insistently ideates female subjects in patriarchal terms (Probyn 1997: 128). Probyn emphasizes the need to grapple with the Self as a construct located at all times in specific sociopolitical circumstances. At the same time, she foregrounds the diversity and mobility of the configurations in which a person might emerge. Probyn is above all intent on examining 'ways of looking at the self that emphasize the levels at which the self actively works in given situations' (p. 132), thus harking back to **Simone de Beauvoir**'s assessment of the situated and embodied subject (see *Chapter 1*). Stressing the principle of diversity as a healthy alternative to Western valorizations of unity, Probyn concurrently maintains that 'the self cannot be seen as an entity that binds women together in the face of racial, sexual, national, and other differences. The self must therefore be seen as a theoretical manoeuvring, not as a unifying principle' (p. 134).

Exposing the dangers implicit in the adoption of a universalizing and/or unifying ethos is one of *Michèle Barrett*'s pivotal concerns. Indeed, she argues that 'Western feminism of the 1970s spoke in a falsely universalized voice' and that subsequent developments have, by contrast, demonstrated a desire to understand and foster diversity among feminist positions (Barrett 1997: 113). Feminism's main aim, in this perspective, is the acknowledgement and cultivation of 'significant differences between national and regional ... development of subjects in various parts of the world' (p. 116).

Patricia Waugh contends that the principle of universalization is spurious because it effaces the inevitably multifaceted and contradictory character of subjectivity in the service of a humanist ethos of uniformity. It is one of feminism's principal tasks, according to Waugh, to highlight and indeed cultivate the subject's intrinsic diversity. She also maintains that exposing the notion of a divided subjectivity is central to **poststructuralist** and postmodernist philosophies and that, to this extent, feminism shares a crucial element with the latter. However, she warns against superficial applications of the concept of self-division to feminist ethics and politics: 'The decentred and fragmented subject of the "postmodern condition" is one which has been created, at least in part, by Postmodernism itself' as a reaction to 'the autonomous subject of Enlightenment thought'. The problem for feminism, in this regard, is that 'the goals of agency, personal autonomy, self-expression and self-determination, can neither be taken for granted nor written off as exhausted. ... Feminism needs coherent subjects' (Waugh 1997: 208). Nevertheless, Waugh suggests that feminism has in common with both **poststructuralism** and postmodernism an 'anti-humanist' thrust, in that it all three refute the authority of the abstract concept of 'Pure Reason' upheld by Enlightenment humanism and stress instead the importance of the material side of experience. Feminist thought, in particular, has often drawn on 'anti-humanist discourses to sharpen its understanding of social processes' and to stress that '"impersonal" historical determinants are lived out through experience'. Feminism, stresses Waugh, is concurrently 'humanist', however, 'in the broader sense of the term' to the extent that it has 'always been rooted in women's subjective experience of the conflicting demands of home and work, family and domestic ties and the wider society' (p. 209).

3. FEMINISM AND ALTERITY

Seyla Benhabib
Carol Gilligan
Sandra Bartky
Gayatri Chakravorty Spivak
Bell Hooks

Seyla Benhabib approaches the relationship between feminism and alterity in a fashion redolent of **Julia Kristeva**'s model (see *Chapter 6*), where an ability to relate to the Other is deemed vital. Central to Benhabib's analysis of alterity is the idea that a willingness to empathize with the Other on the basis of what *Carol Gilligan* terms an *ethic of care* (Gilligan 1982) does not constitute an adequate approach. Indeed, it entails the risk of constructing the 'otherness of the other by projection and fantasy' (Benhabib 1997: 215). An authentic understanding of the Other's needs, values and desires requires the emplacement of institutions and practices that enable these to be fully articulated. Moreover, Benhabib stresses the necessity of distinguishing between 'two conceptions of the self-other relations', namely the 'generalized' Other and the 'concrete' Other. The stance associated with the former 'requires us to view each and every individual as a rational being entitled to the same rights and duties we would want to ascribe to ourselves. In assuming the standpoint, we abstract from the individuality and concrete identity of the other.' The latter modality asks us to see 'each and every rational being as an individual with a concrete history, identity and affective-emotional constitution' (p. 213). Ultimately, 'neither the concreteness nor the otherness of the "concrete other" can be known in the absence of the *voice* of the other' (p. 214).

Sandra Bartky's exploration of alterity underpins the objective of creating a *feminist moral psychology* through which gender tensions may be explored in relation to the ethical issues of difference, shame, guilt and deference, particularly in the context of advanced industrial societies. Various discourses, according to Bartky, have contributed to the marginalization of woman as Other. Harking back to **Monique Plaza**'s critique (see *Chapter 4*), Bartky posits the **Foucauldian approach** (see *Chapter 1*) to the relationship between gender and embodiment as particularly problematic:

Foucault treats the body ... as if it were one, as if the bodily experiences of men and women did not differ and as if men and women bore the same relationship to the characteristic institutions of modern life. ... he is blind to those disciplines that reproduce a modality of embodiment that is particularly feminine. To overlook the forms of subjection that engender the feminine body is to perpetuate the silence and powerlessness of those upon whom the disciplines have been imposed. (Bartky 1988: 63–4)

Gayatri Chakravorty Spivak maintains that, despite their theoretical and methodological differences, both French and Anglo-American feminists have repeatedly failed to address the relevance of their theories to Third-World women, and hence to do justice to the latter's otherness. In 'French Feminism in an International Frame' (Spivak [1981] 1997), in particular, Spivak suggests that Western feminists may even presume that their positions are universally applicable to all female subjects and, as a result, pay scant attention to the 'heterogeneity' and 'discontinuity' of women's conditions across the world. The 'difference between "French" and "Anglo-American" feminism,' Spivak maintains, 'is superficial. ... I see no way to avoid insisting that there has to be a simultaneous other focus: not merely who am I? But who is the other woman? How am I naming her? How does she name me?' Unless these questions are posed and tackled, Third-World women will go on perceiving themselves as mere objects of study, and their 'investigators as sweet and sympathetic creatures from another planet who are free to come and go'. Alternately, they will view the 'feminism' which those fleeting visitors represent as quite irrelevant to their own lives, and 'the liberties it fights for as luxuries' (p. 54).

Furthermore, as a radical postcolonial critic devoted to a **deconstructive** interrogation of both imperialism and decolonization, Spivak is keenly aware of *her own* prismatic and contradictory position as a subject. As Benjamin Graves observes, Spivak is concurrently 'an elite, even esoteric intellectual ... and marginalized as a "Third-World woman", "hyphenated-American", and Bengali exile' (Graves 1998). Thus, analogies can be traced between the texts with which the critic engages and the status of the critic herself as multilayered, patently disunified entities: what **Kristeva** would term *subjects-in-process* (see *Chapter 3*). Following **Jacques Derrida** (see *Chapter 1*), Spivak stresses that the **deconstructive** critic can never fully transcend, or be exempt from, the shortcomings and blind spots of the textual constructs whose positions s/he is committed to question. Indeed, 'Spivak uses deconstruction to address the ways in which she is in fact complicit in the production of social formations that she ostensibly opposes' (Graves 1998). Furthermore, Spivak emphasizes that it is vital to quiz the credentials of postcolonial theory at large rather than simply assume its emancipatory role. For one thing, the idea of *the* postcolonial critic may crystallize into a monolithic type: male, First-World, academic, privileged and hence in danger of viewing postcolonial cultures from an Orientalist perspective that merely replicates the sins of the colonial and imperialist discourses of old. If we are to challenge this reactionary proclivity, we must approach both the colonized body politic and decolonized societies as inherently heterogeneous. Relatedly, for Spivak, adopting the **deconstructive** approach is not tantamount to asserting that 'there is no subject, there is no truth, there is no history'. In fact, it means questioning 'the privileging of identity so that someone is believed to have the truth' and 'persistently looking into how truths are produced' (Interview with Spivak conducted by A. Arteaga; quoted in ibid.). The interrogation of identity promoted by Spivak entails an understanding and acceptance of the heterogeneity not merely of cultural and political organizations but also of each individual subject.

As a paradigmatic instance of the coalescence of racial and sexual alterity, *bell hooks* cites the words and deeds of Sojourner Truth: the nineteenth-century woman who, having 'travelled the long road from slavery to freedom', and having 'bared her breasts to prove that she was indeed a woman' before suspicious white women and men assembled at an 'anti-slavery rally', was not only 'one of the first feminists to call attention to the lot of the black slave woman' but also an ardent proponent of black women's right to embrace diverse subject positions in the face of systems dedicated to reducing them to a singular and uniformly deficient body. 'Unlike most white women's rights advocates,' hooks writes, 'Sojourner Truth could refer to her own personal life experience as evidence for a woman's ability to function as a parent; to be the work equal of man; to undergo persecution, physical abuse, rape, torture; and not only survive but emerge triumphant' (hooks 1982: 159–60). bell hooks concurrently emphasizes the need to recognize the racial specificity of feminist causes. At the same time, she argues that the concept of feminism prevalent in the United States is reductive: feminism is understood monolithically as 'a movement that aims to make women the social equals of men'. Such a definition effaces many feminists' attempts to foreground and appreciate irreducible differences between femininity and masculinity and, no less importantly, ignores the differences that obtain *within* both those categories:

> Since men are not equal in white supremacist, capitalist, patriarchal class structure, which men do women want to be equal to? Do women share a common vision of what equality means? Implicit in this simplistic definition of women's liberation is a dismissal of race and class as factors that, in

conjunction with sexism, determine the extent to which an individual will be discriminated against, exploited, or oppressed. (hooks 1984: 18)

(The concept of *difference-within*, as opposed to *difference-between*, is examined in *Chapter 2* and *Chapter 6*.)

4. FEMINISM AND PSYCHOANALYSIS

Alice Jardine
Jacqueline Rose
Elizabeth Grosz
Marilyn Edelstein
Nancy Chodorow
Martha J. Reineke

According to *Alice Jardine*, 'feminism and psychoanalysis share a central paradox which is shaking up the pedagogue in all of us: they are both *humanist* (concerned with how the "I" is constructed) and, at the same time, and often through the same moves, dramatically *counter-humanist* (decentring the Man in each of us)' (Jardine 1997: 82). It must be stressed, however, that this is just one of many interpretations of the relationship between feminism and psychoanalysis. There is no agreed feminist *line* on this topic in the Anglo-American context any more than there is any such thing in the Francophone world. The paragraphs that follow offer some illustrative positions.

Jacqueline Rose, for example, argues that psychoanalysis can be a useful tool for feminism even though many Anglo-American feminists, particularly left-wing intellectuals devoted to the analysis of the sociopolitical determinants of women's oppression, have rejected psychoanalytic theory on the grounds that it does not supply adequate models of cultural transformation. Rose quizzes this assumption in her own evaluation of Freudian and **Lacanian approaches** (see *Chapter 1*). She argues that those intellectuals, in prioritizing 'a general theory of culture or a sociological account of gender because these seem to lay greater emphasis on the pressures of the "outside" world', neglect to pay proper attention to 'the "internal" complexity and difficulty of psychic life', which psychoanalysis is committed to explore. Yet, the internal dimension does play a vital part in the cultural construction of subjectivity and in inducing feminine and masculine roles and should therefore be considered an appropriate object of study for feminists of diverse orientations (Rose 1983: 10).

Elizabeth Grosz maintains that the most beneficial aspect of psychoanalysis for feminism lies in its emphasis on the *embodied* status of the subject. 'Subjectivity,' Grosz writes, 'has tended to be conceptualized in terms that privilege and affirm the primacy of mind over body' (Grosz 1997: 299). Psychoanalysis, by contrast, focuses on 'the psychosocial signification and lived reality of sexed bodies' rather than on merely 'abstract' conceptions of masculinity and femininity (pp. 299–300). Thus, psychoanalytic theory encourages us to explore the ways in which subjects are constructed *as bodies* in relation to specific sociosexual circumstances. Grosz is especially concerned with the processes through which cultural anxieties come to be inscribed on the body, particularly the female one. Discussing psychosomatic conditions such as hysteria and anorexia nervosa, she contends that 'what psychoanalytic theory makes clear is that the body is literally written on ... at the anatomical, physiological and neurological levels' (p. 308). However, Grosz is dissatisfied with certain aspects of French psychoanalytic feminism and specifically with the theories of **Kristeva** (see *Chapter 3* and *Chapter 5*). In *Sexual Subversions* (Grosz 1989), for instance, she maintains that **Kristeva**'s approach to the body and feminine embodiment is contradictory. Grosz draws attention to **Kristeva**'s 'willingness to describe maternity in biological and physiological terms' and concomitant 'resistance to attributing any female identity to maternity' (pp. 80–1). Therefore, **Kristeva** could be said to both essentialize femininity by linking it closely to the female anatomy and reproductive functions and to further women's marginalization by effacing the specificity of their corporeal experiences.

Marilyn Edelstein offers an alternative interpretation of **Kristeva**'s theories by distinguishing between the figurative significance of the maternal body and the material dimension of maternity:

> Kristeva, like other postmodernists, de-essentializes gender; she treats the *maternal* as metaphorically available to both men and women, but also considers *maternity* as a physiological experience shared by many women. Psychoanalysis itself, practiced by both men and women, becomes, in Kristeva's analyses, a maternal activity, as does much transgressive art. Yet, clearly, her discussion of maternity – including conception, gestation, childbirth, from the mother's point of view – acknowledges the embodiedness, the pain and *jouissance* of real women. (Edelstein 1993: 201)

In *The Reproduction of Mothering* (Chodorow 1978), *Nancy Chodorow* offers an intriguing reassessment of Freudian theory, redolent of **Kristeva**'s approach, that stresses the key role played by the pre-Oedipal stage in our psychosexual development. This stage is particularly important because it shows how babies begin to form relationships with their parents on the basis of gender. In this period of her child's development, a mother experiences two forms of identification: she identifies with her own mother and with her child. Since she is female and so is or was her mother, femininity plays a crucial role in her experience of identification and she is therefore likely to form a closer bond with a girl child than with a boy child. A son, as a result, is encouraged to move away from the mother and to identify with a father figure. Chodorow believes that if men were to play a more active part in childcare, the situation would change. They would develop stronger ties with their daughters and take on a nurturing role. Common understandings of femininity and masculinity would accordingly alter. Like **Kristeva**, moreover, Chodorow places considerable emphasis on the cultural signifi-cance of the phenomenon of motherhood, which she wants to 'be understood historically and contextually, as a reaction to and dialogue with the nearly exclusive Freudian focus on the father and the Oedipus complex' (p. 185). However, in acknowledging points of contact between Chodorow's and **Kris-teva**'s positions, it is simultaneously vital to identity important differences. Chodorow's analysis of the practices through which the cultural system of parenting is constituted indicates that there is a fundamental difference between the experiences of female and male children, and that these lead to the assumption of stereotypical and inflexible gender roles and positions. A radical reformation of parenting would indubitably rectify this situation and supply children with opportunities for the achievement of more balanced and impartial identities.

According to *Martha Reineke*, this perspective differs substantially from **Kristeva**'s:

> although **Kristeva** also focuses on processes by which a subject's needs are constructed, she does not believe that a reconfiguration of the social struc-ture of parenting promises to meet the human subject's most basic desire. Precisely because identity-failure is constitutive in humans – to be human is to endlessly repeat and relive a history of coming to be, without ever wholly accomplishing it – **Kristeva** doubts whether any direct purchase on human identity is possible. (Reineke 1997: 36)

As discussed in *Chapter 3* and *Chapter 6*, the notions of the subject-in-process and of the stranger-within, so pivotal to **Kristeva**'s theories, preclude the possibility of ever arriving at a neatly rounded-off and self-contained selfhood. Our social circumstances may varyingly assist us or hinder us in the ongoing process of coming into being, but they cannot ulti-mately guarantee our success, let alone our happiness.

5. FEMININITY AND THE BODY

Diana Fuss
Kadiatu Kanneh
Sneja Gunew
Laura Mulvey
Teresa De Lauretis
Griselda Pollock
Lynda Nead

Among the main issues explored by French feminist theory that have spawned lively debate in the English-speaking world, one of the most prominent is that of corporeality. Critics are divided over the question of whether emphasis on the specificity of the female body, and on forms of language associated with it, is actually emancipatory. For some, far from constituting a liberating strategy, this focus only serves to perpetuate specious notions of a feminine essence. For others, the enthroning of the female body and of **écriture féminine** as major concerns for feminist philosophers should not be viewed as a retreat into essentialism but as a radical attempt to destabilize conventional views on the relationship between femininity and nature, by showing that femininity is always already a result of cultural descriptions, inscriptions and encryptions: namely, texts. Bodies themselves, in this perspective, can be conceived of as ongoing narratives.

Diana Fuss explores whether or not **Irigaray** can be justifiably accused of essentializing femininity by emphasizing the bodily dimension and argues that **Irigaray**'s 'apparent language of essence' is actually meant to expose as a paradoxical category the construction of woman by Western metaphysics: 'on the one hand, woman is asserted to have an essence that defines her as woman', notoriously asociated with images of passivity and weakness, while 'on the other hand, woman is relegated to the status of matter and can have no access to essence' (Fuss 1989: 72). In this light, **Irigaray** (see *Chapter 5*) could be said to subvert Western definitions of femininity in an ironical fashion, by seemingly imitating their drift. Through her emphasis on the need to liberate and celebrate certain distinctive traits of feminine embodiment and libido, she concurrently demonstrates that those traits do not emanate from a natural substratum untouched by the laws of the Symbolic. In fact, they may only become representable and accessible *as texts*, as forms of language. These, ideally, will be capable of challenging the restrictive norms of patriarchal phallogocentrism. At the same time, in foregrounding the female body, **Irigaray** treats it, too, *as a text* wherein and through which women may articulate not merely matters of physiology but also, more importantly, their places in discourse.

Kadiatu Kanneh, conversely, is suspicious of the import of French approaches to corporeality. Her misgivings ensue from the conviction that the writings of **Irigaray** and **Cixous** (see *Chapter 3* and *Chapter 5*), in particular, ultimately prove complicitous with patriarchal strategies of oppression and exclusion. Moreover, she identifies a distinctively colonialist agenda beneath Cixous's apparent glorification of the *darkness* with which both women and the colonized have traditionally been associated to symbolize their undecipherable alterity. 'The privileging of the body in the writing of Cixous and Irigaray as the radical point for a radical subversion,' writes Kanneh, 'is in many ways ... a dangerous political move' (Kanneh 1997: 292). The celebration of **écriture féminine** as a product of woman 'flying free in the *jouissance* of her own natural self-expression', and of femininity as a nourishing force in 'empathy with nature', does not ultimately emancipate women. Rather, it consolidates their subjection to the sovereignty of the Symbolic, and confirms their entrapment in a state of silence from which they may only temporarily emerge by means of a language that only a few people are willing to comprehend. Thus, according to Kanneh, affirmations of feminine faculties of the kind promulgated by **Hélène Cixous** 'are merely valorizations of spaces into which women may have been coerced by dint of a social world that will not tolerate women as law-givers' (p. 293). In linking the plight of women with that of vilified non-Western cultures on the basis that both categories of subjects have been branded as 'black' and hence 'thrown under a cloak of fear and mystery', **Cixous** is said to be 'in indirect collusion with the deliberate policies of the Western colonial countries which aim to wipe out the achievements and the intricate pasts of the colonized' (p. 295).

However, **Cixous** does not unproblematically use the images singled out by Kanneh to perpetuate the fate of oppression imposed on female and colonized subjects. In fact, in stressing that **écriture féminine** is not necessarily the product of a biologically female author, let alone a Western female author, she intimates that this potentially challenging textual form is available, in principle, to women and men of all colours and classes. Moreover, **Cixous** herself is a multicultural subject (see *Chapter 6*), acutely aware of the psychological rifts induced by multiculturalism. It is hardly likely, in this respect, that she would have wished to reinforce the privileges of colonial rule. In fact, **Cixous**'s work could be read as an encouragement to expand the space of writing as a site in which conventional notions of authorship, authority and authorial ownership are questioned. As *Sneja Gunew* comments, in the wake of **Derridean deconstruction** and its emphasis on the 'play of language', the notion of the 'individual writer' has irremediably lost its traditional significance: 'How, indeed, might anyone be said to "own" a story if in writing we are dealing with a free play of signification?' (Gunew 1988: 111).

Following **Lacanian psychoanalysis**, several theorists have emphasized that practices of seeing and looking play a vital role in *framing the body*. The concept of the gaze, in particular, has been the focus of sustained enquiry in various areas of visual studies. The central assumption upon which a number of psychoanalytic film critics and art historians have been working is that sexuality is intimately linked to structures of power and that the latter, in turn, are inextricable from cultural systems of vision and visuality. The critic and filmmaker *Laura Mulvey* has made a seminal contribution to contemporary debates on the discourse of the gaze in relation to psychoanalysis and sexuality through her examination of the politics and conventions of vision in classical Hollywood cinema. The tradition of popular narrative cinema, according to Mulvey, satisfies the patriarchal unconscious by positing woman as the passive object of the male gaze. Hence, it establishes a structure of power in which woman functions as the *image* and man as the *bearer* of the look. Mulvey maintains that female characters in mainstream Hollywood films are generally controlled by the male gaze on two related levels: the male protagonist objectifies the heroine through his gaze, while the male spectator identifies with the filmic hero and uses his own gaze to frame the heroine as a passive object. In a psychoanalytic frame of reference, the masculine urge for control is said to derive from the fact that woman's lack of the penis alludes to the threat of castration and thus makes her a source of anxiety for the male viewer. (See *Chapter 2* for **Irigaray**'s assessment of the dynamics of the gendered gaze.)

Men may negotiate and, ideally, surmount this anxiety by objectifying the female body through their masterful gaze. Objectification manifests itself in two principal forms and from each a particular stereotype of femininity ensues. On the one hand, woman may be devalued and demonized. This option is most famously exemplified by the stereotype of the *femme fatale*: the vampiric creature ruled by an insatiable appetite and an overpowering desire to drag man into the abyss of unruly passions. The demonic woman fuels male fantasies of containment of the female body ultimately conducive to sadism. On the other hand, woman may be overvalued and idealized. The stereotype of the virginal, unsullied and ultimately self-sacrificial beauty is a popular product of this second strategy of objectification, and bears witness to the male desire to metamorphose woman into a desexualized icon to be placed on a pedestal and contemplated from a distance. This option is termed fetishistic scopophilia: a form of pleasure in looking wherein the deployment of the gaze is combined with the transformation of the perceived image into an artificial object of worship, endowed with quasi-magical powers. The fetishized woman is supposed to compensate for the sense of lack which the male subject experiences in the face of the female Other. Its function is to keep at bay the threat posed by the female anatomy, considered a visible reminder of the possibility of castration, by transcending the reality of the sexual and gendered body (Mulvey 1989).

Teresa De Lauretis argues that in mainstream cinema, only masculine heroes are represented as capable of changing, progressing and crossing frontiers. Woman, in this context, is ideated either as an object of man's desire or as an obstacle hindering the fulfilment of that desire. Female characters that refuse to identify with the subject positions prescribed by this eminently patriarchal model are punished by the conventions of the cinematic apparatus: they fall prey to self-hatred, guilt and insanity and are often condemned to untimely deaths. However, De Lauretis stresses that feminist film theorists should not merely seek to rectify this asymmetrical situation by 'disrupting man-centred vision'. They should also endeavour 'to effect another vision' (De Lauretis 1997: 33) that takes into account the specific cultural and racial identities of different women: 'Radical change requires a delineation and a better understanding of ... *the differences among women.* For there are, after all, different histories of women. There are women who masquerade and women who wear the veil; women invisible to men, in their society, but also women who are invisible to other women' as borne out by the 'invisibility of Black women in white women's films ... or of lesbianism in mainstream feminist criticism' (pp. 34–5). (See *Chapter 2* and *Chapter 6* for detailed discussions of French feminist approaches to *difference.*)

Mulvey's reflections on the cinematic apparatus have been extended by *Griselda Pollock* to the realm of modernist painting. According to Pollock, 'the canonical works' associated with modernism, such as Manet's *Olympia* and Picasso's *Les Demoiselles d'Avignon* imply relations of power of the kind theorized by Mulvey. That is, they assume 'an active mastering gaze subjecting the passive image of woman, fragmented, or dismembered, fetishized and above all silenced'. Thus, modernist painting is not merely about 'individual expression' and 'stylistic innovation': in fact, it is also a 'discourse around the paradoxes and anxieties of masculinity which hysterically and obsessionally figures, debases and dismembers the body of woman' (Pollock 1988: 159). *Lynda Nead*, too, applies the trope of the gaze to the field of painting. In her assessment of the female nude in Western art, specifically, Nead discusses the male urge to restrain a putatively dangerous femininity through the power of the gaze. Nead argues that the artistic genre of the nude, especially in its female form, has traditionally been regarded as the supreme symbol of civilization, aesthetic excellence and technical accomplishment. It is also, however, 'a means of containing femininity and female sexuality'. This strategy of *containment* is motivated by the conviction that women and women's sexuality are intemperate and incompatible with patriarchal law. The female body, specifically, is considered troubling and even obscene insofar as its boundaries are not clearly drawn. Thus, it constitutes a paradigmatic incarnation of the **Kristevan *abject*** (see *Chapter 3* and *Chapter 5*). The nude's primary function, therefore, is to supply aesthetic means of 'controlling this unruly body and placing it within the securing boundaries of aesthetic discourse' (Nead 1992: 2). While the obscene body respects no limits and arouses tumultuous passions, the nude, as represented by high art, offers a sanitized version of the feminine: it frames the flesh, conceals its flaws and, above all, achieves 'a kind of magical regulation of the female body' (p. 7). The male viewer may then enjoy beholding that body without having to confront any reminders of lack.

6. GENDER AND PERFORMATIVITY

Judith Butler
Judith Halberstam
Eve Kosofsky Sedgwick
Teresa De Lauretis

In *Gender Trouble* (Butler 1990), *Judith Butler* endeavours to sever gender categories from putative essences of femininity and masculinity by arguing that gender is not merely a cultural construct but rather a type of performance based on the adoption and display of certain signs and on the ritual repetition of sets of stylized acts. Any gender category entails the possibility of diverse kinds of performativity. Hence, it would be spurious to conceive of woman as an entity endowed with ontological stability and integrity, for whatever "woman" might mean at any one time constitutes a multifaceted and discontinuous signifier. Just as there is no unitary notion of "woman", so, Butler maintains, there cannot be one single understanding of "feminism". Feminist theorists have, by and large, tended to ignore women's diversity by ideating all female subjects as belonging to a species with shared interests and traits, thereby encouraging, as David Gauntlett points out, 'a binary view of gender relations in which human beings are divided into two clear-cut groups, women and men. Rather than opening up possibilities for a person to form and choose their own individual identity, therefore, feminism [has] closed the options down' (Gauntlett 1998). Equality feminism, specifically, has persistently effaced women's diversity by speciously unifying women's disparate concerns under the banner of the pursuit of sexual parity.

It is against this limited perspective that Butler proposes the concept of gender as a shifting variable.

Echoing French critics of a materialist orientation such as **Wittig** and **Delphy** (see *Chapter 2*), Butler rejects the conventional idea that gender positions and, by extension, forms of desire are motivated by sex as a stable substratum and stresses instead the fluidity of gender and desire alike as performative acts: 'There is no gender identity behind the expressions of gender; ... identity is performatively constituted by the very "expressions" that are said to be its results' (Butler 1990: 25). In this respect, Butler's theories also exhibit points of contact with psychoanalytic French feminism by emphasizing the flexible and processual character of subjectivity, as well as the possibility, through the proliferation of gender performances, of subverting the laws of the Symbolic. However, Butler is concurrently critical of psychoanalysis of both Freudian and **Lacanian** derivation, since she perceives it as a grand narrative about the creation of "woman" as a mono-lithic entity. The psychoanalytic discourse 'gives a false sense of legitimacy and universality to a culturally specific and, in some cases, culturally oppres-sive version of gender identity' (p. 329). What Butler sees in the emergence of a gender identity, by contrast, is 'a history of identifications, parts of which can be brought into play into given contexts and which, precisely because they encode the contingencies of personal history, do not always point back to an internal coherence of any kind' (p. 331). Far from ensuing from a set of given corporeal properties, then, gender consists of a fabricated ensemble of narrative effects, a repertoire of codes and costumes analogous to *drag*. Hence, the attribute "masculine" may apply to a female body, and "feminine" to a male one.

In *Bodies That Matter* (Butler 1993), Butler redefines the analysis of gender undertaken in *Gender Trouble* by focusing on the practices through which the heterosexual hegemony forms the *matter* that ultimately constitutes our bodies and is supposed to shape our sexualities and genders. Commenting on the book, Butler states:

> what became important to me in writing *Bodies That Matter* was to go back to the category of sex, and to the problem of materiality, and to ask how it is that sex itself might be constructed as a norm. ... I wanted to work out how a norm actually materializes a body [and] under what condi-tions ... certain biological differences ... become the salient characteristics of sex. In that sense, I'm still in sympathy with the critique of 'sex' as a political category offered by Monique Wittig. (Butler 1994)

The exploration of gender performativity is pursued by *Judith Halberstam* in *Female Masculinity* (Halberstam 1998). In addressing the performative aspects of masculinity, she argues that these are often more difficult to detect than those attached to femininity because they do not always come across as *overtly* performative. Commenting on *Female Masculinity*, Halberstam asserts: 'despite an almost universal concurrence that femaleness does not automatically produce femininity and maleness does not produce masculinity', there is a greater readiness to associate femininity with 'artifice' and 'performativity', which frequently results in an incapacity 'to pry masculinity and maleness apart'. This tendency is partly fostered by the representation of masculinity as 'non-performative or anti-performative (think of Clint Eastwood's laconic roles for example)'. Halberstam argues that it is vital to undertake a rigorous examination of 'the very different meanings of masculinity produced in very different sites', and turns to the phenomenon of female masculinity, specifically, as a means of challenging conventional gender categories. As a hybrid formation, female masculinity neither describes nor prescribes a single identity but rather 'covers a host of cross-identifications: tomboys, butches, masculine heterosexual women, nineteenth-century tribades and sapphists, inverts, transgenders, stone butches and soft butches, drag kings, cyber butches, athletes, women with beards, and the list goes on' (Halberstam 1999).

Eve Kosofsky Sedgwick has challenged the presumed stability of concepts of heterosexuality and homosexuality in ways reminiscent of **French materialist critics'** exposure of the cultural contingency of the meanings attributed to specific forms of erotic desire. **Nicole-Claude Mathieu**'s analysis of the role played by various kinds of homosexuality and transsexuality in processes of enculturement (see *Chapter 2*), for example, finds an analogue in Kosofsky Sedgwick's endeavour to elucidate the status of male-male relations within the socializing regimes imposed upon men and women. In *Between Men* (Kosofsky Sedgwick 1985), she argues that *homosociality* (the type of relationship underpinning institutions such as gentlemen's clubs) has served to legitimize bonds among members of the male sex and, relatedly, consolidated both homophobic and misogynistic attitudes. *Epistemology of the Closet* (Kosofsky Sedgwick 1990) delves further into the issue of how definitions of sexuality contribute to the cultural regulation of the gendered subject by positing two dominant notions of desire. The 'minoritizing' position, on the one hand, aims at stabilizing desire by recourse to the hetero/homo binary. The 'universalizing' perspective, on the other hand, 'regards sexual desire as spanning the whole gamut of opposite-sex and same-sex eroticism, locating bisexual desire at the centre of a broad range of erotic preferences' (Bristow 1997: 208). The latter stance would seem to militate in favour of an understanding of gender and sexuality as mobile phenomena rather than fixed categories rooted in unalterable essences' (Kosofsky Sedgwick 1990). At the same time, it prioritizes an ethos of difference, by underscoring a virtually inexhaustible variety of erotic preferences, over arbitrarily unifying principles of sameness.

The exploration of *other* sexualities is one of the central concerns of *Teresa De Lauretis*, who is reputed to have coined the phrase **"Queer Theory"** (see *Chapter 2*) in the 1990s. No less thought-provoking are her speculations on lesbianism as the expression of erotic drives that can be accounted for by recourse to the Freudian concept of fetishism. Lesbian sexuality is closely related to fetishism insofar as the latter coincides with the displacement of desire from the region of heterosexual intercourse as an aim, and with the substitution of the phallus by an alternative object presumed to yield pleasure. Lesbianism is a deflection of fetishism towards the female subject herself. What is most distinctive about this move is that it does not hinge on the idealization of details or particles of life, as Freudian fetishism is held to do. (Consider the classic case of a lover developing an obsessive attachment to a single aspect or property of the beloved.) In fact, lesbian desire fetishizes the entire body: its anatomical components, gestures, postures, attitudes, vestimentary attributes, and so on (De Lauretis 1994). This position bears affinities to **Wittig**'s conceptualization and fictional depiction of the lesbian body (see *Chapter 3* and *Chapter 5*).

7. TECHNOLOGY AND REPRODUCTION

Carolyn Merchant
Maria Mies and Vandana Shiva
Ynestra King
Paula Gunn Allen
Carol Christ
Rosi Braidotti
Marilyn Strathern
Michelle Stanworth
Sarah Franklin
Anne Balsamo
Donna Haraway

One of the central concerns evinced by anglophone feminist critics since the early 1980s has been the evaluation of the impact of scientific and technological developments on the gendered body. Several theorists engaged in the exploration of these issues evince preoccupations analogous to those expressed by **Tabet** (see *Chapter 4*) in the analysis of cultural and technological interventions into putatively natural phenomena such as procreation. However, to date, the exploration of issues revolving around the relationship between feminism and technology is a much more prominent aspect of Anglo-American feminism than it is of French feminism. It is here discussed, therefore, as a *distinctive feature* of feminist theory in the anglophone world.

Some of the main questions addressed by those writers are: should science and technology be regarded as women's allies or women's enemies? Is the traditional tendency to associate women with nature still valid? If so, does it work in women's favour or against them? Some critics contest the association of femininity with nature by arguing that it has traditionally supplied the basis for the control of femininity by a patriarchal technocracy. Others are keen on maintaining the link between femininity and nature as a way of asserting oppositional identities, capable of challenging the dominance of male technoscience. This view is especially popular among theorists who seek to interweave gender issues and ecological issues. *Carolyn Merchant*, for example, argues that women's connection with nature, in contrast with technology, may aid their emancipation from 'cultural and economic constraints that have kept them subordinate to men'. The alliance of feminism and ecology could therefore lead to a subversive critique of capitalism and of its aggressively competitive and destructive modalities of development and progress. 'Juxtaposing the goals' of feminism and ecology 'can suggest new values and social structures, based not on the domination of women and nature as resources but on the full expression of both male and female talent and on the maintenance of environmental integrity' (Merchant 1980: ix).

Exposing the connection between environmental and patriarchal strategies of exploitation and oppression is the pivotal concern of ecofeminism. As *Maria Mies* and *Vandana Shiva* point out, 'Wherever women acted against ecological destruction or/and the threat of atomic annihilation, they immediately became aware of the connection between patriarchal violence against women, other people and nature' (Mies and Shiva 1993: 14). *Ynestra King*, one of the most influential critics in the domain of ecofeminism, asserts that this movement 'is about connectedness and wholeness of theory and practice. It asserts the special strength and integrity of every living thing.' King adds essentialist connotations to the ecofeminist agenda by stating that women are in an ideal position to understand the violence perpetrated by the patriarchal order on the natural environment, because of their intrinsic nature and cultural experience: 'We have a deep and particular understanding of this both through our natures and our experience as women' (King 1983: 10–11). The ecofeminist perspective stems largely from James Lovelock's *Gaia* principle, according to which the Earth is a physical, living being. Ecofeminist

critics such as *Paula Gunn Allen* (1986) and *Carol Christ* (1989) articulate this
notion in markedly mythological terms by invoking ancient images of Mother
Earth as an all-embracing Goddess. In promoting these ideas and symbols,
many ecofeminists seek to alter patriarchal structures of power. As Victor
Margolin argues:

> For ecofeminists, the narrative of Goddess spirituality has been a powerful
> impetus to political action. They have led and participated in demonstra-
> tions against acid rain, the destruction of the rain forests, the depletion of
> the ozone layer, and the proliferation of nuclear weapons and have, as well,
> been involved in numerous other causes related to a healthy environment.
> (Margolin 1997)

In this respect, ecofeminism is both a form of protest against the often irre-
parable damage inflicted upon the planet's ecology and a means of mobilizing
women as a community whose distinctive identity results from its co-operation with the Earth's living energies.

The reverse, many feminist critics acknowledge technology's inevitability and
even encourage women to promote it. According to these authors, if women
either passively view technology as oppressive or actively rebel against it by
following nature, they merely reproduce an essentialist ethos that uncritically
situates the essence of femininity in nature and that of masculinity in science.
The claim that women have a privileged relation to nature ultimately serves
to perpetuate a metaphysical system that positions women as passive objects
trapped in the *natural condition* of brute matter. *Rosi Braidotti* has made an
especially challenging contribution to these debates by arguing that both
technophobia and technophilia evince narrow-minded mentalities. The
former ultimately amounts to the 'fatal attraction of nostalgia', to a 'flight'
which 'has the immediate effect of neglecting by sheer denial the transition
from a humanistic to a posthuman world'. The latter is no less blinkered if it
simply cultivates a 'phantasy of multiple re-embodiments', the idea that technology promises limitless chances of self-reinvention at no cost. One mourns
the loss of a golden age that probably never existed; the other welcomes the
advent of a golden age that will probably never come to fruition. What Braidotti endorses, alternatively, is the need to confront recent cultural 're-loca-
tions'. We should neither 'mourn the loss of humanistic certainties' nor
fantasize about the vacuous promise of 'polymorphous re-embodiments'.
Much more useful, for Braidotti, is a sustained interrogation of validated
signifying practices, which neither idealizes nor negates the value of the past
but rather continually reassesses the relationship between the past and the
present:

the new is created by revisiting and burning up the old. Like the totemic
meal recommended by Freud, you have to assimilate the dead before you
can move on to a new order. We need rituals of burial and mourning for
the dead, including and especially the ritual of burial of the Woman that
was. ... The answer to metaphysics is metabolism, that is to say a new
embodied becoming. (Braidotti 1996: 25)

While some critics endeavour to dissociate the female body from nature for
fear of perpetuating essentialist positions, others argue for the denaturalization of various dogmatic approaches to nature and the natural. This project
leads to a drastic questioning of three interrelated notions: the naturalness of
reproductive processes; the naturalness of biological life; the naturalness of
the boundary between the natural and the technological. As *Marilyn
Strathern* maintains, novel reproductive technologies do not 'interfere with
nature' but actually with 'the very idea of a natural fact': that is to say, they
compel us to reconceptualize the divide between natural and cultural
phenomena (Strathern 1992: 43). *Michelle Stanworth*, similarly, radically
problematizes the idea of the natural: 'the attempt to reclaim motherhood as
a female accomplishment should not mean giving the natural priority over
the technological – that pregnancy is natural and good, technology unnatural
and bad. It is not at all clear what a "natural" relationship to our fertility,
our reproductive capacity, would look like' (Stanworth 1987: 34). *Sarah
Franklin* foregrounds the collusion of the biological and the technological in
the development of human life by drawing attention to the intriguing image
of the fetus as an autonomous sitter of portraits taken by endoscopic means.
The unborn baby's autonomy, moreover, is underscored by its mother's
absence from its digital representations and by the invisibility of the invasive
tools used for the purpose of visualization (Franklin 1991: 190–204). In this
context, it is becoming increasingly arduous to see how biological growth
could ever be described as wholly *natural*.

Anne Balsamo documents the ubiquity and ineluctability of technology by
concentrating on the relationship between technoscience and issues of gender
and sexuality. For Balsamo, the body upon which various technologies are
routinely deployed is always gendered. Thus, she stresses that while various
technologies of the reproductive body, such as artificial insemination, in vitro
fertilization and embryo transfer, appear to foster the severing of procreation
from intercourse, biotechnology still associates reproduction with the female
body. This notion is paradigmatically encapsulated by the icon of the *artificial womb*. Balsamo is also concerned with other technologies of the body that
emphasize its gendered status. The aesthetic ideals which make muscularity a
vital component of a particular notion of feminine sex-appeal testify to the

gendered status of practices such as bodybuilding. Concurrently, cosmetic surgery, which generally utilizes female bodies as its principal raw materials, promotes technologies that objectify the gendered subject on the basis of the trope of metonymy: 'the physical female body is surgically dissected, stretched, carved, and reconstructed' (Balsamo 1997: 13) with an almost obsessive attention to isolated details, made available by the development of advanced technologies of inner visualization. These constitute gendered mechanisms of surveillance that expose women's bodies to a piercing, conventionally male, medical gaze.

A ground-breaking contribution to debates on the relationship between feminism and technology is indubitably *Donna Haraway*'s 'A Cyborg Manifesto' (1991). This seminal essay develops the constructionist view that nature itself is a cultural fabrication and proposes that feminism should promote a commodious understanding of technology as a multilayered set of practices and discourses, potentially encompassing emancipatory prospects for women. Haraway resorts to the figure of the cyborg, namely 'a cybernetic organism, a hybrid of machine and organism, a creature of social reality as well as a creature of fiction' (p. 149), for two related reasons. Firstly, she wants to suggest that this figure symbolically unsettles certain totalizing notions of subjectivity by virtue of its composite identity. Secondly, she wishes to draw attention to the collapse of traditional boundaries between the natural and the technological. Pursuing these twin aims, Haraway concludes that 'we are all chimeras, theorized and fabricated hybrids of machine and organism' (p. 150). Challenging drastically all principles of totality and unity, Haraway promotes a 'cyborg world' in which men and women can learn to accept and cultivate their 'permanently partial identities and contradictory standpoints' (p. 154). This would lead to a radical debunking of the binary oppositions on which Western culture has tenaciously relied in order to assert the superiority of the Self over the Other, and enforce 'practices of domination of women, people of colour, nature, workers, animals – in short, domination of all constituted as others' (p. 178).

Embracing a markedly anti-essentialist position, Haraway contends that 'there is nothing about being female that naturally binds women. There is not even such a state as being female, itself a highly complex category constructed in contested sexual scientific discourses and other social practices' (p. 155). This implicitly makes the pursuit of equality specious: if there is no such thing as a uniform body of women, it would make no sense to claim that women must be considered equal to men, for it could never be established *which* women should be equal to *which* men.

References

Please note that the original dates of publication of books and articles are supplied in square brackets, where appropriate, in the main body of the text. The bibliographical details given below refer to the specific editions used in the preparation of this book.

It cannot be guaranteed that *all* the website addresses provided are currently available, due to the very nature of the world wide web. However, all sites were active at the time of their consultation (April–August 2000).

Adkins, L. and Leonard, D. (eds) (1996), *Sex in Question: French Materialist Feminism*, London: Taylor & Francis.

Aguiar, M. (1999), 'Feminism in Islamic Africa': http://www.africana.com/Articles/tt_028.htm

Alexander, N. (1999), 'Rending Kant's Umbrella: Kofman's Diagnosis of Ethical Law', in P. Deutscher and K. Oliver (eds), *Enigmas: Essays on Sarah Kofman*, Ithaca: Cornell University Press.

Alphonso, D. R. (2000), 'Sex and Gender/Christine Delphy', in K. Oliver (ed.), *French Feminism Reader*, Oxford and New York: Rowman & Littlefield.

Althusser, L. (1972), 'Ideology and Ideological State Apparatuses', in *Lenin and Philosophy and Other Essays*, London: New Left Books.

Archer, M. (1994), 'What's in a Prefix?', *Art Monthly*, No. 173, February.

Aull, F., 'The Lesbian Body': http://mchip)).med.nyu.edu/lit-med/lit-med-db/webdocs/webdescripts/wittig243-des-html

Balsamo, A. (1997), *Technologies of the Gendered Body: Reading Cyborg Women*, London and Durham, NC: Duke University Press.

Barrett, M. (1997), 'Words and Things: Materialism and Method in Contemporary Feminist Analysis', in S. Kemp and J. Squires (eds), *Feminisms*, Oxford: Oxford University Press.

Barthes, R. (2000a), *Mythologies*, trans. A. Lavers, London: Vintage.

Barthes, R. (2000b), *Camera Lucida*, trans. R. Howard, London: Vintage.

Bartky, S. (1988), 'Foucault, Femininity, and the Modernization of Patriarchal Power', in I. Diamond and L. Quinby (eds), *Feminism and Foucault: Reflections on Resistance*, Boston, MA: Northeastern University Press.

Bartky, S. (1990), *Femininity and Domination*, London and New York: Routledge.

Bataille, G. (1962), *Eroticism*, trans. M. Dalwood, London: Calder & Boyars.

Beauvoir, S. de (1973), *The Second Sex*, trans. E. M. Parshley, New York: Vintage.

Beauvoir, S. de (1984), *Simone de Beauvoir Today. Conversations with Alice Schwartzer, 1972–1982*, London: Chatto & Windus.

Beauvoir, S. de (2000a), 'Introduction to *The Second Sex*', in K. Oliver (ed.), *French Feminism Reader*, Oxford and New York: Rowman & Littlefield.

Beauvoir, S. de (2000b), 'The Woman in Love', in K. Oliver (ed.), *French Feminism Reader*, Oxford and New York: Rowman & Littlefield.

Beauvoir, S. de (2000c), 'The Mother', in K. Oliver (ed.), *French Feminism Reader*, Oxford and New York: Rowman & Littlefield.

Benhabib, S. (1997), 'The Generalized and the Concrete Other', in S. Kemp and J. Squires (eds), *Feminisms*, Oxford: Oxford University Press.

Bernhardt, J. (1996), 'Assia Djebar': http://www.emory.edu/ENGLISH/Bahri/Djebar, html

Braidotti, R. (1996), 'Cyberfeminism with a difference', *New Formations*, No. 29, Autumn: 9–25.

Bristow, J. (1997), *Sexuality*, London and New York: Routledge.

Brooks, A. (1997), *Postfeminisms: Feminism, Cultural Theory and Cultural Forms*, London and New York: Routledge.

Burke, C. G. (1978), 'Report from Paris: Women's Writing and the Women's Movement', *Signs: Journal of Women in Culture and Socsiety*, Vol. 3, No. 4: 843–55.

Butler, J. (1990), *Gender Trouble*, London and New York: Routledge.

Butler, J. (1993), *Bodies That Matter*, London and New York: Routledge.

Butler, J. (1994), 'Gender as Performance', Interview conducted by P. Osborne and L. Segal, *Radical Philosophy*, No. 67: http://www.theory.org.uk/but-int1.htm

Campbell, R. (1999), 'Marjorie Garber and Marguerite Duras – Vested Interests in *The Lover*': http://public.surfree.com/slm249/litcrit.html

Change Collective (1977), *La folie encerclée*, Paris: Segherts/Laffont.

Chanter, T. (1999), 'Eating Words: Antigone as Kofman's Proper Name', in P. Deutscher and K. Oliver (eds), *Enigmas: Essays on Sarah Kofman*, Ithaca: Cornell University Press.

Chawaf, C. (1980), 'La chair linguistique', in E. Marks and I. de Courtivron (eds), *New French Feminisms*, Brighton: Harvester.

Chodorow, N. (1978), *The Reproduction of Mothering*, Berkeley: University of California Press.

Chodorow, N. (1997), 'Feminism and Psychoanalytic Theory', in S. Kemp and J. Squires (eds), *Feminisms*, Oxford: Oxford University Press.

Christ, C. (1989), 'Rethinking technology and nature', in J. Plant (ed.), *Healing the Wounds*, Philadelphia: New Society.

Cixous, H. (1977), 'Entretien avec Françoise van Rossum-Guyon', *Revue des sciences humaines*, No. 168: 479–93.

Cixous, H. (2000a), 'The Laugh of the Medusa', trans. K. Cohen and P. Cohen, in K. Oliver (ed.), *French Feminism Reader*, Oxford and New York: Rowman & Littlefield.

Cixous, H. (2000b), 'Rootprints', from *Rootprints: Memory and Life Writing*, trans. E. Prenowitz, in K. Oliver (ed.), *French Feminism Reader*, Oxford and New York: Rowman & Littlefield.

Cixous, H. (2000c), 'Castration or Decapitation?', trans. K. Oliver, in K. Oliver (ed.), *French Feminism Reader*, Oxford and New York: Rowman & Littlefield.

Cixous, H. and Clément, C. (1987), *The Newly Born Woman*, trans. B. Wing, Manchester: Manchester University Press.

Cobban, A. (1965), *A History of Modern France*, Volume 3: *1871–1962*, Harmondsworth: Penguin.

Collins, M. (2000), *The Keepers of Truth*, London: Phoenix.

'Comparing American and French Feminism' (1998), Presentation to Nicole Vaget's European Studies Seminar, 19 October: http:www.mtholyoke.edu/-jtwood/eurst.html

Conley, V. A. (1984), *Hélène Cixous: Writing the Feminine*, London and Lincoln, NE: University of Nebraska Press.

Conley, V. A., 'Hélène Cixous': http://prelectur.stanford.edu/lecturers/cixous/conley.html

Cornell, D. (1992), *The Philosophy of the Limit*, New York: Routledge.

Cornell, D. (1995), *The Imaginary Domain: Abortion, Pornography and Sexual Harassment*, New York: Routledge.

Cornell, D. (1998), *At the Heart of Freedom*, Princeton: Princeton University Press.

Crowder, D. G. (1994), 'Monique Wittig', in E. Sartori and D. Zimmerman (eds), *French Women Writers*, London and Lincoln, NE: University of Nebraska Press.

De Lauretis, T. (1984), *Alice Doesn't: Feminism, Semiotics, Cinema*, Bloomington: Indiana University Press.

De Lauretis, T. (1994), *The Practice of Love: Lesbian Sexuality and Perverse Desire*, Bloomington: Indiana University Press.

De Lauretis, T. (1997), 'Aesthetic and Feminist Theory: Rethinking Women's Cinema', in S. Kemp and J. Squires (eds), *Feminisms*, Oxford: Oxford University Press.

Deleuze, G. and Guattari, F. (1984), *Anti-Oedipus: Capitalism and Schizophrenia*, trans. R. Hurley and H. R. Lane, London: Athlone/Continuum.

Delphy, C. (1980), 'A Materialist Feminism *is* Possible', *Feminist Review*, No. 4.

Delphy, C. (1984), *Close to Home*, London: Hutchinson.

Delphy, C. (1987), 'Women's liberation: the tenth year', trans. C. Duchen, in C. Duchen (ed.), *French Connections: Voices from the Women's Movement in France*, London: Hutchinson.

Delphy, C. (1995), 'The Invention of French Feminism: an essential move', *Yale French Studies*, No. 87.

Delphy, C. (1996), 'Rethinking Sex and Gender', trans. D. Leonard, in L. Adkins and D. Leonard (eds), *Sex in Question: French Materialist Feminism*, London: Taylor & Francis.

Delphy, C., 'Capitalist exploitation and patriarchal exploitation in the Communist Manifesto: another form of "veiling women"': http://www. internatif.org/EspMarx/Marx_98/Contributions/Contributions

Delphy, C. and Leonard, D. (1992), *Familiar Exploitation: A New Analysis of Marriage in Contemporary Western Societies*, Cambridge: Polity Press.

Derrida, J. (1976), *Of Grammatology*, trans. G. C. Spivak, Baltimore: Johns Hopkins University Press.

Derrida, J. (1981), *Positions*, trans. A. Bass, London: Athlone/Continuum.

Deutscher, P. (1999), 'Complicated Fidelity: Kofman's Freud', in P. Deutscher and K. Oliver (eds), *Enigmas: Essays on Sarah Kofman*, Ithaca: Cornell University Press.

Deutscher, P. and Oliver, K. (1999), 'Sarah Kofman's Skirts', in P. Deutscher and K. Oliver (eds), *Enigmas: Essays on Sarah Kofman*, Ithaca: Cornell University Press.

Djebar, A. (1987), *Sister to Sheherazade*, trans. D. S. Blair, London: Quartet.

Djebar, A. (1993), *Fantasia, an Algerian Cavalcade*, trans. D. S. Blair, Portsmouth, NH: Heinemann.

Droppleman, E. (1985), 'Exposing Norms: Chantal Chawaf's Unruly Écriture Féminine': http://lists.village.virginia.edu/listservs/spoons/frenchfeminism.archive/Lubbock.abstracts/droppleman

Duchen, C. (ed.) (1987), *French Connections: Voices from the Women's Movement in France*, London: Hutchinson.

Duras, M. (1997), *The Lover*, New York: Random House.

Duroux, F. (1999), 'How a Woman Philosophizes', in P. Deutscher and K. Oliver (eds), *Enigmas: Essays on Sarah Kofman*, Ithaca: Cornell University Press.

Duverger, M. (1963), *La Cinquième République*, Paris: Presses Universitaires de France.

Eagleton, T. (1990), *The Ideology of the Aesthetic*, Oxford: Blackwell.

Edelstein, M. (1993), 'Toward a Feminist Postmodern Polèthique', in K. Oliver (ed.), *Ethics, Politics and Difference in Julia Kristeva's Writings*, London and New York: Routledge.

Fallaize, E. (1993), *French Women's Writing*, Basingstoke: Macmillan.

Flick, R., 'Louise Michèle': http://www.spunk.org/texts/anarcfem/sp001098.txt

Foucault, M. (1978), *The History of Sexuality*, Volume I: *An Introduction*, trans. R. Hurley, New York: Random House.

Foucault, M. (1989), *Foucault Live (Interviews, 1961–1984)*, ed. S. Lotringer, trans. L. Hochroth and J. Johnston, New York: Semiotext(e).

Foucault, M. (1994), *The Order of Things*, London: Vintage.

Fouque, A. (1987), Interview for *Le Matin*, trans. C. Duchen, in C. Duchen (ed.), *French Connections: Voices from the Women's Movement in France*, London: Hutchinson.

Franklin, S. (1991), 'Fetal fascinations', in S. Franklin, C. Lury and J. Stacey (eds), *Off-Centre: Feminism and Cultural Studies*, London: HarperCollins Academic.

Fraser, N. (1990), *Unruly Practices*, Cambridge: Polity Press.

Fraser, N. (1996), *Justice Interruptus: Critical Reflections on the 'Postsocialist' Condition*, London and New York: Routledge.

Fraser, N. and Bartky, S. (1992), *Revaluing French Feminism*, Bloomington and Indianapolis: Indiana University Press.

Freud, S. (1913), *Totem and Taboo*, in *The Standard Edition of the Complete Works of Sigmund Freud*, Vol. XIII, ed. J. Strachey, London: Hogarth Press.

Freud, S. (1917), *Mourning and Melancholia*, in *The Standard Edition of the Complete Works of Sigmund Freud*, Vol. XIV, ed. J. Strachey, London: Hogarth Press.

Freud, S. (1975), 'The Dissection of the Psychical Personality', trans. J. Strachey, in *New Introductory Lectures on Psychoanalysis*, Penguin Freud Library, Vol. 2, Harmondsworth: Penguin.

Fuss, D. (1989), *Essentially Speaking: Feminism, Nature and Difference*, London and New York: Routledge.

Galesne, N. and D'Asaro, A. (1995), 'Primary Targets: An Interview with Algerian Feminists': http://www.geocities.com/Wellesley/3321/win6c.htm

Garber, M. (1997), *Vested Interests: Cross-Dressing and Cultural Anxiety*, London and New York: Routledge.

Gauntlett, D. (1998), 'Judith Butler': http://www.theory.org.uk/ctd-butl.htm

Gilligan, C. (1982), *In a Different Voice*, Cambridge, MA: Harvard University Press.

Girard, R. (1977), *Violence and the Sacred*, trans. P. Gregory, Baltimore: Johns Hopkins University Press.

Goldberg Moses, C. (1984), *French Feminism in the Nineteenth Century*, Albany: State University of New York.

Goldstein, C. (1997), 'On *This Sex Which Is Not One*': http://dept.english.u-penn.edu/-jenglish/Courses/goldstein2.html

Gournay, M. de (1622), 'The Equality of Men and Women'; extracts quoted in *Sunshine for Women*: http://www.pinn.net/-sunshine/march1999/gournay2.html

Graves, B. (1998), 'Gayatri Chakravorty Spivak': http://landow.stg.brown.edu/post/poldiscourse/spivak/spivak1.html

Grosz, E. (1989), *Sexual Subversions: Three French Feminists*, Sydney: Allen & Unwin.

Grosz, E. (1994), 'A Thousand Tiny Sexes: Feminism and Rhizomatics', in C. V. Boundas and D. Olkowski (eds), *Gilles Deleuze and the Theater of Philosophy*, New York: Routledge.

Grosz, E. (1997), 'Psychoanalysis and the Imaginary Body', in S. Kemp and J. Squires (eds), *Feminisms*, Oxford: Oxford University Press.

Guertin, C., 'Critical Stings: discourses of subjectivity': http://beehive.temporalimage.com/content_apps@queen_bees/pages/4.html

Guillaumin, C. (1996), 'The Practice of Power and Belief in Nature', trans. L. Murgatroyd, in L. Adkins and D. Leonard (eds), *Sex in Question: French Materialist Feminism*, London: Taylor & Francis.

Guillaumin, C. (2000a), 'The Question of Difference', trans. H. V. Wenzel, in K. Oliver (ed.), *French Feminism Reader*, Oxford and New York: Rowman & Littlefield.

Guillaumin, C. (2000b), 'Race and Nature: The System of Marks', trans. M. J. Lakeland, in K. Oliver (ed.), *French Feminism Reader*, Oxford and New York: Rowman & Littlefield.

Gunew, S. (1988), 'Authenticity and the Writing Cure: Reading Some Migrant Women's Writing', in S. Sheridan (ed.), *Grafts: Feminist Cultural Criticism*, London: Verso.

Gunn Allen, P. (1986), *The Sacred Hoop*, Boston: Beacon Press.

Halberstam, J. (1998), *Female Masculinity*, London and Durham, NC: Duke University Press.

Halberstam, J. (1999), 'Masculinity Without Men', Interview conducted by A. Jagose, *Genders* 29: http://www.genders.org/g29/g29_halberstam.html

Hansen, J. (2000a), 'One Is Not Born a Woman', in K. Oliver (ed.), *French Feminism Reader*, Oxford and New York: Rowman & Littlefield.

Hansen, J. (2000b), 'There Are Two Sexes, Not One/Luce Irigaray', in K. Oliver (ed.), *French Feminism Reader*, Oxford and New York: Rowman & Littlefield.

Haraway, D. (1991), 'A Cyborg Manifesto: Science, Technology and Socialist-Feminism in the Late Twentieth Century', in *Simians, Cyborgs and Women: The Reinvention of Nature*, London and New York: Routledge.

Hartsock, N. (1997), 'The Feminist Standpoint', in S. Kemp and J. Squires (eds), *Feminisms*, Oxford: Oxford University Press.

Hatem, M. (1995), 'Political Liberalization: Gender and the State', in R. Brynen, P. Noble and B. Korany (eds), *Political Liberalization and Democratization in the Arab World*, Boulder: Lynne Reinner.

Hause, S.C. (1987), 'More Minerva than Mars', in M. R. Higonnet and M. C. Weitz (eds), *Behind the Lines: Gender and the Two World Wars*, New Haven and London: Yale University Press.

Hedges, W. (1997), 'Queer Theory Explained': http://www.sou.edu/English/Hedges/Sodashop/RCenter/Theory/Explaind/queer.htm

Hoffmann, E. T. A. (1999), *Life and Opinions of Murr the Tomcat*, ed. J. Adler, trans. A. Bell, London: Penguin.

hooks, b. (1982), *Ain't I a Woman?*, London: Pluto Press.

hooks, b. (1984), *Feminist Theory: From Margin to Centre*, Boston, MA: South End Press.

Houellebecq, M. (2001), *Atomised*, trans. F. Wynne, London: Vintage.

Irigaray, L. (1978), Interview in M.-F. Hans and G. Lapouge (eds), *Les Femmes, la pornographie et l'érotisme*, Paris: Gallimard.

Irigaray, L. (1980), 'When Our Lips Speak Together', trans. C. Burke, *Signs: Journal of Women in Culture and Society*, Vol. 6, No. 1.

Irigaray, L. (1985), *Speculum of the Other Woman*, trans. G. C. Gill, Ithaca: Cornell University Press.

Irigaray, L. (1992), *Elemental Passions*, trans. J. Collie and J. Still, London: Athlone.

Irigaray, L. (1994), *Thinking the Difference*, trans. K. Montin, London: Athlone.

Irigaray, L. (1996), *I Love To You*, trans. A. Martin, London and New York: Routledge.

Irigaray, L. (1999), *The Forgetting of Air*, trans. M. B. Mader, London: Athlone/Continuum.

Irigaray, L. (2000a), *Democracy Begins Between Two*, trans. K. Anderson, London: Athlone/Continuum.

Irigaray, L. (2000b), *To Be Two*, trans. M. M. Rhodes and M. F. Cocito-Monoc, London: Athlone/Continuum.

Irigaray, L. (2000c), 'Women on the Market', from *This Sex Which Is Not One*, trans. C. Porter, in K. Oliver (ed.), *French Feminism Reader*, Oxford and New York: Rowman & Littlefield.

Irigaray, L. (2000d), *This Sex Which Is Not One*, trans. C. Porter, in K. Oliver (ed.), *French Feminism Reader*, Oxford and New York: Rowman & Littlefield.

Irigaray, L. (2000e), 'Body Against Body', from *Sexes and Genealogies*, trans. G. C. Gill, in K. Oliver (ed.), *French Feminism Reader*, Oxford and New York: Rowman & Littlefield.

Jardine, A. (1997), 'Notes for an Analysis', in S. Kemp and J. Squires (eds), *Feminisms*, Oxford: Oxford University Press.

Johnston, C., 'Wittig: *The Lesbian Body*': http://www.queertheory.com/histories/w/wittig_monique.htm

Kanneh, K. (1997), 'Love, Mourning and Metaphor: Terms of Identity', in S. Kemp and J. Squires (eds), *Feminisms*, Oxford: Oxford University Press.

Kaufman, W. (1975), 'Existentialism from Dostoevsky to Sartre', in W. Kaufman (ed.), *Existentialism from Dostoevsky to Sartre*, New York: Penguin Books USA.

Kemp, S. and Squires, J. (eds) (1997), *Feminisms*, Oxford: Oxford University Press.

King, Y. (1983), 'The eco-feminist perspective', in L. Caldecott and S. Leland (eds), *Reclaiming the Earth*, London: The Women's Press.

Klages, M. (1997), 'Queer Theory': http://www.colorado.edu/English/ENGL2012Klages/queertheory.html

Klages, M. (1998), 'Hélène Cixous: "The Laugh of the Medusa"': http://www.colorado.edu/English/ENG2012Klages/cixous.html

Klages, M. (1999), 'What is Feminism (and why do we have to talk about it so much)?': http://www.colorado.edu/English/ENG2012Klages/1feminism.html

Kofman, S. (1973), *Camera Obscura*, Paris: Galilée.

Kofman, S. (1982a), *Le respect des femmes (Kant et Rousseau)*, Paris: Galilée.

Kofman, S. (1982b), 'The Economy of Respect: Kant and Respect for Women', trans. N. Fisher, *Social Research*, Vol. 49, No. 2.

Kofman, S. (1984), *Autobiogriffures*, Paris: Galilée.

Kofman, S. (1985), *The Enigma of Woman: Woman in Freud's Writings*, trans. C. Porter, Ithaca: Cornell University Press.

Kofman, S. (1986a), *Nietzsche et la scène philosophique*, Paris: Galilée.

Kofman, S. (1986b), 'Autobiographical Writings', *SubStance* , Nos 49/50.

Kofman, S. (1988a), *The Childhood of Art*, trans. W. Woodhull, New York: Columbia University Press.

Kofman, S. (1988b), 'Sarah Kofman: Interview with A. Jardine', in A. Jardine and A. M. Menke (eds), 'Exploding the Issue: French Women Writers and the Canon? Fourteen Interviews', *Yale French Studies*, No. 75.

Kofman, S. (1993), 'Subvertir le philosophique *ou* Pour un supplément de jouissance', Interview conducted by E. Ender, *Compar(a)isons*, Vol. 1.

Kofman, S. (1996), *Rue Ordener, Rue Labat*, trans. A. Smock, London and Lincoln, NE: University of Nebraska Press.

Kofman, S. (1999a), 'Mirror and Oneiric Images: Plato, Precursor of Freud', *The Harvard Review of Philosophy*, Vol. VII.

Kofman, S. (1999b), 'The Imposture of Beauty: the Uncanniness of Oscar Wilde's *The Picture of Dorian Gray*', in P. Deutscher and K. Oliver (eds), *Enigmas: Essays on Sarah Kofman*, Ithaca: Cornell University Press.

Komarovsky, M. (1950), 'Functional Analysis of Sex Roles', *American Sociological Review*, Vol. 15, No. 4.

Kosofsky Sedgwick, E. (1985), *Between Men*, New York: Columbia University Press.

Kosofsky Sedgwick, E. (1990), *Epistemology of the Closet*, Berkeley: University of California Press.

Kristeva, J. (1974), 'La femme, ce n'est jamais ça', *Tel Quel*, Vol. 59, Autumn.

Kristeva, J. (1977), *About Chinese Women*, trans. A. Barrows, London: Marion Boyars.

Kristeva, J. (1980), *Desire in Language: A Semiotic Approach to Literature and Art*, trans. T. Gora, A. Jardine and L. Roudiez, New York: Columbia University Press.

Kristeva, J. (1984), *Revolution in Poetic Language*, trans. M. Waller, New York: Columbia University Press.

Kristeva, J. (1986a), 'A New Type of Intellectual: The Dissident', in T. Moi (ed.), *The Kristeva Reader*, New York: Columbia University Press.

Kristeva, J. (1986b), 'Stabat Mater', in S. R. Suleiman (ed.), *The Female Body in Western Culture*, Cambridge, MA: Harvard University Press.

Kristeva, J. (1988), 'The Speaking Subject', in *On Signs*, ed. M. Blonsky, Baltimore: Johns Hopkins University Press.

Kristeva, J. (1989a), 'Interview with S. Sellers', *Women's Review*, Vol. 12.

Kristeva, J. (1989b), *Black Sun: Depression and Melancholy*, trans. L. Roudiez, New York: Columbia University Press.

Kristeva, J. (1991a), *Strangers to Ourselves*, trans. L. Roudiez, New York: Columbia University Press.

Kristeva, J. (1991b), *Lettre ouvert à Harlem Désir*, Paris: Gallimard.

Kristeva, J. (1992), *The Samurai*, trans. B. Bray, New York: Columbia University Press.

Kristeva, J. (1996a), 'Julia Kristeva Speaks Out', Interview conducted by R. Guberman, in R. Guberman (ed.), *Julia Kristeva: Interviews*, New York: Columbia University Press.

Kristeva, J. (1996b), 'The Ethics and Practice of Love', Interview conducted by F. Collin, in R. Guberman (ed.), *Julia Kristeva: Interviews*, New York: Columbia University Press.

Kristeva, J. (1996c), 'On *New Maladies of the Soul*', Interview conducted by C. Francblin, in R. Guberman (ed.), *Julia Kristeva: Interviews*, New York: Columbia University Press.

Kristeva, J. (1996d), 'Cultural Strangeness and the Subject in Crisis', Interview conducted by S. Clark and K. Hulley, in R. Guberman (ed.), *Julia Kristeva: Interviews*, New York: Columbia University Press.

Kristeva, J. (1996e), 'Feminism and Psychoanalysis', Interview conducted by E. H. Baruch, in R. Guberman (ed.), *Julia Kristeva: Interviews*, New York: Columbia University Press.

Kristeva, J. (1996f), 'Avant-Garde Practice', Interview conducted by V. Kolocotroni, in R. Guberman (ed.), *Julia Kristeva: Interviews*, New York: Columbia University Press.

Kristeva, J. (1996g), 'Reading and Writing', Interview conducted by S. Gavronsky, in R. Guberman (ed.), *Julia Kristeva: Interviews*, New York: Columbia University Press.

Kristeva, J. (2000a), 'Women's Time', trans. A. Jardine and H. Blake, in K. Oliver (ed.), *French Feminism Reader*, Oxford and New York: Rowman & Littlefield.

Kristeva, J. (2000b), 'From Filth to Defilement', trans. L. Roudiez, in K. Oliver (ed.), *French Feminism Reader*, Oxford and New York: Rowman & Littlefield.

Kuhn, T. (1962), *The Structure of Scientific Revolutions*, Chicago: Chicago University Press.

Lacan, J. (1977), *Écrits – A Selection*, trans. A. Sheridan, London: Tavistock.

Lamarche, P. (1999), 'Schemata of Ideology', in P. Deutscher and K. Oliver (eds), *Enigmas: Essays on Sarah Kofman*, Ithaca: Cornell University Press.

Lechte, J. (1990), *Julia Kristeva*, London and New York: Routledge.

Leclerc, A. (1980), *Parole de Femme*, in E. Marks and I. de Courtivron (eds), *New French Feminisms*, Brighton: Harvester.

Leclerc, A. (1987), 'Woman's Word', in C. Duchen (ed.), *French Connections: Voices from the Women's Movement in France*, London: Hutchinson.

Le Doeuff, M. (1989), *The Philosophical Imaginary*, trans. C. Gordon, London: Athlone/Continuum.

Le Doeuff, M. (1998), *Le sexe du savoir*, Paris: Aubier.

Le Doeuff, M. (2000), *Hipparchia's Choice*, extracts, trans. T. Selous, in K. Oliver (ed.), *French Feminism Reader*, Oxford and New York: Rowman & Littlefield.

Le Doeuff, M. (2001), Contribution to the Conference on 'Knowledge and Learning for a Sustainable Society' (Göteborg, Sweden, 12–14 June: http://www.gmv.gu.se/Le_Doeuff.htm

Lessep, E. de (1980), 'Heterosexuality and Feminism', *Questions Féministes*, February.

Lethem, J. (2000), *Motherless Brooklyn*, London: Faber & Faber.

Lévi-Strauss, C. (1969), *The Elementary Structures of Kinship*, trans. J. H. Bell and R. Needham, London: Eyre & Spottiswoode.

Lowe, L. (1993), *Des Chinoises*: Orientalism, Psychoanalysis, and Feminine Writing', in K. Oliver (ed.), *Ethics, Politics and Difference in Julia Kristeva's Writings*, London and New York: Routledge.

Lyotard, J.-F. (1984), *The Postmodern Condition: A Report on Knowledge*, trans. B. Massumi, Manchester: Manchester University Press.

McAfee, N. (1993), 'Abject Strangers: Toward an Ethics of Respect', in K. Oliver (ed.), *Ethics, Politics and Difference in Julia Kristeva's Writings*, London and New York: Routledge.

McGreevy, M. (1997), 'Review of M. A. Simons (ed.) (1995), *Feminist Interpretations of Simone de Beauvoir*', University Park, PA: The Pennsylvania State University Press: http://www.apa.udel.edu/apa/archive/newsletters/v96n2/feminism/debeuvo.asp

McMillan, J. F., 'The Coming of Women's Suffrage': www.tasc.ac.uk/histcourse/suffrage/coredocs/coredoc3.htm

McMillan, J. F. 'Opposition to Women's Suffrage': http://humanities.uwe.ac.uk/corehistorians/suffrage/coredocs/coredoc2.htm

Mann, T. (1947), 'Freud and the Future', trans. H. T. Lowe-Porter, in *Essays of Three Decades*, London: Secker & Warburg.

Margolin, V. (1997), 'The politics of the artificial': http://mitpress.mit.edu/e-journals/Leonardo/isast/articles/margolin.html

Marks, E. and Courtivron, I. de (eds) (1980), *New French Feminisms*, Brighton: Harvester.

Martin, B. (1988), 'Feminism, Criticism, and Foucault', in I. Diamond and L. Quinby (eds), *Feminism and Foucault: Reflections on Resistance*, Boston, MA: Northeastern University Press.

Marvin, C. (2000), 'Simone de Beauvoir': http://www.trincoll.edu/depts/phil/philo/phils'beauvoir.html

Mastrangelo Bové, C. (1984), 'The Politics of Desire in Julia Kristeva', *Boundary 2: A Journal of Postmodern Literature*, Vol. 12.

Mathieu, N.-C. (1996), 'Sexual, Sexed and Sex-Class Identities: Three Ways of Conceptualizing the Relationship Between Sex and Gender', trans. D. Leonard, in L. Adkins and D. Leonard (eds), *Sex in Question: French Materialist Feminism*, London: Taylor & Francis.

Mead, M. (1935), *Sex and Temperament in Three Primitive Societies*, New York: William Morrow.

Merchant, C. (1980), *The Death of Nature*, San Francisco: Harper Row.

Messaoudi, K., 'Una donna in piedi: Interview': http://www.mondadori.com/libri/yesterday/messaoudi/scheda.html

Michel, A. (1959), *Famille, industrialisation, logement*, Paris: Centre National de Recherche Scientifique.

Mies, M. and Shiva, V. (1993), *Ecofeminism*, London: Zed Books.

Mitterbacher, D., 'Monique Wittig: The Myth of Woman': http://anglistik.uibk.ac.at/-billb/books.htm

Moi, T. (1985), *Sexual/Textual Politics*, London and New York: Methuen.

Moi, T. (1997), 'Feminist, Female, Feminine', in S. Kemp and J. Squires (eds), *Feminisms*, Oxford: Oxford University Press.

Moi, T. (1999), *What Is a Woman? And Other Essays*, Oxford: Oxford University Press.

Morgan, D. (1999), '"Made in Germany": Judging National Identity Negatively', in P. Deutscher and K. Oliver (eds), *Enigmas: Essays on Sarah Kofman*, Ithaca: Cornell University Press.

Morrison, T. (1997), *Beloved*, New York: Knopf.

Mortimer, M. (1996), 'Assia Djebar's *Algerian Quartet*: A Study in Fragmented Autobiography', *Research in African Literature*, Vol. 28, No. 2: http://iupjournals.org/ral/ral28-2.html

Moruzzi, N. C. (1993), 'National Abjects: Julia Kristeva on the Process of Political Self-Identification', in K. Oliver (ed.), *Ethics, Politics and Difference in Julia Kristeva's Writings*, London and New York: Routledge.

Mouffe, C. (1993), *The Return of the Political*, London: Verso.

Mouffe, C. (ed.) (1999), *The Challenge of Carl Schmitt*, London: Verso.

Mulvey, L. (1989), *Visual and Other Pleasures*, London: Macmillan.

Murphy, S. (1998), 'On Drucilla Cornell': http://www.cddc.vt.edu/feminism/Cornell.html

Myrdal, A. and Klein, V. (1956), *Women's Two Roles: Home and Work*, London: Routledge & Kegan Paul.

Nead, L. (1992), *The Female Nude: Art, Obscenity and Sexuality*, London and New York: Routledge.

Oakley, A. (1985), *Sex, Gender and Society*, London: Gower.

Offen, K. (1988), 'Defining Feminism: A Comparative Historical Approach', *Signs: Journal of Women in Culture and Society*, Vol. 14, No.1: http://humanities.uwe.ac.uk/corehistorians/suffrage/document/offen.htm

O'Grady, K. (1996), 'Guardian of Language: An Interview with Hélène Cixous': http://bailiwick.lib.uiowa.edu/wstudies/cixous/index.html

Oliver, K. (1993), Introduction to K. Oliver (ed.), *Ethics, Politics and Difference in Julia Kristeva's Writings*, London and New York: Routledge.

Oliver, K. (2000), 'Preface: French Feminism in an American Context', in K. Oliver (ed.), *French Feminism Reader*, Oxford and New York: Rowman & Littlefield.

Picq, F. (1987), 'The MLF: run for your life', in C. Duchen (ed.), *French Connections: Voices from the Women's Movement in France*, London: Hutchinson.

Plaza, M. (1978), '"Phallomorphic Power" and the psychology of "woman"', *Ideology and Consciousness*, No. 4, Autumn, 4–36.

Plaza, M. (1996), 'Our Costs and Their Benefits', trans. D. Leonard, in L. Adkins and D. Leonard (eds), *Sex in Question: French Materialist Feminism*, London: Taylor & Francis.

Pollock, G. (1988), *Vision and Difference: Femininity, Feminism and the Histories of Art*, London and New York: Routledge.

Power, E. (2001), *Medieval Women*, London: The Folio Society.

Probyn, E. (1997), 'Materializing Locations: Images and Selves', in S. Kemp and J. Squires (eds), *Feminisms*, Oxford: Oxford University Press.

Prosser MacDonald, D. (1995), *Transgressive Corporeality*, Albany: State University of New York Press.

Radice, B. (1974), *The Letters of Abelard and Héloïse*, Harmondsworth: Penguin.

Reineke, M. J. (1997), *Sacrificed Lives*, Bloomington and Indianapolis: Indiana University Press.

Reynolds, S. (1996), 'Irresistible Force or Movable Object?', in *France Between the Wars: Gender and Politics*, London: Routledge: http://humanities.uwe.ac.uk/corehistorians/suffrage/document/reynoc16.htm

Richards, E. J. (1994), *Book of the City of Ladies by Christine de Pisan*, New York: Persea Press; extracts quoted in *Sunshine for Women*: http://www.pinn.net/-sunshine/march1999/pizan3.html

Rose, J. (1983), 'Femininity and Its Discontents', *Feminist Review*, No. 14.

Roussel, P. (1820), *Système physique et moral de la femme*, in *Complete Works*, ed. J. L. Alibert, Paris: Alibert.

Sartre, J.-P. (1978), *Being and Nothingness*, trans. H. E. Barnes, New York: Quokka Books.

Schafer, R. (1983), *The Analytic Attitude*, New York: Basic Books.

Scherman, T. H. on Toni Morrison's *Beloved*: http://www.neiu.edu/-partm/dep/profs/scherm/html/finalwkey.htm

Showalter, E. (1988), 'Feminist Criticism in the Wilderness', in D. Lodge (ed.), *Modern Criticism and Theory*, London and New York: Longman.

Smith, P. (1996), *Feminism and the Third Republic*, Oxford: Clarendon Press.

Smith, S. and Watson, J. (eds) (1996), *Getting a Life: Everyday Uses of Autobiography*, Minneapolis: University of Minnesota Press.

Smyth, C. (1992), *Lesbians Talk Queer Notions*, London: Scarlet Press.

Spivak, G.C. (1997), 'French Feminism in an International Frame', in S. Kemp and J. Squires (eds), *Feminisms*, Oxford: Oxford University Press.

Stanworth, M. (1987), *Reproductive Technologies*, Cambridge: Polity Press.

Stavro-Pearce, E. (1999), 'Transgressing Sartre: embodied situated subjects in *The Second Sex*': http:h2hobel.phl.univie.ac.at/-iaf/Labyrinth/Estravo.html

Steinem, G. (2001), 'Foreword' to E. Ensler, *The Vagina Monologues*, London: Virago.

Stone, S., 'Transgender': http://www.sandystone.com/trans.html

Strathern, M. (1992), *After Nature*, Cambridge: Cambridge University Press.

Swift, R. (1995), 'Interview with Khalida Messaoudi', *New Internationalist Magazine*: http://www.thirdworldtraveler.com/Heroes/Khalida_Messaoudi.html

Tabet, P. (1996), 'Natural Fertility, Forced Reproduction', trans. D. Leonard, in L. Adkins and D. Leonard (eds), *Sex in Question: French Materialist Feminism*, London: Taylor & Francis.

Turner, B. (1984), *The Body and Society*, Oxford: Blackwell.

Viennot, E. (1987), 'Feminism and political parties: the impossible union', trans. C. Duchen, in C. Duchen (ed.), *French Connections: Voices from the Women's Movement in France*, London: Hutchinson.

Waugh, P. (1997), 'Modernism, Postmodernism, Gender: The View From Feminism', in S. Kemp and J. Squires (eds), *Feminisms*, Oxford: Oxford University Press.

Weedon, C. (1987), *Feminist Practice and Poststructuralist Theory*, Oxford: Blackwell.

Weir, A. (1993), 'Identification with the Divided Mother: Kristeva's Ambivalence', in K. Oliver (ed.), *Ethics, Politics and Difference in Julia Kristeva's Writings*, London and New York: Routledge.

Whitford, M. (1991), *Luce Irigaray: Philosophy in the Feminine*, London: Routledge.

Wills, C. (1992), 'Mothers and Other Strangers', *Women: A Cultural Review*, Vol. 3, No. 3.

Wittig, M. (1964), *L'Opoponax*, Paris: Editions de Minuit.

Wittig, M. (1973), *The Lesbian Body*, trans. D. Le Vay, Boston: Beacon Press.

Wittig, M. (1996), 'The Category of Sex', trans. M. Wittig, in L. Adkins and D. Leonard (eds), *Sex in Question: French Materialist Feminism*, London: Taylor & Francis.

Wittig, M. (2000a), 'The Straight Mind', in K. Oliver (ed.), *French Feminism Reader*, Oxford and New York: Rowman & Littlefield.

Wittig, M. (2000b), 'One Is Not Born a Woman', in K. Oliver (ed.), *French Feminism Reader*, Oxford and New York: Rowman & Littlefield.

Wittig, M. (2000c), 'Homo Sum', in K. Oliver (ed.), *French Feminism Reader*, Oxford and New York: Rowman & Littlefield.

Woodhull, W. (1988), 'Sexuality, Power, and the Question of Rape', in I. Diamond and L. Quinby (eds), *Feminism and Foucault: Reflections on Resistance*, Boston, MA: Northeastern University Press.

Woolfe, K. (1998), 'It's not what you wear: fashioning a queer identity', in D. Atkins (ed.), *Looking Queer: Body Image and Identity in Lesbian, Bisexual, Gay and Transgender Communities*, New York and London: Harrington Park Press.

Ziarek, E. (1993), 'Kristeva and Levinas: Mourning, Ethics, and the Feminine', in K. Oliver (ed.), *Ethics, Politics and Difference in Julia Kristeva's Writings*, London and New York: Routledge.

Index